THE GERMAN THEATRE

G. E. LESSING

By courtesy of Mary Evans Picture Library

THE
GERMAN
THEATRE

A SYMPOSIUM

Edited and introduced by
RONALD HAYMAN

LONDON : OSWALD WOLFF
NEW YORK : BARNES & NOBLE BOOKS

© Oswald Wolff (Publishers) Ltd. 1975

© in the compilation and introduction Ronald Hayman

Published by
Oswald Wolff (Publ.) Ltd., London
and
Harper & Row, Publishers, Inc., New York
Barnes & Noble Import Division

U.K. 0 85496 364 2
U.S. 0 06 492759 8

Made and printed in Great Britain by
The Garden City Press Limited
Letchworth, Hertfordshire SG6 1JS

CONTENTS

		page
RONALD HAYMAN Introduction		7

I   Dramatic Literature from Lessing to the Present

1	GERTRUD MANDER Lessing and His Heritage	13
2	H. M. WAIDSON and T. M. HOLMES The Shakespearean Strain	27
3	LADISLAUS LÖB Domestic Tragedy—Realism and the Middle Classes	59
4	JOHN OSBORNE Anti-Aristotelian Drama from Lenz to Wedekind	87
5	NICHOLAS HERN Expressionism	107
6	STUART PARKES West German Drama Since the War	129

II   European Cross-Currents

7	HILDE SPIEL The Austrian Contribution	151
8	ARRIGO SUBIOTTO The Swiss Contribution	171
9	CLIVE BARKER Theatre in East Germany	189
10	RONALD HAYMAN Brecht in the English Theatre	201

III   Structure and Theatrical Practice

11	PETER FISCHER Doing Princely Sums—Structure and Subsidy	215
12	KLAUS VÖLKER The New Theatre Buildings	235
13	VOLKER CANARIS Style and the Director	247

Bibliography	275
Notes on Contributors	279
Index	281

INTRODUCTION

In 1955 Brecht was still almost unknown in the English-speaking world. Today he is generally acknowledged to be a key figure in 20th century theatre: in England he has been one of the dominant influences on both playwriting and production style ever since 1956, when his Berliner Ensemble paid its first visit to London. But we are still just as ignorant of his theatrical background as we used to be of his own work. Without even thinking about it, we discount the tradition from which he emerged; or if we do think about it, our excuse for dismissing it is that since he was reacting against it, he couldn't have taken much from it.

Certainly it can be argued that he owed less to German playwrights of the 19th and early 20th centuries than to English playwrights of the Elizabethan and Jacobean periods, and indeed his main contribution to modern British drama was in encouraging playwrights to return to the mould shaped by Marlowe, Shakespeare and Ben Jonson, jettisoning methods of plotting derived from Ibsen and methods of construction based on the unities of time, place and action and derived ultimately from Aristotle, more directly from Scribe and the ideal of the *pièce bien faite*. Strange though it might seem that we needed a German writer to teach us this elementary lesson in the history of English Drama, a study of the past shows that cross-fertilization is characteristic of the relationship between the two theatrical cultures. If Brecht is probably the most important playwright in the British theatre since the war, Shakespeare is certainly the most important playwright in the German theatre since the Renaissance.

The chapter in this book on 'The Shakespearean Strain' by Professor H. M. Waidson and Mr T. M. Holmes refers to the travelling companies of English actors that were active in 17th century Germany. As well as their adulterated Shakespearean performances, they presented rough and ready versions of Greene, Peele, Marlowe and Kyd, inspiring imitation from German writers like Duke Heinrich Julius of Brunswick and, more important, encouraging a professional theatre to come into existence alongside the didactic theatrical activities of the Church. Latin, French, Italian and Dutch elements were also important in the beginnings of German drama. Commedia dell' arte troupes, too, were touring the country and Andreas Gryphius (1616–64) who was probably the best of the German Baroque dramatists, spoke seven languages and spent twelve years travelling abroad. The most important influences seem to have been Shakespeare, Seneca, Corneille and Joost van Vondel.

The theatrical barrenness of the early 18th century and the discontinuity between the Baroque Drama and the Neo-classical Drama that emerged towards the middle of the century are usually explained, rather unsatisfactorily, in terms of the disruption that followed the Thirty Years War. In any case, the climate of the new rationalism was inimical to the drama of unrestrained passion, and Johann Christoff Gottsched, the pundit of German neo-classicism, was anti-Shakespearean. Unable to point to any native models of the classical virtues, he turned to French and Danish playwrights— Corneille, Racine and Ludwig Holberg (1684–1754). Gertrud Mander's chapter 'Lessing and His Heritage' shows how Gotthold Ephraim Lessing (1729–81) broke through to laying the foundations for an autochthonous classicism—but partly by reinstating the Shakespearean model that Gottsched had rejected.

The turbulent dramas of the *Sturm und Drang* (Storm and Stress) movement that held sway from about 1760 till about 1785 were still more Shakespearean than Lessing's in their orientation. This violent reaction against the restraints of rationalism and neo-classicism involved Goethe (1749–1832) and Schiller (1759–1805) as well as Jakob Michael Reinhold Lenz (1751–92) who believed that the powers of the unrestrained imagination could be unlimited and that a true natural genius (like Shakespeare or Goethe) was capable of creating a universe no less real than the universe around us. The *Sturm und Drang* movement took its name from a play by Maximilian Klinger (1752–1831) which was written in Shakespearean prose and contained a scene adapted from *Romeo and Juliet*. Klinger's earlier attempt at a Shakespearean tragedy, *Otto* (1774) had been prompted by the example of Goethe's *Götz von Berlichingen* (1773) a play about the 16th century knight, who became more heroic and Hamlet-like in Goethe's characterization, championing the victims of the oppressive aristocracy and finally being destroyed because, like

Othello, he has a free and open nature, too generous to suspect that others have a greater capacity for foul play. The play first bounced back into English in a translation by Sir Walter Scott, and, in 1963, in an adaptation by John Arden, *Ironhand*. It also provided Jean-Paul Sartre with the basis for his play *Le Diable et le bon Dieu* (1951).

Shakespeare continued to be important to both Goethe and Schiller as they moved out of their *Sturm und Drang* romanticism towards a more classical maturity. The blank verse of Schiller's *Wallenstein* trilogy (1789–99) is bluntly Shakespearean, and his translation of *Macbeth* (1800) attempts to classicize and moralize Shakespeare's tragedy. Goethe went further towards digesting what he took from Shakespeare, but *Faust* (Part One 1808, Part Two 1832) which subsumes and resolves all the disparate tendencies of his earlier work, is more a dramatic poem than a play, as Goethe is more a poet than a dramatist.

Important though they are in the development of German drama, the plays of Lessing, Goethe and Schiller are limited by their dependence on Shakespeare, and although they are regularly revived in German theatres, they do not have much appeal today to non-German-speaking audiences. The German playwright most undeservedly neglected outside German-language theatres is Kleist (1777–1811) while Georg Büchner (1813–37) and Frank Wedekind (1864–1918) are currently enjoying a belated and long-deserved recognition in this country. Of the German-language playwrights to emerge since the war, the best known are still the two Swiss dramatists Max Frisch (born 1911) and Friedrich Dürrenmatt (born 1921). Peter Weiss was born in Germany in 1916 but left the country in 1934 and lived in Sweden from 1939; while Peter Handke, who was born in 1942, is an Austrian. Now that Germany is split into two states, with very little theatrical give-and-take between them, the cross-currents between the separate German-speaking sectors are more complex than ever before. Playwrights, directors and actors can move between the sectors or migrate from one to another, while there is a good deal of influence exchanged between the playwrights and directors of the Swiss, Austrian and West German theatres. The East German theatre is more isolated, but, as Volker Canaris shows in his essay, directors trained by Brecht in the Berliner Ensemble have become important and influential when they have come away to live in the West, while Stuart Parkes's essay shows that several of the play-wrights doing the best work in the West have also come from the East. The human traffic is one-way only: few if any artists leave the West to live in the East; but there is some imitation of Western styles and techniques. The cross-currents cannot possibly be charted in their totality, and they inevitably fluctuate in their force, but the book contains chapters by Hilde Spiel and Arrigo Subiotto, examining the Austrian and Swiss contributions to the German theatre, past and present, while Clive Barker presents a view of the situation in East Germany.

There have also been cross-currents with other continental theatres. The important Austrian playwright Franz Grillparzer (1791–1872) was writing under the shadow of Lope de Vega; and Ibsen exerted a strong influence on the German Naturalists Gerhart Hauptmann (1862–1946) and Carl Zuckmayer (born 1896) though their work also had roots in the German tradition of Domestic Tragedy, which Ladislaus Löb has described in his chapter; while the Expressionists owed a great deal to Strindberg, as Nicholas Hern demonstrates in his chapter on them.

The method of this book is more impressionistic than historical or encyclopaedic. It is not intended to be comprehensive: there are many phases in the development of German drama that are not illuminated, many important plays and playwrights that are not even mentioned, while there are a few key plays—like Wedekind's *Frühlings Erwachen* (*Spring Awakening*)—which recur in several chapters, approached from different angles for different reasons. My objective has been to collect a series of essays each of which is intelligibly complete in itself but which add up to put the present situation of the German theatre into the perspective of its past. Far from wanting to obscure the evidence of differing viewpoints in the contributors— or to choose contributors who would agree with each other—I feel that the book gains from the gamut of attitudes expressed. There are academics and journalists, critics and theatre practitioners among the writers, some of whom are English, some German. Some of the Germans are based in Germany, some in England.

Obviously no one book can say more than a small part of what there is to say about the German Theatre, and I hope this one, by focusing on so many questions from so many angles, will arouse more curiosity than it satisfies.

I

DRAMATIC LITERATURE
FROM LESSING TO THE PRESENT

Gertrud Mander: LESSING AND HIS HERITAGE

Every German schoolchild is taught that Gotthold Ephraim Lessing (1729–81) was the founder of the German theatre. This is of course one of the terrible simplifications of the personality-centred textbook approach. For how on earth could one man, however determined and talented, undertake alone a task like that, which would have involved theorizing and organizing as well as making the actual product? What the statement suggests is that Lessing—critic as well as playwright and a theoretician who himself tried out the viability of his theories —is *the* big and recognizable figure in a landscape swarming with smaller figures. He clarified and put into words a powerful trend of the time and articulated guidelines, found classifications, issued admonitions and passed judgment, where others merely fumbled and groped for the right words or acted in more practical ways by building theatres, forming acting troupes, and setting up academies. A kind of theatre existed before Lessing made himself into the fervent spokesman of renewal—a provincial, financially unstable, actor-based version of the English strolling players on the one hand and the court theatre on the other, which was mostly doing opera or was totally dependent on foreign products. Yet a different kind of theatre was just about to emerge on the bourgeois literary scene from the vulgar and merely popular plane on which it had existed since the end of the Thirty Years War. When Lessing encountered this first really serious and regular kind of theatre, an actors' troupe based in Leipzig, headed by the famous actress Karoline Neuber, the young student of theology, philosophy and medicine decided to give up his half-hearted ambition of making a career in the university or the church (like his father) and to take up writing full-time as a playwright and freelance journalist and critic.

The first evidence of this was a play, the comedy *Der junge Gelehrte* (*The Young Scholar*), which was performed by the Neuberin troupe in

1748 and was in some ways a tribute to their well-meant activities, which young Lessing appreciated and enjoyed, though he was deeply critical of the troupe's famous *spiritus rector*, Professor Gottsched, who preached the French gospel of the unities, prompted the banishment of Harlequin from their stage and insisted on an all-French or French-inspired repertoire.

Lessing was a truly 18th century figure, a man completely of his time, yet with a vision and a will that reached far into the future. It is fashionable to call him a revolutionary since his aims for the theatre, the writer, and the actor expressed the ambitions of the rising and mutinous educated middle classes in Germany which, at the time, were in silent or defiant opposition to their feudalist and despotic rulers. And yet Lessing, the learned, Classics-trained scholar, is in a way almost as model-dominated and rule-obsessed as his enemy Johann Christoph Gottsched (1700–66), because to him the classical writers represent the absolute standard against which all contemporary ideas and products have to be measured. They are the repositories of the truth—Truth is Lessing's most important concept, often teamed with Nature against Beauty, Art or Manners. However, he did not want the artist and writer to follow the Ancients blindly or mechanically, but to find truly national and contemporary interpretations and equivalents.

This recommendation brought Lessing the reputation of a good patriot—a two-edged compliment considering some of the people who did the labelling and their notions of what good patriotism should be: 19th century chauvinists or 20th century Nazis. But this is certainly not Lessing's fault. Anyone who reads his works at all carefully will discover that his nationalism was not an uncritical devotion to all things German; it was a cautious and well-reasoned identification with the national idea (for lack of a unified nation), it was a perspective into the future of a country that had never achieved nationhood and was split up into many hostile political units.

Lessing's lively and restless temperament and independent, inquiring mind was eminently well suited to the task of formulating a practicable theory of the theatre and of putting the theory to the test by writing plays. Apart from occasional lapses into antiquarianism and philosophical casuistry, his thinking and writing style combined lucidity and passion, common sense and directness, wit and simplicity, a combination (normally considered un-German) that was made possible at this juncture in German cultural history by the prevailing enlightenment in attitudes and ideals, particularly the belief in reason. Lessing's suggestions for the social and aesthetic reform of the ailing, provincial German theatre—only one of the many causes he took up in the course of his relatively short life—are based on this reasonableness that is attuned to simplicity and to an emphasis on essentials. The rationalist Lessing fights on two fronts—against the pedants (like Gottsched) and against the enthusiasts (the writers of tearful plays and nature poems). He assumes (or rather calls for) a similar reasoning and thinking attitude in the makers and the consumers of theatre—the actor and the spectator. In questions of form and style the rational approach is evident, too. There is a strong interest in classification (of genres, but also of possible subjects as in comedy or of gestures in acting, and Lessing even thought of devising a system of punctuation to ease the task of the actor).

This leads to his important '*Grenzziehungen*'—his clear structural distinctions between the functions and the possibilities of different artistic media, of which the theatre, as the most complex and multifaceted, is assigned the most important and immediate social and educative role. Where Molière—whose ideas and predilections come closest to Lessing's, particularly as regards comedy—always stressed the entertainment aspect of his craft, Lessing, the son of a Lutheran pastor, the ex-theology student and fervent disciple of the Classics, introduces a moral and social dimension into the discussion on functions. It is an eminently bourgeois approach. And of course it is again mainly French in origin, derived from the Encyclopaedist Diderot and from the classical French comedy.

Lessing's anti-French stance, which is so strongly emphasized in the textbooks, needs to be examined more closely for its negative and positive ingredients. For all the talk about Shakespeare, who is held up to contemporary and future playwrights as a shining example of the truly popular and national dramatist, it has to be remembered that the basis of Lessing's thought is not and could not have been Anglo-Saxon—he never even saw a Shakespeare play performed on stage—but French: Enlightenment, bourgeois, rationalist, in short, everything Molière and Diderot stood for. Shakespeare's sublime disregard for rules and unities is the stick for beating the pedants, the mechanical imitators with their stiff, rhyming Alexandrines.

But nothing was further from Lessing's orderly and objective mind than to recommend an absolute disregard for rules and unities. He wanted to expose the courtly theatre of the French with its grand artificiality and mechanical structure as a misunderstanding of Aristotle's dicta on the theatre. What he saw, through slightly biased eyes, was a schematized, stylized, abstract kind of theatre that stressed superficial rules of style and structure at the expense of truth and nature. Being a polemicist with a quick and dialectic turn of mind, Lessing drew his contrasts deliberately and not without exaggerations. Shakespeare is to be his paragon, as a truly popular dramatist, like the Greeks, who employed reasonable rather than strict forms. Yet he is not held up as a model to be followed blindly and slavishly. Lessing insisted that Shakespeare would have to be modified for the Germans, and this advice was put into practice by the first German Shakespeare producer and actor, Friedrich Schröder, in Hamburg, when he played Shakespeare's tragedies with happy endings. 'Shakespeare,' says Lessing, 'to judge by the precepts of the Ancients, is a much greater tragic poet than Corneille, although the latter knew the Ancients well and the former hardly at all. Corneille approximates to them in the mechanical arrangements and Shakespeare in essentials. The English-man achieves the aim of tragedy almost all the time, strange and idiosyncratic as his methods may be, and the Frenchman almost never, though he follows conscientiously in the Ancients' footsteps...'

The reason Lessing gets so hot under the collar about Gottsched and his Frenchified taste is that he wants to teach the Germans to be themselves and to feel that they have a common, a national identity. 'We haven't as yet got a theatre in which we can understand ourselves as one nation. Nor do the French... since their tragedy is court-centred.' What Gottsched tried to do, according to Lessing, was not to improve the existing German theatre, but to create a com-pletely new theatre, a Frenchified theatre, without ever bothering to find out whether this fitted the German mentality. In Lessing's view, German theatre of the past had been closer to the English taste than to the French: 'In our tragedies we want to see more and think more than what the timid French tragedy offers us to see and to think, we are more deeply impressed by the great, the terrible, the melan-choly than by the proper, the affectionate, the enamoured, and too much simplicity tires us more than too much complication... If Shakespeare's masterpieces had been translated into German with some modest changes, he would have been a better influence than this over-exposure to Corneille and Racine that we get. Also, he would probably have encouraged minds totally different from the minds encouraged by the French influence. A genius can only be kindled by a genius and best by the kind of genius that seems to be indebted to nothing and nobody but nature and does not intimidate by the laborious perfections of art.'

Lessing cannot be held responsible for the misreading of these (and other) opinions of his on Shakespeare by a younger generation that was rebelling against rationalism and all closed systems—the *Sturm und Drang* writers (who included the young Goethe). Their notions of Shakespeare's original genius became the basis of the principal romantic idea—the absolute freedom of the individual artist. Lessing held up his concept of the artistic rule that is derived from direct observation of great works of art against their libertarian—not to say anarchist and subjective—approach to creativity. He abhorred the wild talk among these latter-day enthusiasts about 'abolishing all rules and conventions in order to allow every writer to invent his own art'. This earned him the reputation of having failed to encourage the rising generation of dramatists and writers, particularly Goethe, or to have seen their real merit because he was envious and spiteful since they did not follow his precepts.

That he did not in fact see merit and genius where it was, is true (nor did Goethe in the young writers of his time). Yet it is an unfair judgment—as unfair as the nationalist interpretation. From Lessing's point of view the subjective and individualistic *Sturm and Drang* drama and novel (for instance *Die Leiden des jungen Werthers* which he felt needed a critical commentary by the author) was faulty because it offended against reason and his definition of realism as aiming for general truths. The comparison of Lessing's *Faust* fragment with Goethe's *Faust Part I* is instructive in this respect: the former has a 'positive' hero whose unbounded thirst for knowledge and truth (in the service of mankind) embodies the bourgeois values at their most progressive, whereas the latter, with its dissatisfied and alienated hero, is the tragedy of the bourgeoisie at a later stage, when it had begun to doubt reason, the value of knowledge and the possibility of progress.

If Goethe had intended to write an anti-Lessing work (something he would never have done, indebted as he was to the older man), this would have been it. *Faust*, though cast in the formula of the popular theatre so treasured by Lessing—doggerel, medieval setting, lyrical immediacy, spurning of the unities of time and place in favour of unified character and plot—had a message that contradicted the revolutionary bourgeois enlightenment optimism. The enemy is not, as in Lessing's plays, the despotic feudal overlord or the unenlightened, unreasonable, unnatural fellow-human being; the enemy is within: the hero is a split character because his world is split into ideal and reality. Experience and perception no longer find reason their un-failing guide, the moral and social rules of the mid-18th century have lost their apparently universal and lasting validity.

Thus Lessing is dated, in a sense, before he has written his last word. But only in a limited sense, in the optimistic rational search for general truths and rules. In other aspects—his conception of dramatic charac-ter as natural, i.e. true to life, his insistence on the realistic against the artificial and mechanical, on the use of personal and actual ex-perience and contemporary subjects etc.—he has never been doubted or refuted. His searching inquiry into the meaning and function of art, particularly that of the theatre, started a debate in Germany that has never come to rest, a debate for (or, in the case of Brecht, against) Aristotle's definition of the theatre as a public institution with social and educative functions apart from its role as entertainment.

In this sense Lessing's aesthetic theories amounted to a national event. The vast influence he exerted on most German writers coming after him proves that he had set something in motion of genuine social significance. He was the first to think in terms of functions and effects rather than content and style alone, and it is certainly not accidental that Goethe's Werther reads Lessing's *Emilia Galotti* before he commits suicide—much as Lessing would have hated the thought of being a teacher of despair.

Though Lessing's restless mind ranged over a wide field of subjects in the fashion of the time, which would have called him a philosopher rather than a critic, he is remembered mostly for his theories on the theatre and for his plays. The former determined the shape of German playwriting to come, the latter gloriously exemplified the former, proved their validity and still belong to the basic repertoire of con-temporary German theatre because of the freshness, profound psy-chology, and realism of their characters and their political and humanitarian messages, which are forever topical. It is important to remember that in a certain sense Lessing was a playwright before he turned critic and theoretician. During his student days in Leipzig (1746–8)—which was then considered a kind of German mini-Paris— he discovered a love for the theatre that distracted him from his theological studies, much to his parents' chagrin.

He was fortunate to be there at the very moment when the bourgeois German theatre was born—a concept that became dear and central to Lessing's thought in years to come, coupled with that of the national theatre. Gottsched's cleaning-up of the completely declassée, unprofessional, and unliterary German stage of the day has been underrated, since it is always seen through the highly polemical, deliberately loaded comments of Lessing, whose *bête noire* was Gottsched. Lessing had many *bêtes noires*. In spite of his fierce honesty, truthfulness, and personal disinterestedness, he was not above being unfair when he felt strongly about something and pushed a cause hard—in this case the fight against mechanical rules in favour of natural and realistic ways of dramatic presentation. What happened in Leipzig under the eyes of young Lessing, fresh from the provinces and new to the ways of the great world, was a drastic reform of acting styles and playwriting. Gottsched favoured and introduced such unknown novelties as rehearsing a play and making actors learn their parts by heart instead of extemporizing in the fashion of the *commedia dell'arte*, and he generally brought the theatre into line with serious and polite literature, which meant for him French Literature, French tragedy, and the comedy of manners. It also meant regular theatre as against the rough-and-ready tumble and the baroque shapelessness of the popular play. And it meant getting rid of Harlequin, the ubiquitous figure on the popular German stage, the symbol of unruliness and low entertainment. Later on, Lessing will talk about the expulsion of Harlequin that was symbolically enacted on the stage of the Neubersches Theater, as 'the greatest harlequinade of them all', and, via Shakespeare and the Greeks, ask for a return to the popular theatre of the past.

During his second stay in Leipzig (when he tried even to rescue the failing Neubersches Theater by lending it his savings—his one and only attempt at involving himself financially in the theatre) a lot of his thoughts on the future of the German theatre must have been germinating. Yet the very first products of his avid theatre going

were plays—first the comedy *Der junge Gelehrte* (*The Young Scholar*)
that was performed by Frau Neuber in 1748 and written very much in
the taste of the time. Another, later in Berlin, followed (*Die Juden*,
The Jews), and many fragments and projects of plays some of which
never materialized, while others took years before they were finished.
The most interesting project of the Berlin years, when Lessing had
become a journalist and editor of magazines and books, was the idea
of writing up a political *cause célèbre* of the day : the arrest, torture,
and execution of the outspoken Swiss journalist Samuel Henzi and
his friends by a despotic, oligarchic government in Berne, a plan that
got no further than one and a half acts, stiffly written (and in Alexandrines, a metre Lessing would soon replace with blank verse). Yet the
dramatic fragment constitutes a landmark in the theatre in that it
dares—in 1749—to project a contemporary subject and a bourgeois
hero straight on to the stage, and in the form of tragedy, a genre
which so far, according to a convention derived from Aristotle, had
been reserved for the sufferings of the great. If finished, this would
have been the first documentary play in history. The idea alone is of
momentous importance : Lessing has seen clearly that the theatre
can and should be a political instrument, that it must be a platform
in the cities from which the writer educates the public socially and
politically.

His next political play, *Minna von Barnhelm*, completed after the
Seven Years' War, is a comedy and uses invented characters. Yet the
events of the day—or rather of yesterday, since the play is set in the
war—are sensed in every word, and its contemporary immediacy
seems to have been overwhelmingly felt. Even now it has a liveliness
and authenticity of atmosphere and mood which are rare in the
theatre. What the public made of it is a different matter. Unlike
Samuel Henzi, which seems to have been an unequivocal plea for
freedom of expression and condemnation of the arbitrary methods of
government by the princes of the day, *Minna von Barnhelm* managed
to be different things to different people. This most famous of German
comedies was taken by most contemporaries to be a pro-Prussian
patriotic play—even by young Goethe, who welcomed it enthusiastic-
ally as 'truly contemporary, a true product of the Seven Years' War
which drew the whole nation's attention to the significant public
events'.

There is certainly much more to it than that, though it might seem enough in view of what was offered by other theatrical fare. For instance, it contains a lot of hidden criticism of a political scene in which an omnipotent monarch arbitrarily decides the fate of his subjects—including one Herr Lessing whom he never forgave an unintended offence against M. Voltaire and who is thus considered unworthy of the post of court librarian, although influential people warmly recommend him; an unknown Frenchman is preferred. The comedy is muted, as in Molière's *Le Misanthrope*. It is full of serious social or personal matter and agonising soul-searchings. Lessing's Protestant heritage makes itself strongly felt. It is an aspect of this and of all his works that makes for their continuing interest. The dramatic character is not a type (as in classical and much classicist comedy). Nor is it an embodiment of superhuman emotion (as in French tragedy). It is, according to a definition in the later work *Hamburgische Dramaturgie*, strongly individualized and possesses an 'inner probability' by acting 'not according to the book but as in real life'. Samuel Henzi *was* a real-life character in the historical sense, Minna and Tellheim, Franziska and Werner *are experienced* as real-life people such as only Molière or Shakespeare had put on the stage before.

The play grew out of a five-year stint as secretary to a Prussian General, von Tauentzien, in occupied Breslau. This was Lessing's most prosperous time financially, and he not only collected his thoughts for the major work on aesthetics *Laokoon* (a study on the varying representational techniques of the different media, precursor of the less academic and antiquarian *Hamburgische Dramaturgie*) but also observed life in the centre of the political stage. The fact is that Lessing, who has the reputation of being a bookworm, a man of theories, of general definitions, and systematic thought, was always guided by concrete personal experience. His plays are drawn as much from his observation of contemporary life and human nature as from thinking about the sayings of the immortal Aristotle, and they are carefully tailored to the practical requirements and possibilities of the stage.

Much later, in the isolation of his court librarian's existence at Wolfenbüttel (near Brunswick) Lessing writes another political play, this time a bourgeois tragedy. In *Emilia Galotti* a classical subject is set in an Italian court and made to carry Lessing's own melancholy experience of princely government. It is tragic because it portrays the bourgeois citizens' total dependence on their sovereign's whims. Short of revolution there is only murder or suicide for the bourgeois of honour and integrity who has been wronged by his prince—the prince in the play attempts to seduce Galotti's virtuous and virginal daughter Emilia. The spirit of impotence and of defiance felt by the bourgeoisie at the time is given eloquent expression, though the play is perhaps a little sentimental to our taste. There is none of the detached, stylized grandeur and horror of French tragedy, but a direct appeal to the pity and fear of a spectator who tomorrow might be in a similar plight himself. Lessing realized his ideal of bourgeois tragedy as against the courtly tragedy of the French in the sense in which he explained it in his *Hamburgische Dramaturgie* : 'The names of princes and heroes will give nothing but pomp and majesty to a play but they do not produce emotion. The misfortunes of people whose circumstances resemble our own most closely will naturally touch us most profoundly, and if we pity kings it is because they are human beings and not because they are kings. Even though their rank makes their mishaps more important, it does not make them more interesting. Whole nations may be involved in them, and yet our sympathy needs an individual object and a nation is far too abstract a concept for our emotions to get engaged.' After seeing the play, Herder, a great friend and admirer of Lessing's, called for a theatre 'where works of this kind would be shown once a week', to make the citizen more aware and teach him to think about his situation.

This is true to the thinking of Lessing, in which the much-debated concept of catharsis is for the first time taken to mean an affect produced in the spectator and is not merely related to the passions presented on the stage. Lessing's definition was that catharsis amounted to a transformation of these passions into virtuous actions on the part of the audience : 'from the purified passions comes the power of thinking, the healing power of art, whereby reason and virtue are seen to be identical'. Goethe called the play 'a decisive step forward towards the indignant moral opposition against tyrannical despotism'. And yet the Austrian Emperor refused to be moved and commented cheerfully : 'Never in my life have I laughed as much in a tragedy.' Which only goes to prove Lessing's point about the unbridgeable gap between the ruler and the ruled, and about the arrogant insensitivity and unreasonableness of the aristocracy and royalty of the time.

Small though his actual output as a playwright may have been, Lessing showed himself in his plays as a masterly political analyst and dialectician, a careful and shrewd craftsman, and a very interesting psychologist. His characters, measured as they are against the high enlightenment standards of virtue, are by no means simple or one-dimensional. The virtuous are always struggling and are always intensely vulnerable. The vicious are shown to be trapped tragically in their class, their upbringing or the political system, and the happy endings of *Minna* and *Nathan der Weise* (*Nathan the Wise*)—Lessing's last play in which he preaches universal tolerance in religious and racial matters—are narrow escapes and ideal philosophical solutions.

Because of his advocacy of reason, of bourgeois emancipation, of realism and the positive hero, Lessing has become the darling of Marxist literary criticism. Nobody owes more to him than Bertolt Brecht, in spite of his anti-Aristotelianism. Yet for all his emphasis on realism, Lessing was putting forward not a simple doctrine of endorsing reality, but rather an outline for the future; and he was for ever aware of a threat—both constitutional and social—to man's rationality and goodness. That he managed to stick to his belief in the educability of man, in his ability to act reasonably and to exercise tolerance is a remarkable feat, considering the treatment he got in an unfree age as an upright freethinker and as a dependent on patrons and princes. If anyone ever lived what he preached, it was Lessing, who defined the true dramatic character as a character who never acts without intention and thus teaches the spectator to think. Like his Faust, he was motivated by one powerful drive—the search for truth and knowledge. To this he sacrificed a more comfortable and almost certainly more outwardly brilliant career in the university or church, the prospect of domesticity, and material security; for it he constantly risked his reputation and, at times, even his personal security. This is the red thread that runs through his checkered career of theology student, freelance literary journalist, magazine and book editor, secretary, playwright, dramaturg and theatre critic, author of polemical academic pamphlets, of learned philosophical and theological discourses, of open letters to eminent personalities, of fables and epigrams, librarian, and instigator of important new departures in the literature and thought of his country.

The most intriguing aspect of his personality and his influence lies in the interaction of theory and practice. These are the two equally important expressions of one mind, there is no lecturing in the plays,

no special pleading in the theorizing. The plays were written to set
an example, no doubt, an example of the bourgeois drama, the
bourgeois comedy, the bourgeois tragedy, yet they were also the
spontaneous expressions of a born dramatic writer. The theories are
usually triggered by an occasion: a book or ideas put forward by
somebody else, the lucky chance of being offered a platform from
which to make himself heard (in Berlin the *Letters Concerning Modern
Literature*, in Hamburg the *Hamburgische Dramaturgie*) or personal
and spiritual experiences (as the religious polemics which occupied the
last years of his life and culminated in the 'dramatic poem' *Nathan
der Weise*). His argumentative, witty mind excelled in dialogue. When
not writing dialogue for the stage he writes in the form of letters or as
if talking to an imaginary partner in a conversation, an opponent in
a debate. Thus, weighing the pros and cons, if only as a method of
argument, as a stratagem, like Socrates, he arrives at his conclusions,
carrying the reader with him as no abstract learned discourse or
dogmatic manifesto will ever do.

The most important work, apart from the plays, is the *Hamburgische
Dramaturgie*. It is the product of a dismal failure—an attempt at
setting up—in 1767—a subsidized, national theatre by a group of
enterprising Hamburg businessmen—and it is again an illustration of
the way in which Lessing managed to coin gold out of the most
unpromising, untoward circumstances. He had been called to Hamburg, as Germany's foremost playwright and critic, to help the enterprise off the ground, and had been offered the post of writer-in-
residence. He came as its critic-in-residence instead, to reserve himself some freedom, the freedom of the observer, and not to be told
what to write or what to do. Twice weekly he was to write a piece
reviewing the performances on stage, but also, according to the purpose of the magazine, ambitiously called *Hamburgische Dramaturgie*,
he was to put down his thoughts on theatre in general, on acting,
writing for the stage, building up a repertoire of plays, educating an
audience and so on. In fact, he was meant to contribute on his part to
the 'improvement of German theatre' as much as the actual performances on the stage. In other words one hoped that the presence of
Germany's foremost theatre writer would ensure the success of the
venture.

The national theatre was an idea very much to Lessing's taste: it
was to be a theatre not dependent, as the court theatre, on an aristo-

cratic patron who acted as a censor nor, as the strolling companies and the handful of private theatres, on the vagaries of a paying public, whose vulgar taste dictated the choice of plays, an enterprise not dominated by box office concerns or the arbitrary taste of a high-ranking individual. This seemed to be the perfect answer at last to Lessing's demands for a truly bourgeois, truly indigenous German theatre. Yet the narrow-mindedness and petty rivalries of the bene-factors and the indifference of the audience killed the project after little more than a year. As Lessing had put it in 1760: 'We have no theatre, we have no actors, we have no spectators. The Frenchman at least has a stage, the German has hardly a hut.' Yet this new tomb-stone on the rough road to a viable German theatre is different from all the earlier ones in that it planted an idea which was to persist for years and even centuries to come: the idea of the serious national theatre supported by an educated audience and subsidized by an impartial body, a scene of real action, an arena of topical ideas, a focusing point for true theatrical talent. Very soon there would be attempts in Mannheim to found another national theatre, this time successfully, and Lessing was again asked to participate; but the negotiations got stuck and petered out. While the Hamburg stage was run by the actor manager Friedrich Schröder (privately, yet in many ways as Lessing would have wanted it), Mannheim staged the first play by another truly national dramatist, Friedrich Schiller's *Die Räuber* (*The Robbers*) a contemporary and highly explosive subject. It was a revolutionary theatrical and political event. Lessing, unfortunately, had died a year before. What would he have said about this idiosyncratic sapling from his very own tree?

To return to the 'Hamburgische Dramaturgie', the only enduring product of the fated and unfortunate project in Hamburg. After a few months of happy week-by-week reviewing, mostly with an eye on acting styles and pursuing the aim of establishing the fundamental rules of this art, he found that the actors objected to his close analyses of their work and threatened to walk out. From then on Lessing con-fined his articles to general discussions which may have been to the benefit of posterity. There would not be another treatise on the theatre as profound and influential in Germany until Brecht. How-ever much the plays of Goethe, Schiller, Kleist, or Grillparzer—to name only the great classical dramatists—might deviate from the findings and precepts of Lessing, they are all products of a total absorption of his ideas in the cultural climate of the time. No German play worth its salt would again strive to be regular in the French sense or merely entertaining. The 'new' unities of character and plot, defined in terms of truth to nature or 'realism', have not been doubted until the expressionist and the absurdist theatre put out their anti-realist and more subjective ideas.

Yet most important and influential of all proved to be Lessing's emphasis on the social function of the theatre, its role in the life of the German nation as a 'moral institution', as first his enemies and then Schiller would define it, as a place where 'the spectator is purified of his passions and made to think' (or changed, as Brecht later had it). To the non-German who expects his theatre primarily to be entertaining, this is probably the most German aspect of Lessing's theatrical gospel. Yet the gaiety and briskness of Lessing's own plays and his blunt insistence on immediacy and interest of plot and charac-ter should make the foreign sceptic reconsider his prejudice against the apparent overseriousness of our legendary *praeceptor Germaniae*. Lessing is less dogmatic than Brecht, than Goethe, or Schiller, the three other theoreticians and great creative minds of the German theatre; he is perhaps the wittiest and certainly the most economical and lucid stylist of them all. On stage and on the printed page he never bores—something that cannot be said with honesty of the other illustrious three. Whatever he did was unexpected and dramatic. He set ideas in motion, stirred up hidden troubles, made people think, laugh and feel disturbed. This last is, perhaps, his most valuable and most enduring achievement.

2

H. M. Waidson and T. M. Holmes: THE SHAKESPEAREAN STRAIN

Although rough and ready popular plays based on Shakespeare were performed in Germany by English travelling companies through much of the 17th century,[1] the literary reception of the great English dramatist was delayed until nearly half way through the 18th. Writing in 1682 of John Dryden's drama criticism, D. G. Morhof admits that he has seen nothing of Shakespeare, Beaumont or Fletcher, the playwrights whom Dryden discusses. Andreas Gryphius's *Herr Peter Squentz* (1657) seems to have taken the names of 'Squentz' and 'Butäin' only indirectly, via Daniel Schwenter, from a version of *A Midsummer Night's Dream*, perhaps performed as an intermezzo by one of the English troupes. The eventual impact of the authentic Shakespeare on mid-18th century Germany was, however, profound and powerful, contributing to a tremendous upsurge of critical polemic, creative inspiration, and cultural and social awareness.

J. G. Robertson sees in the seventeenth of Lessing's *Briefe, die neueste Litteratur betreffend* (*Epistles concerning the Most Recent Literature*) of February 16, 1759 'the most daring appreciation of Shakespeare to be found in any German writer before the *Sturm und Drang*'.[2] Yet Robertson speaks of Lessing's 'paradoxical assertion ... that Shakespeare was a more faithful observer of the laws of Aristotle than Corneille' (p. 245), whereas Lessing makes no mention of any 'laws' in this context. Lessing's point is that Shakespeare fulfils the final purpose of tragedy without adopting the ways and means of the Greeks. His own 'characteristic' approach may seem 'strange' compared with the classical tradition, but nevertheless it usually works. Shakespeare is judged alongside classical tragedy only insofar as both are great examples of the genre; and he may be said to be a good Aristotelian only as regards Aristotle's indication of the fundamental aim of tragedy. Where Aristotle prescribes regulations for the attainment of that end, Shakespeare diverges from him, deploying his own fund of tragic methods and materials.

The same view of Shakespeare's genius is crystallized in a passage from Lessing's *Philologischer Nachlaß* (*Philological Bequest*) which Robertson cites (p. 249 n.) without commenting: 'A great deal is said about Shakespeare's defects ... I believe that I can provide a reason for nearly every one of these defects. He incurs them in order to achieve the principal object and produce all the more vivid an emotional effect on the audience.' Lessing's admission of the word 'defects' is surely ironical, for if Shakespeare's transgressions of the classical canon are precisely the means by which he attains 'the principal object' they cannot be judged failings.

Invoking the unitary criterion of aesthetic impact Lessing dissolves the typical dilemma of the neo-classical critics, who are inclined to weigh Shakespeare's indubitable effect uneasily against his grave infractions of the literary rules. This attitude may be exemplified in German criticism by C. M. Wieland the first systematic German translator of Shakespeare[3], who writes 'Je l'aime avec toutes ses fautes' (to Zimmermann, April 24, 1758). Book X of Wieland's novel *Agathon* (1766–7) opens with a digression on Shakespeare in which Wieland observes that his irregularities have often been criticized, but that his intuitive portrayal of human characters has no equal since Homer.[4] He clearly attributes to Shakespeare's drama all the shortcomings of the *Haupt- und Staatsaktionen* which were often in reality corrupt versions of Shakespeare's dramas, first introduced into Germany at the end of the 16th century by the English travelling players, and suitably simplified and vulgarized for performance to popular German-speaking audiences.[5] As late as 1784 Wieland says in his journal *Der teutsche Merkur*, 'Shakespeare's plays are for the most part *Haupt- und Staatsaktionen*'. Lessing on the other hand deplores the 'nonsense, bombast, filth, and vulgar mirth' of the old popular stage (seventeenth 'Literaturbrief') without suggesting the remotest comparison between this tradition and Shakespeare's drama, for as we have seen, Lessing confirms the logical structure of Shakespeare's creativity, establishing his alleged faults as integral moments in his aesthetic achievement.

Lessing's assessment of Shakespeare is not, of course, disinterested. He suggests in the seventeenth 'Literaturbrief' that Shakespeare's genius may inspire a recrudescence of German creative writing. He asserts that the German people will find Shakespeare much more to its liking than French tragedy, for Shakespeare offers more complexity, more spectacle, weightier impressions and emotions—and more occasion for thought. What is the reason for the Germans' preference in this matter? The answer we may infer from Lessing's aesthetic writings turns as much on the great historical issues of his time as on questions of literary taste.

In order to construe this answer we have to revert to the Shakespeare digression in Wieland's *Agathon*, which Lessing quotes and comments on in section LXIX of his *Hamburgische Dramaturgie* (1767–8). The digression takes the form of a mock vindication of the *Haupt- und Staatsaktion*. Wieland proposes, tongue in cheek, that such monstrosities may be justified on the ground that they mirror the confusion and absurdity of real life. The particular relevance of this satire to contemporary German conditions is conveyed by the ironical hesitancy with which Wieland suggests that the dramatic farrago (the *Mischspiel*, as Lessing terms it) might be thought to reflect not only personal but also ('if we may be permitted to say so') *political* affairs. Wieland implies that the petty leviathans of the German political scene are run like real-life *Haupt- und Staatsaktionen*, with villains or poltroons in the majestical roles, and clowns, pimps, and knaves meddling in the business of the state. It is a calamitous situation that admits of neither organic development nor sensible initiative.

Lessing appreciates the satirical point of the passage he cites. For the sake of the argument, however, he replies to this defence of the *Mischspiel* as if it were meant to be taken seriously. He does not deny that art consists in the imitation of nature, but he objects that the *Mischspiel* reproduces only one half of nature; it leaves out of account human subjectivity and the human faculties, which make possible a coherent perception of the outer world. This cognitive and volitional activity protects us from falling prey to a promiscuous host of impressions, and enables us to participate, at least indirectly, in the overall sense and scheme of creation. The dramatic mélange presents only confused snatches of reality and does not enable us to reach a higher perception that would transcend and pattern the particulars we glimpse.

Shakespeare's art, Lessing intimates, is of a quite different order. Contrasting C. F. Weisse's and Shakespeare's *Richard III* in section

LXXIII of the *Hamburgische Dramaturgie*, he likens Shakespearean drama to a *camera obscura* into which the landscape painter peers 'in order to learn how all nature's facets are projected on to a *single* plane'. One cannot borrow piecemeal from Shakespeare, for he offers an integral, all-embracing vision, with every detail incorporated in the grand contours of historical drama. Shakespeare surveys the plenitude of nature and history, rendering it coherent and communicable. Whereas Weisse's *Richard III* presents us wth starkly isolated elements of cruelty and evil, the scale and structure of Shakespeare's drama would seem to fulfil Lessing's demand that such impressions be subordinated to an ultimate vision of Providence : 'The whole fashioned by this mortal creator [i.e. the poet] should be a silhouette of the whole of the eternal Creator and accustom us to the thought that all things are resolved for the best therein, as they are in the work of art' (Section LXXIX).

The serious drama cannot content itself with depicting such discontinuous aspects of life as the odious crimes of Richard III or the stagnation and buffoonery of German duodecimo absolutism. Art moves beyond these fragments to the teleological patterning of reality; it is not mesmerized by the instant, but surveys a prospect of development and meaning. The implication is that the Germans will appreciate and profit from Shakespeare inasmuch as the scope and vitality of his drama may aid them to visualize the reactivation of their own history in a framework far transcending the closed, corrupt political world of their present time. But it would seem misleading to speak of a people simply *contemplating* its own national revival; it is clear that such a perspective would be inseparable from the actions and purposes of those involved. Seen in this light the Shakespearean precept has relevance not merely for historical epistemology but also for a progressive social *praxis* in Germany.

In his essay *Shakespear* (1773) Herder sets out to explode the frame of reference of traditional Shakespeare controversy, within which even Shakespeare's supporters had always felt obliged to qualify their admiration by conceding that he contravenes the rules. Instead of judging Shakespeare by extraneous norms, Herder wants to teach us to see him for what he is. Only then shall we appreciate how Shakespeare fulfils in his own way as perfectly as Sophocles the one 'rule' of tragedy, the aim of conveying a 'particular emotional impact' through engaging the imagination of the audience. To this end Herder applies a comparative historical approach to Shakespeare, pioneered in Germany in the *Briefe über Merkwürdigkeiten der Literatur* (*Epistles on Curiosities of Literature*, 1766–7) of H. W. von Gerstenberg, who had drawn in turn on the work of contemporary French and English critics like Brumoy and Hurd. Herder contrasts the historical origins of Greek and Shakespearean drama, demonstrating in this way the irrelevance of criteria derived from the former for an appreciation of the nordic bard. Whereas Greek drama epitomizes the essential simplicity of the political, cultural, and religious forms of life in which it is sited, Shakespeare's drama reflects the multifarious and problematic existence he encountered in a totally different epoch. Shakespeare's dramas are not unified along a single strand of action, but follow the trajectory of a complex event of world-historical proportions. He penetrates the diffuse, shifting fullness of his age and renders it panopticon: 'A world of dramatic history; but the creator gives us the vision and the viewpoint to scan its breadth and depth.'

Shakespeare's plays are seen as the massive 'ruins of chivalry', witness to the dissolution of the old feudal order. The guilt and suffering of the characters are intrinsic to this momentous historical event. The significance of the process is not, however, exhausted in the tragic destiny of the participants, for the dark symbols trace the 'radiant locus of a divine theodicy'. It is important to see this positive dimension of Herder's reading of Shakespeare not as a spiritual consolation but as a concrete social prospect, and to grasp this point we must understand the emphasis Herder lays on Shakespeare's roots in the people of England. The interest in the common people which we find in much *Sturm und Drang* literature is connected not only with an awakening taste for the unspoiled vitality of their art but also with the belief that the people alone were capable of creating the *material* basis for a German national revival. The circle around Herder and Goethe in Frankfurt propagated the economic ideas of the French physiocrats, who taught that nature, or the land, was the sole source of wealth, the class of smallholders the real producer of surplus value. Herder is drawn to folk poetry as the expression of life in close and vigorous interaction with nature, and it seems reasonable to suppose that in collecting German folksongs he is conscious of documenting the well-springs of both cultural and economic creativity in his own land. Herder considers Shakespeare a popular writer who draws his materials from English folksongs, ballads, romances and popular chronicles. Herein is the reason for the enormous difference between Shakespeare's strength and the vapidity of French literature, which is a 'lady of the metropolis' remote from the vibrant culture of the countryside.[6] Whereas the *tragédie classique* is bound in the rigid ethos of the old ruling class, Shakespeare's dramas are an undismayed record of the violent demise of that regime, seen as it were by the bearers of the future, a people already capable of directing and utilizing the revolutionary flux.

The political and economic underdevelopment of 18th century Germany, however, implied a depressed and unenterprising peasantry. There was in Germany no such sturdy yeoman farmer class as existed in France and more especially in England, and upon which physiocratic theory was predicated. The very social backwardness that made the younger German intellectuals so receptive to progressive currents of thought was just as likely to condemn their enthusiasm to impracticability. This dilemma is reflected in the literature of the *Sturm und Drang*, which delights in Shakespeare's world of action and movement but portrays in its own dramatic works idealists and sentimentalists thwarted in their practical ambitions. F. M. Klinger, contemporary and friend of Goethe in Frankfurt in the early seventeen-seventies, uses motifs from *King Lear* in his first play *Otto* (1775), while others of his dramas of that decade also show his liking for Shakespearean dramatic structure and situations, including *Sturm und Drang* (1777) with its lovers between inimical families and its melancholy irony against a background of the American War of Independence. But Klinger's *Die Zwillinge* (*The Twins*, 1776) was recognized as a powerful expression of the frustration of his generation; Guelfo's narrow circumstances in this drama turn his longing for greatness to pathological envy and malice.

The young Goethe's play *Götz von Berlichingen* (1773) may be seen as meeting in some respects Herder's wish for a German creative response to the mighty stimulus of Shakespeare, but it reveals an underlying divergence from Herder's Shakespeare model, determined by the uneasy conjuncture in German ideology and history outlined above. In his address *Zum Schäkespears Tag* (*For Shakespeare's Name-Day*, 1771) Goethe tells how Shakespeare's thrilling example set him free at a stroke from imprisonment in the classical rules to discover a spontaneous, natural creativity. James Boyd calls *Götz* 'the first direct result of his Shakespeare worship' and details the

. .

manifold points of correspondence with a wide range of Shakespeare's principal plays.[7] Herder had rounded off his essay on Shakespeare by encouraging Goethe to complete, for the sake of their now sadly degenerate Fatherland, this 'monument to Shakespeare' wrought in Germany's own history and language. Roy Pascal notes, however, that neither in the speech *Zum Schäkespears Tag* nor in *Götz* do we detect the sense of a divine teleology so important for Herder's understanding of Shakespeare.[8] Shakespeare's plays, Goethe declaims in his speech, 'turn all upon the hidden point (which no philosopher has seen and defined) in which the specific quality of our ego, the assumed freedom of our will clashes with the necessary course of the whole'. The necessity that triumphs here is not designated divine and might indeed be identified with the age of deceit and decadence which finally crushes the ingenuous, independent spirit of Götz. It has been argued on the other hand that the very choice of historical theme in *Götz*, together with the association of the principal figure with the lower classes and the restless, genre-breaking form and tempo employed for these new types of content, represent in themselves a crucial ideological advance. In the last analysis, however, this message is seriously qualified under the sheer weight of adversity. Götz's dying invocation, 'Freedom! Freedom!', echoes ambiguously across a social and moral devastation in which even the people have betrayed his trust. Some hope is perhaps transmitted obliquely in Lerse's words to Götz, 'Woe to posterity if it heed you not!' The play ends with no concrete symbol of renewal, but with this epitaph, which may or may not serve as salutary provocation for the future.

Goethe's *Egmont* (1775–88) is also indebted to Shakespeare, drawing particularly on his portrayal of the noble, popular and gigantic figure of Julius Caesar. The composition of the play spans a far-reaching transition in Goethe's development, and after the opening the 'thronged Elizabethan stage' tends to give way to more intimate and 'classical' scenes.[9] The drama ends with the suppression of political freedom, but a dream vision of liberation inspires Egmont to a confident, heroic posture, out of keeping with the circumstances but vindicated by the 'triumphal symphony' that follows the curtain. The spirit of Egmont lives on, but, unlike Julius Caesar's, it is not seen translated into seething political reality. The promise of regeneration is conveyed by the incorporeal agencies of music and allegory, and not through the activity of the people, who figure prominently at the start but are dispersed and demoralized by the close. We may perhaps see in this development a step towards the theatrical symbolism which Goethe preferred in later life to the density and vitality of Shakespeare's style. Looking back in 1825 on his earlier career, Goethe congratulates himself on having got Shakespeare out of his system in *Götz* and *Egmont*, for he feels now that Shakespeare's impact may overwhelm the writer who is exposed to him too often (conversation with Eckermann, December 25).

Goethe's move to the court at Weimar in 1775 marks a turning point in his attitudes to art and society. The fusion of titanism and populism, projected yet questioned too in the literature of the *Sturm und Drang*, he now abandons as a practical concept for national resurgence. Progress is to be pursued henceforth indirectly, in practice through cameral influence, in art through intimation of the ideal. The older Goethe's insistence that Shakespeare expresses the vigorous national history of England brings out the gulf that separates their worlds, and thus provides the rationale for his peculiar handling of Shakespeare on the Weimar stage. From 1791 Goethe took charge of the reorganized Weimar court theatre and cultivated a harmonious and decorous style of production extending even to the performance of Shakespeare's dramas. A good example was his production of Schiller's very free version of *Macbeth* (1800), in which he further enhanced Schiller's ennobling treatment of the witches by casting beautiful young girls in the parts and instructing them in slow and impressive incantation. There was also his 'amazing travesty' of *Romeo and Juliet* presented in 1812 on the basis of A. W. Schlegel's translation.[10]

The discussions of Hamlet in Goethe's *Wilhelm Meisters Lehrjahre* (*Wilhelm Meister's Apprentice Years*, 1795–6) suggest a unifying theme of the play: 'a great deed is enjoined upon a soul incapable of carrying it out' (Book 4, Chapter 13). But the dramatic integrity Wilhelm stresses does not in his view symbolize a universal teleology. The historical perspective of Shakespearean drama is grimly and laconically characterized: 'One generation is mown down and another one springs up' (Book 4, Chapter 15). For all its vitality and psychological profundity Shakespeare's dramatic world is seen as reducible to a succession of brutal incidents lacking any promise of development. In his *Shakespeare und kein Ende* (*Shakespeare and No End*, 1813–26) Goethe deems Shakespeare 'untheatrical' since in his opinion no action is theatrical which is not symbolical, which does not refer to some deeper level of meaning. Goethe's conception of symbolical drama is exemplified perhaps in his own *Iphigenie auf Tauris* (1787) in which a train of violence and evil is terminated by the heroine's resonant act of trust. The future is vouchsafed, not as it was for the younger Herder in the energetic detail, mass, and movement of Shakespeare's realism, but in the sublime morality of an idealized individual. This turn from Shakespeare may itself be taken as symbolizing the historical sequestration of Weimar's coterie classicism, its virtual withdrawal from the public sphere to an unconquerable realm of the spirit.

But Shakespeare also penetrated at this time to rather humbler levels of cultural consciousness. A tribute to his impact in J. J. Eschenburg's translation is to be found in *Etwas über William Shakespeares Schauspiele* (*Something about William Shakespeare's Plays*) by the Swiss peasant-farmer and yarn pedlar Ulrich Bräker. These rapturous but not uncritical commentaries on thirty-six plays were written in 1780, but not published until 1877.

In his medical dissertation on the interaction of body and mind (1780) the young Friedrich Schiller takes Shakespeare's Cassius, Richard III, and Lady Macbeth as clinical examples, treating these dramatic figures as fully realized human beings. This implicit acknowledgment of the profound veracity of Shakespeare's character drawing places Schiller in a critical tradition going back at least as far as Pope's statement that 'every single character in Shakespeare is as much an individual as those in life itself' (1725). J. E. Schlegel, Wieland, and Gerstenberg all ascribe a pivotal importance to this aspect of Shakespeare's art, and J. M. R. Lenz in his *Anmerkungen übers Theater* (*Observations on the Theatre*), written about 1771, contrasts Shakespeare's tragedies, in which 'the hero alone provides the key to his own fate', with Greek tragedy, in which an external fate decrees the dramatic nexus. All Shakespeare's characters, says Lenz, whatever their social status, 'feel warm blood beating in their hearts'. Schiller's earlier works, especially his first drama *Die Räuber* (*The Robbers*, 1781) abound in Shakespearean characteristics. The deformed Franz Moor, a sophistic villain, has touches of Iago and obvious affinities with Richard III. His brother Karl oscillates between impassioned revolt on the fearful scale of Shakespeare's activists, and a brooding hesitancy that recalls Hamlet. The plight of their father,

Old Moor, is reminiscent of Gloucester. This emphasis on Shake-spearean range and vividness of character has a political significance; *Die Räuber* drew upon a story by C. F. D. Schubart entitled *Zur Geschichte des menschlichen Herzens* (*On the History of the Human Heart*, 1775), which the author had recommended as proof that Germany too could produce great characters and actions despite the 'form of government that enjoins on the German a merely passive condition'. The enormity of the drama denotes an attempt to trans-cend the restrictive pettiness of German circumstances and match the intensity of Shakespeare's world. 'Give me an army of fellows like me,' cries Karl Moor, 'and out of Germany shall spring a republic that will make Rome and Sparta look like nunneries.'

At the end of the drama, however, Karl is made to realize how perilously close he has come to destroying the entire fabric of the moral world. The stirring impulse to violent renewal is seen at length pessimistically, deflected and distorted in the gross medium of the age. A suppressed foreword explains that *Die Räuber* necessarily violates both theatrical and ethical propriety in order to give a true copy of life, but by 1784 Schiller has clearly distanced himself from the strident tone of this play, and declares in the prospectus for his journal, the *Rheinische Thalia*, that its excesses were born of the tension between genius and subordination, that they are symptomatic and not truly mimetic. This prompt apostasy indicates Schiller's gravi-tation away from the discouraging terrain of a specific political struggle. He now styles himself a 'citizen of the world', anticipating his ascension to an Olympian cosmopolitanism alongside Goethe—and under the patronage of the Duke of Weimar.

In his treatise *Über naive und sentimentalische Dichtung* (*On Naive and Sentimental Poetry*, 1795–6) Schiller discerns in retrospect a deep gulf that had always existed between Shakespeare's sensibility and his own. He had found in Shakespeare's representations of human life a certain 'coldness', as for instance in the ruthless juxtaposition of deeply moving and comical incidents (in his translation of *Macbeth* he replaced the porter's bawdy humour wth a pious song). He now sees this contrast of temperaments as exemplifying an historico-typo-logical distinction between 'naive' and 'sentimental' poetry. The naive poet like Shakespeare is at one with nature, creating intuitively and impersonally from within it; the sentimental poet is aware, as Schiller was himself, of being dislodged from this state, and projects forfeit nature as a conscious ideal, to be infinitely pursued but never finally repossessed.

But there is nothing of Herder's 'folk poetry' in Schiller's concept of the naive. He does not now regard Shakespeare as an exponent of the 'naturalism' that he criticises in, for example, the poetry of G. A. Bürger. Indeed he comes to speak of Shakespeare's 'abstractions' from reality, as when he distills a few ideal voices from 'the mass and the mob' in *Julius Caesar* (to Goethe, April 7, 1797). In *Richard III*, too, Shakespeare had 'represented what could not be presented' and 'used symbols where nature cannot be depicted'. The play is dominated by an 'exalted nemesis' that draws it close to Greek tragedy (to Goethe, November 28, 1797). Schiller's sense of a kinship between Shakespeare and Sophocles influenced the conception of his *Wallenstein* trilogy (1798–9). The first part, *Wallensteins Lager* (*Wallenstein's Encampment*), features a Shakespearean crowd in the form of the Imperial army, but already in the *Prolog* (written for the reopening of the Weimar court theatre in 1798) this mass is seen explicitly as a component of Wallenstein's tragic destiny, functionalized as the occasion of his *hubris*:

> It was his power that seduced his heart,
> The picture of the camp explains his crime.

Schiller even suggested in his essay *Über den Gebrauch des Chors in der Tragödie* (*On the Use of the Chorus in Tragedy*, 1803) that a classical chorus would heighten the artistry of Shakespeare's drama by arresting the flow of events and expatiating on their underlying significance.

Schiller proposes a view of Shakespeare that would qualify him for Goethe's 'symbolical' theatre, minimizing the elements of force, pace, and quiddity that Herder had so vividly evoked in his essay on the English dramatist. His view should be seen in relation to the political structure that sustained Weimar classicism. The dramaturgical policies of a state theatre like that of the Weimar court naturally reflected the political attitudes of its absolutist patron; 'depth' on the Weimar stage was no doubt much preferable to disruption, especially after the experience of the French Revolution.

In 1803 Goethe produced *Julius Caesar* in A. W. Schlegel's translation, which had a deep effect on Schiller, 'buoying up' work on his last drama *Wilhelm Tell* (1804). His dramatization of the Swiss national uprising exudes a Shakespearean feeling of variety and activity, with the corporate and individual crisis reverberating in nature itself. Inevitably though it lacks the radical, shattering force Herder attributed to Shakespeare, for it celebrates a conservative and legitimist movement, which Schiller by implication contrasts with the French Revolution in the verses he sent with the play to Karl Theodor von Dalberg.

Friedrich Schlegel's treatise *Über das Studium der griechischen Poesie* (*On the Study of Greek Poetry*, 1797) is an important document of the gestation of Romantic literary theory. His contrast between 'ancient' and 'modern' types of literature parallels Schiller's classification of 'naive' and 'sentimental' and prefigures the definition of 'classical' and 'romantic'. For Schlegel Shakespeare represents 'the pinnacle of modern poetry'. There is a complete reversal of Schiller's allocation of Shakespeare to the 'naive' category; Schlegel insists that Shakespeare is 'never objective, but mannered throughout,' by which he means that the author's intention, imagination, and individuality always dominate the mere subject-matter of his art. The common people, Schlegel thinks, have appreciated only the realistic aspect of Shakespeare's dramas and missed the crucial 'philosophical' dimension. In the lectures Schlegel gave in Vienna in 1812 entitled *Geschichte der alten und neuen Literatur* (*History of Ancient and Modern Literature*) he modified his earlier assessment of Shakespeare. Shakespeare's representation of life, he now states, too often takes the form of an unanswered 'riddle', a knot of confusions and complications. The solutions or deeper meanings we glimpse fleetingly in this 'old nordic' writer await full realization in the future in some 'higher poetry' revealing the 'hidden life of the very soul of man and nature', and inspired at least as much by the 'lyrical', transfiguring art of Calderon as by Shakespeare himself.

Friedrich's brother August Wilhelm Schlegel, whose uncle Johann Elias had made a not insignificant contribution to the understanding of Shakespeare in Germany a generation earlier, was to become a key-figure in the story of the German appreciation of the English dramatist. His essay *Etwas über William Shakespeare bei Gelegenheit 'Wilhelm Meisters'* (*Something about Shakespeare in the Context of Wilhelm Meister*, 1796) reviews in percipient detail Goethe's approach to Shakespeare in this novel, gives his own enthusiastic and judicious summary of the dramatist's qualities, and anticipates his own method

of working as translator. The seventeen plays that Schlegel translated
into German are in 'secular literature, perhaps the mightiest of all
miracles that has ever been accomplished by a translator of the
German language', Emil Staiger writes;[11] he also makes reference
to criticism that Schlegel's language is often too soft, too lyrical, too
dependent on atmosphere and lacking in the strong accents of the
Renaissance poet, though he does not accept these strictures as reasonable. Schlegel's closeness to the original Staiger also commends, while
he finds that 'over his German Shakespeare there lies a soft romantic
aura, something that . . . from afar recalls the taperings of idealistic
thinking'. The style and atmosphere of Schlegel's translations made a
substantial contribution to the dramatic writing of Kleist, Grillparzer,
Hebbel and Otto Ludwig, Staiger further states. Seven lectures are
devoted to Shakespeare in Schlegel's *Vorlesungen über dramatische
Kunst und Literatur* (*Lectures on Dramatic Art and Literature*, 1809),
four of which give a clear, informative and elegantly expressed commentary on the individual plays. The personality of Hamlet, he
explains, he sees in a less favourable light than did Goethe; Schlegel
proceeds to give chapter and verse to back up his view. In the historical
plays Shakespeare nearly always succeeds in combining concentrated
excerpts with a living sense of unfolding. Othello is 'a tragic
Rembrandt'. 'As in *Macbeth* terror reaches its highest peak, so in
King Lear the subject of pity is treated exhaustively.' The fairies
and witches illustrate Shakespeare's closeness to folk-poetry and to the
secret motive-forces of nature. Form must be conceived organically
with Shakespeare, as in nature; at different times and places the
spirit of poetry requires other forms (Schlegel is following Herder
here). The plays of Shakespeare and his contemporaries are, from the
classical point of view, neither tragedies nor comedies, 'they are just
romantic plays'. Schlegel's definition of the romantic, in the context
of Shakespeare, points to indissoluble mixtures, the blending of
opposites, the fragmentary, a drive towards chaos that comes nearer
to the secret of the Universe. If classical Greek tragedy can be recalled
in a group of sculptured figures, romantic drama is a picturesque
painting which gives colours and rich background as well as the more
sensitive inwardness revealed in its portrayal of facial expression.
Schlegel's appreciation of Shakespeare is warm and unequivocal:

For me he is a profound artist, not a blind, wild-running genius.

He links together all that is high and deep in his being, and the strangest, indeed apparently most incompatible qualities exist in him peacefully side by side.

Where the actually tragic element comes in, all irony certainly stops; but from the confessed humour of comedy onwards until the point where the submission of mortal beings beneath an unavoidable fate requires strict seriousness, there is a crowd of human conditions which, it is true, may be regarded with irony without confusing the eternal boundary-mark between good and evil.

But let no one lay hand on Shakespeare's works in order to change anything essential about them: such action always punishes itself.

Ludwig Tieck gives an affectionate and thoughtful fictional portrait of Shakespeare in a sequence of three tales. The first, *Das Fest zu Kenelworth (The Festivities at Kenilworth*, 1828), is a short story which acts as a prologue to the two more extended narratives that are to follow, rather as the one-act prelude ushers in the two five-act dramas of Schiller's *Wallenstein*. As a boy of eleven William would like to go with others from Stratford to the unique celebrations at Kenilworth in honour of the Queen's visit. His father, unappreciative of the arts and of festivities that he considers frivolous, arouses fear and frustrations in the youngster that are only partially allayed by his mother and friends such as the Hathaways. The first part of *Dichterleben (Poet's Life*, 1826) takes place when Marlowe is working on his 'devil's tragedy' and Shakespeare is confirming his reputation with the presentation of *Romeo and Juliet*. Shakespeare is contrasted with Robert Greene and Marlowe. While the younger man is to them a quiet stranger who can make unexpectedly brilliant speeches about the desirability of blending wit and lightness with heroism and passion or about England's historic role, these more established figures on the contemporary literary scene are above all concerned with their own affairs. Greene needs to be reconciled to his wife, while for Marlowe relationships with women are subordinate to his burning ambitions as poet. Marlowe, after experiencing the impact of *Romeo and Juliet*, comes to realize that he is no longer the leading figure among playwrights of his time; his violent death is contingent upon the loss of his self-confidence as a writer. The creative artist is seen here by Tieck as threatened by dark forces, though essentially these are aspects of his own nature which he cannot control; yet his way of life contains a fineness and open vitality which are shown in contrast to the deluded narrowness of Arthington, an adherent of a fanatical sect which features in a sub-plot.

The second part of *Dichterleben* is sub-titled 'The Poet and his Friend' (1831). If as a small boy Tieck's William was emotionally vulnerable, at the time of the encounters with Greene and Marlowe he was more self-sufficient and apparently unproblematic. Now, a little time after the deaths of Greene and Marlowe, Shakespeare's deepest feelings are absorbed in his friendship for the eighteen-year-old Henry, Earl of Southampton. He says to him:

> ... forgive me that you are too precious to me, that I love you too intensely; too unnaturally, most people would say, too exaggeratedly, unhealthily, madly. And this is how it may be, for after all I do not see this sort of friendship among other people.

The poet recounts to Southampton the more significant phases of his earlier life—the continued hostility of his father to his artistic interests, the unplanned intimacy with Johanna Hathaway that led to an uncongenial marriage which soon broke down. Tieck's reconstruction of the poet's Stratford past provides an inset-story of considerable sensitivity. Southampton's visit to Shakespeare's family and the subsequent reconciliation between father and son are rather less convincing. However, the implication is that the writer has now faced and overcome, as far as he can, the emotional problems left from his youth, and that his friend Southampton has played a felicitous part here. For Shakespeare now, as for the two other poets previously, fate and human frailty threaten with passionate distress; Southampton has an affair with Rosaline, the dark widow with whom Shakespeare is in love. This motif is somewhat contrived, but the author neatly shows Shakespeare as narrowly avoiding a fate like Marlowe's when he is involved in a somewhat parallel situation. Tieck did not take his fictionalized account of his hero beyond this point. It was not necessary that he should; these are the poet's years of apprenticeship, and from now onwards it can be assumed that the pattern of maturity, as in the traditional German novel of individual development, has been established.

Heinrich von Kleist's first drama *Die Familie Schroffenstein* (1803) is based on a *Romeo and Juliet* situation, and reflects the influence of a number of Shakespeare's other plays, while the unfinished *Robert Guiskard* embodied, in Wieland's view, a fusion of Greek and Shakespearean tragedy. In Kleist's last play *Prinz Friedrich von Homburg* (1810) the Prince's abject fear of execution in Act III, associated with the nadir of his sense of loyalty and honour, is strikingly reminiscent of the behaviour of Claudio, condemned to death in *Measure for Measure*. There is also a more general, structural and thematic similarity between these two tragi-comedies, since both resolve tense antagonisms centred on the problem of authority into a texture of reconciliation.

Franz Grillparzer began to study Shakespeare after 1817 but soon sensed, as Goethe had done, the danger of being imaginatively dominated. In 1822 he wrote, 'Shakespeare tyrannizes my spirit, and I want to be free. I thank God that he is there, and that I have been fortunate enough to read him again and again and absorb him. But now I strive to forget him.' There are correspondences in characters and materials between Grillparzer and Shakespeare, the similarities for instance between Shakespeare's Juliet and Hero in *Des Meeres und der Liebe Wellen* (*Waves of the Sea and of Love*, 1831), or the large and varied historical canvas of *König Ottokar* (1825). Often, however, Grillparzer lays an un-Shakespearean emphasis on analysing states of mind at the expense of full-blooded dramatic action. The Emperor Rudolf II in *Ein Bruderzwist in Habsburg* (*Fraternal Strife in the House of Habsburg*, 1872) surely epitomizes what has been described as the underlying tragedy of both Grillparzer and his dramatic characters—an introspective nature unequal to the demands of life.

It is hardly surprising, therefore, that of all Shakespeare's plays *Hamlet* made the deepest impression on Grillparzer. The Romantics, adapting the view of this drama given in Goethe's *Wilhelm Meisters Lehrjahre*, had established Hamlet as the typically 'modern' hero of the intellect, whose predicament symbolized 'the boundless discrepancy between thought and action' (F. Schlegel). Schopenhauer had inscribed Hamlet's name in the hagiology of pessimism, seeing in him a pure reflectiveness, redeemed from the blind will to life. But the eighteen-thirties and forties produced a violent attack by progressive writers on this apotheosis of inert perspicacity. Gutzkow's fantasy drama *Hamlet in Wittenberg* (1832) depicts Hamlet as a radical student whose capacity for action is fatally impaired when he meets up with Faust and Mephisto, representing the unpolitical heritage of German Idealism. In Freiligrath's poem *Hamlet* (1844) 'Germany is Hamlet', debilitated by bookishness and haunted by the ghost of assassinated liberty. In 1849 Gervinus took Hamlet as a symbolic explanation of the defeat of the 1848 revolution; the Germans had concentrated on cultivating mind and spirit to the neglect of grappling with outer realities.

C. D. Grabbe's essay *Uber die Shakespearo-Manie* (*On the Shakespeare Mania*, 1827) also represents an attack on the Romantics' reception of Shakespeare. Only in its translations, especially of Shakespeare, had the Romantic movement in Grabbe's opinion produced a lasting achievement; these translations tended to substitute for original creative writing. Grabbe also criticized Shakespeare himself, pointing for example to bombastic and bizarre features of character and language. While this unsympathetic approach may be understandable as an attempt to demystify the Romantic Shakespeare cult, which had stressed Shakespeare's consummate artistry, it seems exaggerated in view of the debt to Shakespeare evident in Grabbe's own dramas. *Titus Andronicus* was clearly the model for his *Herzog Theodor von Gotland* (1822), while the fragmentary *Marius und Sulla* derives much from *Coriolanus*. *Napoleon, oder die hundert Tage* (*Napoleon, or the Hundred Days*, 1831) is a remarkable drama, not directly dependent on any of Shakespeare's plays, but displaying characteristics we might call Shakespearean in a deeper sense. There is the technique of conveying exposition and development by means of dramatic incidents rather than reportage. Even the battle scenes are meant to be acted out, with the great commanders moving among the ranks of fighting men. This image itself suggests another Shakespearean trait; for all his charisma and strength of character Napoleon does not dominate the play monolithically. He is seen from many contradictory angles and his destiny is interwoven with a broad and complex set of historical motions.

'Of all the German dramatists of the 19th century', writes L. M. Price, 'Büchner was the most closely related to Shakespeare' (p. 229). In his fragmentary novella *Lenz* (published 1839) Georg Büchner expresses his own aesthetic views through the *Sturm und Drang* dramatist. Idealism is arraigned for its contemptuous treatment of pulsating human life. True realism is said to be found in Shakespeare, in folksong, and sometimes in Goethe (the implied setting of the story in 1778 indicates that this is a reference to Goethe's earlier works). The realism championed here is democratic and dynamic, extending insight and compassion to the most humble, inarticulate people, and embracing, in a series of changing pictures, the movement and mutability of circumstances. Many of the direct echoes of Shakespeare in Büchner's plays come from *Hamlet*, but Büchner was far removed from pessimistic élitism of the Romantic Hamlet myth. Leonce, the idle, melancholy prince in the comedy *Leonce und Lena* (published 1850) seems conceived as a parody on the Romantic view, identifying with Hamlet's 'Would not this, sir, and a forest of feathers . . .' in a dream-laden, sentimental atmosphere ludicrously unlike the tense situation (Act III, scene 2) in which these words are spoken in Shakespeare. The hero in *Dantons Tod* (*Danton's Death*, 1835) is passive and sceptical where he is called upon to be decisive, but these symptoms have political rather than existential significance, suggesting, against a vivid and precise historical background, Danton's disillusionment with the aims of the bourgeois revolution. The drama *Woyzeck*, which Büchner left unfinished when he died in 1837, gives indignant, poignant, and intimate expression to the plight of an exploited wretch, such as Lear encountered in his clairvoyant madness on the heath.

From a starkly contrasting standpoint Nietzsche admires the assertive strength of Shakespeare's 'raw, hard, granite-like men' and regrets that such characters are so few and far between in his own time. Nietzsche's view seems to parallel the predilection for heroic, monumental, isolated figures in much German literature in the years following the foundation of the empire.

For several decades Hauptmann admired and was influenced by Shakespeare, and embodied various aspects of this respect into his own writing. The two scenes of the 'induction' to *The Taming of the Shrew* provided Hauptmann with material which he could develop into the full-length comedy *Schluck und Jau* (1900). Jau, the counterpart of Christopher Sly, talks in Silesian dialect, and is provided with a boon-companion Schluck. Hauptmann makes full use of the farcical humour inherent in the situation, but also develops the more problematic aspects of Jau's role—his doubts about his identity, and about dreaming and waking, as well as the emergence of an aggressive urge as he comes to feel more at ease in the guise of a lord. Karl, the member of the gentry who is largely responsible for the practical joke at Jau's expense, finally learns the lesson that the gap between himself and the fellow whom he is ridiculing is in fundamental essentials smaller than he had thought.

Hauptmann's *Indipohdi* (1920) is a colourful verse drama which succeeds in combining contemplative lyricism with effective action in a milieu of exotic adventure. Its themes include tensions of love and hate, with the possibility of reconciliation; there are conflicts in family relationships, while the struggle between father and son is also closely associated with power to rule a wider group. The civilizing influence of an isolated expatriate in a remote society and some particulars of the plot recall Goethe's *Iphigenie auf Tauris*; but that substantial analogies to *The Tempest* are to be seen is indicated at once by Hauptmann's calling the central figure of his play Prospero. After having withdrawn from the anxieties of public life in Europe, this figure sees himself as old and looking forward to an uneventful death; his practice of magic is one of self-absorbed, lonely creation which can appear as a substitute for a sense of living purpose. The natives of the tropical island press him to be their king, and soon after the arrival of his children Ormann and Pyrrha and the relationship with the young Tehura present Prospero with calls to immediate participation in the life of the community around him. After believing that his life was to continue in a pattern of ascetic renunciation, he finds himself being drawn back to kingship and to a possibility of renewed youth. With Tehura's support Prospero overcomes his anger against Ormann and renounces power so that his son may rule, while committing himself to a self-sacrificing death (reminiscent of Hölderlin's Empedokles). In his monologue at the opening of act three Prospero speaks of the created world as awe-inspiring and terrible, prodigal in its succession of births and deaths, paradoxical in its combinations of waking and dreaming, cruelty and kindness, suffering and happiness. The central problem of Prospero at this point is the part played by killing in the lives of men and animals. Later in the play Tehura's belief in reconciliation leads him to find inward harmony, with appreciation above all of the quality of patient suffering. *Indipohdi* has its various literary associations (Goethe's *Faust*, for instance, too) and at the same time is a unified, coherent drama in its own right, bearing the clear stamp of Hauptmann's personality as a creative writer. The title *Vor Sonnenuntergang* (*Before Sunset*, 1932) indicates the author's wish to form a link here with his own early play and the contemporary realism of his naturalistic works of the eighteen-nineties; he can see himself spanning thereby the years between his own youth and later years. As in the case of *Indipohdi*, Hauptmann introduces motifs from Shakespeare and Goethe. A preliminary title for the play was 'The new Lear', and the conflict between the seventy-year-old Clausen and his children leads to the father's sense of loneliness and despair when he realizes the intensity of the estrangement. The relationship that develops between Clausen and the girl Inken Peters has of course no analogy with *Lear*, and has been seen as having Goethe's expressions of feeling for Ulrike von Levetzow as literary forebear. The younger generation is in general more hide-bound than the vigorous, unconventional parent, and the play contains social satire at the expense of the monied middle class of the nineteen-twenties. It is less stark than either *Vor Sonnen-aufgang (Before Sunrise)* or *King Lear* in its overall approach, and Clausen's life during the course of the action has evident elements of vigour and fulfilment.

Hauptmann described his play *Hamlet in Wittenberg* (1935) as an attempt to supplement the work of the poet retrospectively:

> I felt attracted to presenting the world-famous Danish prince and his *Sturm und Drang* period in the town of Luther.

In Wittenberg Hamlet is surrounded by friends, but he is melancholy and reluctant to join in expected student activities. His loyal friend Horatio explains that Hamlet is here largely because his uncle Claudius wanted him away from Denmark; Rosenkranz and Güldenstern are here too, as spies in Claudius' service. The prince's belief is that suffering and tears come before action; he would be glad to live a simple life, away from cares of the world. The main action centres upon Hamlet's falling in love with the gypsy-girl Hamida. The events leading to their union in act four are, however, not compellingly dramatic. To Hamlet Hamida appears as 'child, folksong, lute, song, poet'; he has led her, he believes, from the underworld to the world of light. It is, however, a short-lived relationship; Hamida pines to be back among her own people, while Hamlet realizes that affairs of state require his return to Denmark, and in this context rational considerations are supported by appearances of the ghost of his father. 'Suffering is the lot of all that has been created, the lot of creation', Hamlet reflects. Hauptmann's hero is not disposed to quick, impetuous reactions and changes of mood, and the Wittenberg environment seems less laden with threats and tensions than that of Shakespeare's Elsinore. Hauptmann's preoccupation with *Hamlet* also found expression in other contexts. There is a presentation of *Shakespeare's Tragic Story of Hamlet, Prince of Denmark* (1930). The German version offered here is on the whole that of Schlegel-Tieck, with some cuts and changes. The speech 'To be or not to be' appears in Act V, and Hauptmann's last act also includes a suggestion by Hamlet that he might well withdraw voluntarily from the Danish scene and return to Wittenberg. Hauptmann's Hamlet emerges as a purposeful, active figure. The German author includes various analyses and comments on *Hamlet* in his novel *Im Wirbel der Berufung* (*In the Maelstrom of Vocation*, 1936). The action centres upon preparations for a summer production of *Hamlet* under princely patronage by the Baltic coast in North Germany; the time is before 1914. A turbulence of crises of personal relations and of health accompanies Erasmus Gotter, the inspiring mind behind this particular production. He insists that *Hamlet* is a play for acting, and not primarily for reading, as Goethe had suggested; that 'Hamlet is not Orestes'; that his production should bring out the tension and action between Claudius and Hamlet; that the Ghost has to be given emphasis as a major force too. In answer to an inquiry from the German Shakespeare Society in 1915, Hauptmann had declared that it was permissible, indeed should be required, that the appreciation of Shakespeare should continue during the war, since an international understanding of the highest products of the human mind should be encouraged at all times. A speech of 1927 ('Shakespeare-Tagung in Bochum') refers to Shakespeare as being also a German national possession; Hauptmann envisages the English dramatist as writing his works with a sense of higher mission, even though this task almost brought about his collapse. Hauptmann's attitude to Shakespeare is particularly sensitive to the delineation of suffering in the latter's work; Aeschylus and Shakespeare he regarded as the two greatest tragedians of world literature.[12]

Hofmannsthal approaches Shakespeare with a rhapsodic, cultivated flow of appreciation in his essay on Shakespeare's kings and gentlemen ('Shakespeares Könige und Herren', 1905). 'The atmosphere in Shakespeare's work is aristocratic nobility', he writes, where arrogance and politeness interweave, and where life can be glorified. In a fictitious dialogue on characters in the novel and in the drama (*Uber Charaktere im Roman und im Drama*, 1902) Hofmannsthal makes

Balzac distinguish between figures in novels and the characters in some of Shakespeare's plays. The essay 'Shakespeare und wir' ('Shakespeare and ourselves', 1916) emphasizes the continuous tradition of preoccupation with Shakespeare on the part of German actors and producers. If in some of Hofmannsthal's early poems and one-act plays, such as *Der Tor und der Tod* (*Death and the Fool*, 1893), there is a mood of dream and fantasy reminiscent of Shakespeare and Calderon, there are two later dramas which derive with some closeness from English models—*Jedermann* (*Everyman*, 1911) and *Das gerettete Venedig* (based on Otway's *Venice Preserved*, 1905). Stefan George's major expression of admiration for Shakespeare the poet is found in his translation of the *Sonnets* of 1909, in a version offering much starkness and subtlety; in his introduction George describes as central to the sonnets 'the passionate devotion of the poet to his friend', while their essential content consists of 'the worship of beauty and the glowing impulse towards immortalization'.

Rudolf Alexander Schröder, as friend and contemporary of Hofmannsthal and George, shared their cultivated respect for the traditions of world literature. It is, however, in the nineteen-forties, in the course of the last period of his life, that he wrote a number of essays which, sensitive and informed as they are, can be thought of in the context of the writing of the 'inner emigration' of that time. Schröder has a tendency to bring Shakespeare closer to German audiences (these were usually public lectures) by referring him to the late 18th century Central European approach, as when it is assumed that *A Midsummer Night's Dream* will be less familiar than Mozart's *Magic Flute*. His essay on *Hamlet* of 1948 sees the Prince as too undecided and inactive to be termed a hero. 'The only truly active person is fate itself'; but Schröder sees a hope of grace in the ending. *The Tempest* he describes sympathetically, and *Measure for Measure*. His considered comparison of Goethe and Shakespeare was written for the Goethe bi-centenary of 1949; while criticizing Goethe's attitude to Shakespeare in a number of utterances in his later years, he identifies himself warmly with the interpretation of Shakespeare in *Wilhelm Meisters Lehrjahre*. In writing about the translating of Shakespeare, Schröder points to a number of linguistic problems, and believes that every new translator of Shakespeare stands on the shoulders of the Schlegel-Tieck achievement, that he can only hope to improve it and get closer to the original while working within its framework.

Brecht wrestled with Shakespeare at intervals from the early years of his play-writing until late in his life. The preoccupation was in the fields both of dramatic theory and of creative writing. In 'Sollten wir nicht die Ästhetik liquidieren?' 'Should we not liquidate Aesthetics?' (June 2, 1927) Brecht states that he 'expected from sociology that it should liquidate the drama of today'. Although the basis of the modern repertoire has been given to us in 'the great Shakespearean dramas', with the passing of time and the changes in society these no longer have any effect today. As for drama after Shakespeare, there is little point in talking about it, since it is without exception weaker. Brecht's fragment 'Gespräch über Klassiker' (about 1929) asserts that the German classics met their death in the war of 1914–18; the classics, including the English classics, need to be dismantled and reassembled, as happened with Marlowe's *Edward II*, which Brecht cites as an example of rewriting in order to replace the false, bourgeois-idealistic admiration of greatness by the cool detachment of distance. It is in 1939, in a lecture given at Stockholm 'Über experimentelles Theater,' that Brecht probably uses the word *Verfremdung* (alienation) for the first time as a conscious slogan or technical term. In this paper he chooses *King Lear* to illustrate this point. A traditional performance of the play, he tells us, would show the anger of Lear at his daughter's ingratitude as natural and generally human; an alienated approach, however, would present Lear's actions as peculiar and remarkable, as a social phenomenon not to be taken for granted. *Der Messingkauf* (*The Buying of Brass*), mostly written between 1939 and 1940, an extended work of dramatic theory, frequently refers to Shakespeare, who here seems to be the one playwright of the past who can be considered as still vitally relevant to Brecht's vision of drama in the present and the future.

Major plays of Brecht's belonging to this period can be seen as having features that are Shakespearean and also reminiscent of the *Sturm und Drang* movement. The presentation of the biography of an outstanding personality (*Life of Galilei, Mother Courage*) may be cited, or the multiple action of *The Caucasian Chalk Circle*; further there are such features as the abrupt transition from high seriousness to comedy, the apparent discontinuity of single episodes within an overall unity, the juxtaposition of varying styles (prose, blank verse, folksong and ballad), a widely ranging diversity of setting, or the use of a stage that dispenses with detailed realism of decor. In the

Messingkauf, Brecht's philosopher sees Shakespeare's plays as depicting the transition from feudal to capitalist society. The subject of tragedy is the downfall of a feudal figure; Hamlet has lost confidence in feudal domination because as a student at Wittenberg he has absorbed middle-class ideas. The emotional situations portrayed in older plays, that is, those of Shakespeare and the Greeks, are barbaric and unreal and their plots are incredible, Brecht says in his last major work of dramatic criticism, *Small Organon for the Theatre* (1948). Here too he repudiates empathy by attacking an audience's willingness to be identified with unsuitable heroes such as Oedipus or Othello.

It was while he had a contract with the Munich theatre 'Deutsche Kammerspiele', in 1923, that Brecht found himself confronted in a major way by the challenge of Elizabethan drama. Ernst Schumacher[13] recounts that experimental productions of Shakespeare and other established dramatists were in the air at the time; Max Reinhardt put on *Hamlet* in a circus in 1920, and *Richard III* was produced with abstract decor. There was a proposal that Brecht should produce *Macbeth*, but he turned to the less familiar *Edward II* of Marlowe as the basis for his own free adaptation (Lion Feuchtwanger collaborated with Brecht here). The mellifluous regularity of Marlowe's verse is replaced by the often clipped, caustic and colloquial free verse of Brecht; poetic quality is undoubtedly present in many places, but it is Brecht's poetry, not Marlowe's. Instead of five acts there is a succession of scenes, with headlines by way of plot-summary, and with precise dating and timing before each scene where relevant. Brecht 'tidies up' the action of the earlier play as a practical producer who feels at liberty to change his original freely. One way in which he does this is by introducing motifs from Shakespeare (*Macbeth*, *Richard III*, for example) into Marlowe's action. There does not seem to be any parodistic approach to Marlowe's play on Brecht's part; Edward and Mortimer, at different points in the action, are given heroic proportions, and indeed Brecht allows Edward more opportunities to acquire stoic grandeur than does Marlowe. A few years later Brecht adapted *Macbeth* (1927) and *Hamlet* (1931) for radio, though it seems that only fragments of the texts are available; he was considerably censured at the time for the liberties he took with the original works.

Two full-length plays of Brecht from the nineteen-thirties are for the most part original creations, while deriving significant features of plot and characterization from Shakespeare. Both are satirical works, but their satire is topical political caricaturing of Hitler and National Socialism; Shakespeare's 'raw material' is being used for an ulterior end. *Die Rundköpfe und die Spitzköpfe* (*The Round Heads and the Pointed Heads*, first performed in Copenhagen, 1936) originated in a project of 1931 which was apparently of a purely literary character, a German adaptation of *Measure for Measure*. In its action *Die Rundköpfe und die Spitzköpfe* is one of Brecht's most complicated plays, as well as being over-long for a normal evening's performance. The background of Peru has something of a fairy-tale character, while the criticism may also be allowed that the play does not take National Socialism and its racial theories with sufficient seriousness. The Viceroy (Shakespeare's Duke Vincentio) discusses with his minister Eskahler (Escalus) his plan to allow Angelas (Angelo) to deputize for him. The Viceroy will remain aware that the fundamental struggle will be between rich and poor, the capitalists and landlords being pitted against the masses; but Angelas, the equivalent of Hitler, can become a useful catspaw to the Viceroy, because he leads a movement of some popularity and with his racialist theories can distract the people from what should be their main target, the ruling classes. For Brecht, Isabella's wish to enter a convent and to remain a virgin is a matter for unfavourable contrast with the role of Judith, the working girl for whom prostitution is a living to be considered in economic terms. The policies of the dictator are shown as ridiculous and incompetent, and Angelas is relieved when the old master, the Viceroy, comes back; the analogy with Hitler, however, is hardly convincing.

Der aufhaltsame Aufstieg des Arturo Ui (*The Avoidable Rise of Arturo Ui*, written in 1941) resembles *The Round Heads and the Pointed Heads* in being a polemic against National Socialism that is presented in an indirect and grotesque manner, against an exotic background that introduces the remote and the fantastic—gang warfare involving the greengrocery traders of Chicago. A further deliberate alienation device is to be the presentation of the action in the manner of an Elizabethan play. In introducing the characters, the announcer of the Prologue compares Ui specifically with Richard III, while in Scene 7 Ui hires old Mahogonney, a down-at-heel actor, to teach him oratory. The vehicle used is Mark Antony's 'Friends, Romans, countrymen' speech in *Julius Caesar*; there is the implication that the grand manner of the classical idealist German conception of

Shakespeare cannot be taken seriously today, while Brecht's conception of Julius Caesar as Roman gangster and businessman is developed
in his prose work *Die Geschäfte des Herrn Julius Cäsar* (*The Business
Affairs of Mr Julius Caesar*). A complicating factor is that while
writing the play in German verse, Brecht was aware that it would
then have to be translated into English, if it were to be produced in
the United States while he was resident there. The historical events
which the dramatist wishes to bring to our notice are some of those
involving Hitler and those close to him from about 1929 to 1938.
From Brecht's own point of view, the urge to expose and attack
Nazism, it is unfortunate that the play concludes with Ui at a moment
of triumph. It was not performed during the author's lifetime, and
was first published posthumously; it is undoubtedly a work of considerable subtlety.

A performance of *Coriolanus* in Berlin impressed Brecht in 1925,
though not until 1951–2 did he give detailed attention to the plan of
adapting it for the stage. It is understandable that the play would
present a challenge to an author who had made class conflicts a
frequent theme in his works. It is not surprising either that Brecht's
adaptation should not only make cuts and alterations for the sake of
economy of action but should also fundamentally change the interpretation of the plot. A Coriolanus who can say without irony 'Alone
I did it' would hardly have the approval of Brecht and his collaborators. The tribunes and people of Rome are to be shown in worthier
light, and it must be made clear that 'society must and can protect
itself from hybrid claims of the individual' (Manfred Berger, *Theater
in der Zeitenwende*, vol. 2, p. 329). Brecht did not, however, produce
his *Coriolanus*. The Berlin Ensemble staged it in 1964, and it has
been claimed (Berger, ibid.) that in this production there was a high
degree of success in blending the Shakespearean theory of the passions
with Brecht's 'theatre of the scientific age'.

Brecht's concern with Shakespeare has itself been given dramatic
form by Günter Grass in *Die Plebejer proben den Aufstand* (*The
Plebeians Rehearse the Uprising*, 1966), where the Boss is engaged in
rehearsing *Coriolanus* until he is interrupted by representatives of the
revolt of June 1953 in East Berlin who would like to obtain his
support. The Boss is portrayed like Brecht and has a number of his
words and traits, and indeed emerges as a unique and idiosyncratic
individual, master in his theatre environment, even if he would like

to use this as a means of escape from political decision. Hints and snatches of *Coriolanus* provide a play within a play; actors playing parts as rebellious Romans are jostled by contemporary Berliners who have no wish to be play-acting at this moment. Grass's irony neatly and affectionately shows that Brecht's attitude can be relativized too. At the same time, as the Boss, Brecht has now been mythologized as a central figure in a German drama of some importance, where he may play a role more akin to Hamlet's than to Coriolanus'.

The personnel manager Richard Egli, in Dürrenmatt's *Frank der Fünfte* (*Frank the Fifth*, 1960), introduces this 'opera of a private bank' with an opening speech to the audience which claims that modern business methods are as hair-raising and therefore as dramatically and artistically interesting as a Baroque spectacle. The figures to be introduced in the work are 'no less great and bloody/than the heroes of Shakespeare'. Crime is shown satirically as requiring great efforts of self-denial; Egli and his fiancée look to marriage and family life as an unattainable idyll. Böckmann, the accountant, discovers that he has cancer. Frank, ruthless dynastic ruler of the bank, is ultimately liquidated by his son Herbert who replaces him, with the condonement of the state.

Dürrenmatt's first adaptation of a Shakespeare play, *King John* (*König Johann*, 1968), indicates that modern author's sense of alienation from the issues of medieval dynastic strife.[14] There are relatively few changes in the first three acts. The Bastard Faulconbridge has a central role; it is he who intervenes to plead with the kings of England and France that they should not fight, so that carnage may be spared. Johann and Philipp recognize that they have much in common, that they are business rivals who are driven to press each other hard, but that they belong together in their interests and attitudes. The Bastard remains in spirit outside the concerns of his own social group. His lover, Blanka of Castile, upbraids him as 'the very greatest of all fools', but it is he who has the adaptability and alertness to supply Johann with a policy. As Prince Arthur's guard the Bastard replaces Shakespeare's Hubert. On his death-bed Johann curses the Bastard for having given him consistently bad advice:

> You brought nothing but misfortune,
> In improving the world, you only made it
> More damned.

Under the new regime of Pembroke, the Bastard is offered a title
and position, but he prefers to renounce participation in affairs of
state and to live quietly in the country :

> I pushed
> My way into the world of the powerful,
> Attempted to guide it to a better aim.
> But stupidity was drawing the carriage of fate.
> And chance.

If Shakespeare's Bastard is above all an English patriot, seeing people
and rulers as united, Dürrenmatt's character regards all feudal powers
with scepticism and would like reason, patience and humane sympathy to replace violence.

Dürrenmatt sub-titled his version of *Titus Andronicus* 'a comedy
after Shakespeare'. Most of the horrors of the original are retained,
and much of the plot too. There are nine scenes, which are an effectively pared down rendering of the earlier work, with the addition of
occasional new motifs. Expansive language, with illustrative imagery
and epithets, can be radically pruned. Shakespeare's Titus says (I, 1) :

> Hail, Rome, victorious in thy mourning weeds !
> Lo, as the bark that hath discharged her fraught
> Returns with precious lading to the bay
> From whence at first she weigh'd her anchorage,
> Cometh Andronicus, bound with laurel boughs,
> To re-salute his country with his tears,
> Tears of true joy for his return to Rome.

Dürrenmatt's equivalent to this is :

> Rome, victor in mourning clothes,
> With tears Andronicus approaches you
> Wearing the laurel wreath.

Aaron is much less of a plotter and ruthless villain in Dürrenmatt's
play; he is allowed to leave Rome with his child to return to his state
of nature in Africa :

> Therefore are we again what we once were,
> Not slaves of Rome, but free cannibals.

Publius becomes a humble veteran loyal to Titus, while the clown (IV, 3) describes himself as 'a Christian peasant-farmer' who believes in St Sebastian. Saturnicus sees himself in the role of poet as well as emperor. Lucius is not allowed to survive, but in the final scene he too is killed (after Lavinia, Tamora, Titus and Saturnicus) by the Goths' leader Alarich, who concludes the play with reflections on cosmic transience and meaninglessness. Dürrenmatt gives added emphasis to the themes of justice, judgment, execution and revenge, which are present in Shakespeare's play. Marcus Andronicus is much aware of his professional office of judge, and endeavours to be balanced and just amidst the violence around him; Dürrenmatt's Saturnicus orders him to be hanged. The chances of the survival of the fair-minded approach to problems of state are much less here than in *König Johann*.

Martin Walser's *Der schwarze Schwan* (*The Black Swan*, 1964) takes as its main theme the tension between fathers and children that is accentuated by a son's anguish and shame on behalf of a father who does not feel guilty when the son believes he should. Rudi Goothein discovers that his father, a surgeon, was directly involved in concentration camp activities during the early nineteen-forties. Rudi's girl-friend Irm is the daughter of Goothein's former concentration camp colleague, Liberé, who is now in charge of a private mental hospital where Rudi is sent, quite without malice, by his father for treatment and observation. The play ends with Rudi's suicide as a form of self-sacrificing gesture. At an earlier stage in the action Rudi makes one definite attempt to shock the older generation into what he considers a sense of responsibility. He, directing a group of fellow-patients in the hospital, puts on a play that is intended to remind Liberé and Goothein of their guilt and to provide the final conviction to Rudi that the older generation is guilty. German post-war economic recovery is interpreted as a form of activity intended to banish any possible sense of guilt about the past.

In his essay 'Hamlet als Autor' ('Hamlet as Author', 1964) Walser writes that it was not until he had completed his play and a friend had read it that he realized to what an extent the shade of Hamlet had been invoked. He makes the point that a German born between 1933 and 1945 may well find himself in the psychological situation of Hamlet, and indeed will be envious of him because the father of Shakespeare's hero was on the side of the victims. Throughout the play Rudi is frustrated in his wish to persuade the people around him, though there is finally an indication that his father has been moved by what has happened. Rudi is convincing as a victim, but the two older men dominate the play, and for all their complicity in past misdeeds they become interesting human figures. Walser relates (in 'Hamlet als Autor') that 'one grows up with Shakespeare as one grows up in a landscape; it is not until later that one realizes in what kind of landscape one has grown up'.

The lively stimulus of Brecht's drama, and of his approach to Shakespeare, may well have introduced an element of ferment which is still continuing to make a vital impact, whereas the effect of earlier German dramatists' evocations of Shakespeare is now probably mainly historical. Dürrenmatt, Grass and Walser belong to an era that comes after Brecht. Their contemporary Peter Hacks may be cited finally as another writer whose plays in the nineteen-fifties and after have also given testimony to a continuing, indeed renewed, Shakespearean strain. If he is thought of as beginning in the school of Brecht, he has developed his own independent manner as dramatist, and as a critic he has wished to go beyond him too.

Essays written in the German Democratic Republic between 1959 and 1966 (*Das Poetische*, Frankfurt, 1972) affirm drama as one of the great arts from which totality may be expected; its themes should be important and capable of being transformed into art; its protagonists are to be politically significant people or else intelligent people with new and significant passions. Shakespeare can be the model to help dramatists inaugurate a period of 'classical drama' in which theatrical pomp indicates riches that have been or may be achieved, and where an outstanding hero is a celebration of human possibilities. 'The history of the realistic play in Germany is the history of the assimilation of Shakespeare' (p. 47). The dramatist, Hacks wrote in 1960, will not be limited by naturalistic narrowness, but will make full use of his medium, deploying fantasy, abstraction, brilliance and virtuosity. 'The classical play ... proclaims its good opinion of the world throughout the use of beautiful, great art forms' (p. 36). If Shakespeare is seen as classical in some such sense as this, he can be a model that Hacks could evoke in his encouragement in the nineteen-sixties of a drama of the future. Hacks' brief tribute to Shakespeare in 1964 ended with the following words (p. 83), which are here quoted to form a conclusion to the present very limited outline of a few aspects of a great theme :

I personally did not understand Shakespeare until very late. It was only that each time I began to do something in a really first-class way, I noticed that Shakespeare had done it better. We know a certain amount more about the world than Shakespeare did. We hardly know more about man, and we still do not even know the half of what he knew about art.

The sections referring to the 18th and 19th centuries are mainly the work of T.M.H., while H.M.W. is principally responsible for our material on the Romantics and for the section concerning the 20th century.

NOTES

1. After the Thirty Years War the companies calling themselves 'English players' were all German, but retained the texts from the repertoire of the original English troupes (Roy Pascal, *German Literature in the Sixteenth and Seventeenth Centuries*, Introductions to German Literature, 2 (London, 1968), pp. 65–6).
2. *Lessing's Dramatic Theory* (Cambridge, 1939), p. 247.
3. See Laurence Marsden Price, *Die Aufnahme englischer Literatur in Deutschland* (Berne and Munich, 1961), pp. 240 ff.
4. In what is probably the first German critical text on Shakespeare, *Vergleichung Shakespears und Andreas Gryphs* (*A Comparison of Shakespeare and Andreas Gryphius*, 1741), J. E. Schlegel suggests that Shakespeare deviates from the classical rules because his plays are structured around characters and not around plots. In attributing to Shakespeare a method adapted to his purpose, Schlegel takes a step in Lessing's direction and away from the then very influential Gottsched, who rejected Shakespeare as totally formless.

5. The *Hauptaktion* or 'main event' in the programme of the travelling players came to be called the *Haupt- und Staatsaktion* because it was full of 'state scenes' involving people of rank and consequence (W. H. Bruford, *Theatre, Drama and Audience in Goethe's Germany*. London, 1950, p. 20).

6. Herder, *Von Ähnlichkeit der mittlern englischen und deutschen Dichtkunst* (*On the Similarity of Medieval English and German Literature*, 1777) and *Über die Würkung der Dichtkunst auf die Sitten der Völker in alten und neuen Zeiten* (*On the Effect of Literature on the Customs of the Nations in Ancient and Modern Times*, 1781).

7. *Goethe's Knowledge of English Literature* (Oxford, 1932), pp. 5–16. See also Walter F. Schirmer, 'Shakespeare und der junge Goethe', *Publications of the English Goethe Society (P.E.G.S.)*, N.S. 17 (1947), 26–42.

8. 'Constancy and Change in Goethe's Attitude to Shakespeare', *Publications of the English Goethe Society*, N.S. 34 (1964), 153–74 (pp. 160–1).

9. Ronald Gray, *Goethe. A Critical Introduction* (Cambridge, 1967).

10. Bruford, op. cit., p. 319.

11. August Wilhelm Schlegel, *Kritische Schriften*, edited by Emil Staiger (Zürich and Stuttgart, 1962), p. 17.

12. Felix A. Voigt and Walter A. Reichart, *Hauptmann und Shakespeare* (Goslar, 1947, 2nd edition), p. 122. See also H. F. Garten, 'Gerhart Hauptmann and Hamlet'. In: *Affinities. Essays in German and English Literature*, edited by R. W. Last (London, 1971).

13. Ernst Schumacher, *Die dramatischen Versuche Bertolt Brechts, 1918–33* (Berlin, 1955), p. 80.

14. See also A. Subiotto, 'The "Comedy of Politics": Dürrenmatt's *King John*'. In: *Affinities. Essays in German and English Literature*.

3

Ladislaus Löb: DOMESTIC TRAGEDY—REALISM AND THE MIDDLE CLASSES

'A literary form which from being one of the most effective weapons of the middle class developed into the most dangerous instrument of its self-estrangement and demoralisation' : this is how Arnold Hauser characterizes European domestic drama in the 18th and 19th centuries, citing in support of his argument the assumption 'that the faithful reproduction of facts leads automatically to the dissolution of social prejudices and the abolition of injustice.'[1] One may object that at the present level of our knowledge, generalizations about the interaction of society and art must be largely hypothetical, that the concept of a 'middle class' is itself controversial, and that in all events Hauser overstates his case. Nevertheless, most critics agree that the changing features of domestic drama reflect changes in the circumstances of the middle classes as well as a movement towards increasing artistic realism. The purpose of this essay, therefore, is to investigate the presentation of middle-class problems and the evolution of realistic methods in a number of domestic tragedies, which are commonly considered the outstanding German examples of the singularly popular domestic genre.

The term 'bürgerliches Trauerspiel', used by all German commentators, derives from the French 'tragédie bourgeoise', which dates back to a letter written by Michel Linant to Pierre Robert Le Cornier on November 10, 1733; it first occurs, applied to Voltaire's *Nanine*, in the German translation of the second of two French articles—both entitled *Theatralische Neuigkeiten aus Paris* (*Theatrical News from Paris*)—in the journal *Beiträge zur Historie und Aufnahme des Theaters* (*Contributions to the History and Advancement of the Theatre*) published in 1750 by Lessing and Mylius. 'Tragédie bourgeoise' is the subtitle provided for Lillo's *The London Merchant* in the French translation of 1748 by Pierre Clément, and is rendered as 'bürgerliches Trauerspiel' in the subtitle of Henning Adam v. Bassewitz's 1752 German adaptation of Clément. In 1755 'bürgerliches Trauerspiel' appears as the subtitle of Lessing's *Miss Sara Sampson*, thereby becoming fully established in the German critical vocabulary. A French alternative, either replacing or accompanying 'tragédie bourgeoise', is 'tragédie domestique', found notably in the third of Diderot's *Entretiens sur Le fils naturel* (*Conversations on 'The Natural Son'*) of 1757, but very rarely matched by the German equivalent 'häusliches Trauerspiel'. The most frequent English designation, occasionally supplanted by 'middle-class tragedy' or 'bourgeois tragedy', is 'domestic tragedy' : while the genre itself originated in Elizabethan England, the precise English formula seems to have been adopted only in the course of the 19th century; it is, however, foreshadowed by earlier writers such as Addison who, in *The Spectator* of April 14, 1711, praises Thomas Otway, the author of *The Orphan*, for incorporating 'something familiar and domestic in the fable of his tragedy'. The variations in French and English terminology illustrate overtly and specifically the complexity of both the aesthetic and the social situation, which is somewhat obscured by the many-faceted but single term 'bürgerlich' in German.

The 18th century was the period in which the middle classes, or the Third Estate, emancipated themselves from the hangovers of feudalism and rose to a position of importance under aristocratic absolutism. In England their sphere of influence included politics from an early date; in France they completed their political ascendancy through the 1789 Revolution. In fragmented Germany, on the other hand, their significance remained largely restricted to economic and cultural matters. It is this mixture of middle-class self-assertion and repression which can be recognized in the works of 18th century playwrights. Georg Lukács proves most representative of one school of interpreters in maintaining that 'domestic drama was the first to arise from a conscious class-conflict; to aim at expressing the feelings and thoughts of a class which was fighting for freedom and power, and its relation to the other classes'.[2] The opposite view is epitomized by Lothar Pikulik, who, linking domestic drama with the allegedly 'non-middle-class phenomenon of Sensibility', sees 'no conclusive proof that its ideal of humanity was sociologically connected with one particular class.'[3] The truth, as usual, lies between the extremes. Domestic drama in the mid-18th century makes no direct reference to any class-struggle, and later its advocacy of middle-class values is tempered with criticism. At the same time its attitudes correspond to an ideology which is commonly associated with the middle classes. Karl S. Guthke seems to strike the right balance : ' "Bürgerlich" means not a class but a way of life, a mentality. This does not, however, prevent domestic tragedy, even in its first phase, from being carried by the "Bürgertum" and its ideals.'[4]

A fundamental axiom of literary theory up to the middle of the 18th century was that tragedy, to quote the *Versuch einer Critischen Dichtkunst* (*Essay in Poetics*, 1730) by the Neo-Classicist, Johann Christoph Gottsched, must aim at 'arousing sadness, terror, pity and admiration in the spectators by depicting the misfortunes of the great' (Part I, Section 1, Chapter x). This view was challenged in England by several Elizabethan and Jacobean writers, but it was George Lillo who brought about the decisive change through *The London Merchant* (1731). In the 'Dedication' Lillo argues that the moral lesson which endows tragedy with 'dignity' will be more effective if it emanates from the portrayal of common people, who constitute the majority of society :

> If princes, etc., were alone liable to misfortunes arising from vice or weakness in themselves or others, there would be good reason for confining the characters in tragedy to those of superior rank; but, since the contrary is evident, nothing can be more reasonable than to proportion the remedy to the disease.

In the Prologue he praises his predecessors in replacing the 'awful pomp' of tragedies about 'Princes distrest . . . The fall of nations, or some hero's fate' by 'humbler' topics and techniques, also found in his own play :

> Forgive us then, if we attempt to show,
> In artless strains, a tale of private woe.
> A London 'prentice ruin'd is our theme . . .

The play itself conforms to the theory by using commoners as heroes and by teaching rational virtue through the unadorned but senti-mental presentation, in prose, of private suffering; it transcends the theory by exalting the political significance of middle-class business-men, who are said to 'contribute to the safety to their country as they do at all times to its happiness' and who are awarded near-aristocratic honours for their successful financial and diplomatic operations:

> As the name of merchant never degrades the gentleman, so by no means does it exclude him. (Act I, Scene i)

The London Merchant—and to some extent Edward Moore's *The Gamester* (1753)—exerted a great influence on Continental dramatists. On the one hand it promoted what Peter Szondi, referring to the ideas of Max Weber, describes as 'that inward-directed asceticism which in the 17th and 18th centuries helped to make the victory of middle-class capitalism, and consequently of the middle classes themselves, possible.' On the other hand it fostered, above all in Germany, a concentration on individual emotion which may have been both a cause and an effect of the continued civic reticence of the middle classes: 'The "Bürger" accepts his impotence under absolutism by retiring into a private world over which social and political conditions appear to have no control.'[5]

Lillo's impact reached Germany both directly and by way of France. The most celebrated French model, in the field of theory as well as practice, was Diderot. His major theoretical innovation consisted in the establishment of two intermediate types of drama, located between traditional derisory comedy and heroic tragedy. As he puts it in Chapter II of his treatise *De la poésie dramatique* (*On Dramatic Poetry*, 1758), the first type—based on the existing 'sentimental comedy', which was written chiefly by Nivelle de la Chaussée in the seventeen-thirties and forties, and which proceeded through tear-jerking vicissitudes to a happy and moral ending—was that of 'serious comedy, which has as its object virtue and the duties of man'; the second type—mainly demonstrated by Lillo but yet to be attempted by a French author—was that of a 'tragedy which would have as its object our domestic mishaps'. Diderot's most concise statement occurs in the third of his critical dialogues entitled *Entretiens sur Le fils naturel*, in the form of a list of demands addressed to contemporary dramatists and headed by calls for the 'creation of domestic tragedy' and the 'improvement of serious comedy'. These demands have social as well as aesthetic implications. The respectful treatment of commoners and their private problems posited with both new types of drama indicates a growing middle-class self-awareness, also suggested by the priority given to 'occupations' over 'characters'; when a previous passage recommends the exploration of 'all the relationships : the father, the husband, the sister, the brothers', the emphasis shifts to the family, which indeed provided the focal point of most domestic dramas and of middle-class society itself. At the same time the recognition of such social factors is a feature of realism, which is further adumbrated in the list through the plea for the expression of— Rousseauesque—feeling by means of 'mime' and 'tableaux' rather than by means of artificial rhetoric and histrionic sensations, and which is summed up, together with other connotations, in the closing item :

To introduce real tragedy into the lyric theatre.

An extremely significant move towards realism is finally seen in Chapter X of *De la poésie dramatique*, where Diderot declares his preference of prose to the ubiquitous Alexandrine :

I have sometimes asked myself whether domestic tragedy could be written in verse; and, without quite knowing why, I have answered that it could not.

Diderot's own plays, *Le fils naturel* (1757) and *Le père de famille* (*The Father of the Family*, 1758) partly contradict his theories : they neglect questions of occupation and seem stylized rather than realistic in method. But they are written in prose; they deal with the private relations of lovers and of parents and children in an earnest manner, stressing the importance of the family and its supposed centre, the father; although their protagonists belong to the gentry the virtues they teach in the typical rationalist-cum-sentimental fashion of the period are those normally credited to the middle classes. Diderot never wrote a domestic tragedy, but his two serious comedies greatly influenced the progress of domestic drama in general.

In Germany, Lessing was acutely aware of English and French developments, although the beginnings of his own domestic drama preceded those of Diderot, which he translated in 1759–60. The supreme German writer of the Enlightenment, he also precipitated the emergence of the movements of *Sturm und Drang* and *Klassik* (Weimar Classicism), chiefly through his appreciation of the genius of Shakespeare and his reinterpretation of Aristotle's concept of Catharsis. In his struggle against Gottsched's Neo-Classical rules he engaged the support of both French sentimental comedy and English domestic tragedy, which he describes with approval in the first of his *Abhand-lungen von dem weinerlichen oder rührenden Lustspiele* (*Treatises on the Tearful or Touching Comedy*, 1754):

> Comedy was raised and tragedy lowered by several degrees. On the one hand it was felt that the world had long enough laughed and hissed at absurd vices in comedy, and might now be allowed also to weep and derive a noble pleasure from the gentle virtues in it. On the other hand it was considered improper that only rulers and persons of exalted status should arouse our terror and pity in tragedy; consequently heroes were sought from among the middle ranks and set upon the tragic buskin, which they had previously worn only in order to be ridiculed.

Lessing subscribes to the tenets of Rationalism in expecting moral instruction from tragedy but he advances far into—and beyond—the realm of Sensibility in arguing that tragedy must above all else produce a psychological effect—an effect which, according to a passage in the prefatory essay of *Des Herrn Jakob Thomson sämtliche Trauerspiele* (*The Complete Tragedies of Mr James Thomson*, 1756), is admirably achieved by Lillo in *The London Merchant*:

> And these tears of compassion and humane emotion are the sole purpose of tragedy, or it can have none.

The evocation of pity and fear in tragedy relies on the spectators' sympathy for the characters. Sympathy is the more likely to occur the more the spectators have in common with the characters. In the fourteenth article of the *Hamburgische Dramaturgie* (1767–9) Lessing therefore rejects aristocratic protagonists and heroic themes, demanding that concentration on private humanity which is the hallmark of early domestic tragedy:

> The names of princes and heroes can lend pomp and majesty to a play, but they contribute nothing to our emotion. The misfortunes of those whose circumstances most resemble our own, must naturally penetrate most deeply into our hearts, and if we pity kings, we pity them as human beings, not as kings . . . our sympathy requires an individual object and a state is far too much an abstract conception to touch our feelings.

The interest in individual rather than class issues is, incidentally, highlighted by Lessing's contemporary Johann Gottlob Benjamin Pfeil, who sets his domestic tragedy *Lucie Woodvil* (1756) among upper-class people, and who in his treatise *Vom bürgerlichen Trauerspiele* (*On Domestic Tragedy*, 1755) defines the genre as one which deals with 'the affairs of some private persons', explaining the occasional appearance of noblemen among its heroes by the fact that 'middle-class' attitudes could be determined by education no less than social standing :

> There is a certain intermediate order between the mob and the great. The merchant, the scholar, the aristocrat, in short whoever has had an opportunity to improve his heart or to enlighten his intellect, belongs to it.

It has been claimed that Lessing, as a writer of domestic tragedy, was preceded by Andreas Gryphius in *Cardenio und Celinde* (written in 1648–9), Johann Elias Schlegel in *Canut* (*Canute*, 1746), Christian Leberecht Martini in *Rhynsolt und Sapphira* (published in 1755 but extant in 1753) and even Gottsched in *Sterbender Cato* (*The Dying Cato*, 1732). All those plays, however, depart from the genre either in outlook or in style. Lessing was the first German playwright to fulfil all the relevant criteria in *Miss Sara Sampson* (1755), which is consequently the first genuine domestic tragedy in the language.

Miss Sara Sampson, set in England, shows the influence of *The London Merchant* and Samuel Richardson's novel *Clarissa Harlowe*. It has some psychological subtleties and may reveal, perhaps un-consciously, a critique of the beliefs it affirms on the surface; but on the whole it is a sentimental and melodramatic lesson about the dangers of abandoning duty and honour for passion. While designed chiefly to create pity for the fallen but appealing heroine, the episodes are heavily didactic. The dissipated prodigal Mellefont bitterly regrets robbing Sara of her innocence; Mellefont's former mistress Marwood proves as capable of murder as of sexual abandonment; Sara is constantly in tears over her elopement with Mellefont and her betrayal of her father. Repentance, gratitude and love—mainly between parent and child—are extolled, as is the divine quality of forgiveness. The entire action is interpreted, in the dialogue itself, as a demonstration of Enlightenment morality—steadfast in Sir William Sampson, who is said to survive in order to guide others; fragile in Sara, who is said to die in order to avoid total corruption :

God must let the virtue which has been tested remain long in this world as an example; only the weak virtue which would perhaps succumb to too many temptations is quickly raised above the dangerous confines of the earth (Act V, Scene x)

After *Miss Sara Sampson* the use of prose in tragedy, the comparatively realistic milieu and the serious treatment of private family affairs became the stock-in-trade of all domestic dramatists. The prototypes of good but assailable heroine, self-indulgent seducer, depraved mistress and venerable father were adopted on innumerable occasions. The conflict of conscience and the heart—expressed through the clash and reconciliation of young lovers with paternal authority—was re-enacted again and again. The moral values, the new dignity and the basically passive conduct of the protagonists—who are aristocratic in name but 'middle-class' in attitude—were copied for many decades. Despite its flaws, then, the first of German domestic tragedies was also novel and powerful enough to prove one of the most influential.

While Lessing's masterpieces, *Minna von Barnhelm* (1767) and *Nathan der Weise* (1779) have affinities with Diderot's serious comedy, *Emilia Galotti* (1772) is another domestic tragedy, no less influential and more aesthetically satisfying than *Miss Sara Sampson*. The problems and methods of the earlier play are again in evidence, and the typical 'dramatis personae' reappear, with the addition of a foolish mother, a high-handed ruler and an unprincipled official. Lessing, in his letter of January 21, 1758 to Christoph Friedrich Nicolai, maintains that he deliberately planned to omit all matters of state from his 'bürgerliche Virginia', since the private aspects of the story were tragic enough in themselves. Nevertheless, the play has a bearing on German politics, which is hardly disguised by the Italian setting.

The veteran officer Odoardo Galotti, an enemy of courtly depravity and a representative of patriarchal integrity, is brave, honest and proud; Emilia, who—in the somewhat contrived rational manner of the whole work—persuades him to kill her rather than letting her lose her innocence, glorifies the ideal of sexual purity. Besides the praise of such middle-class virtues, however, the play initiates that criticism of the middle classes whch became central to subsequent domestic drama. Claudia's pleasure at the Prince's interest in her daughter exemplifies middle-class snobbery. Odoardo displays the sour censoriousness often associated with middle-class fathers in life as on stage. His readiness to fight the Prince for his rights—

> Short-sighted voluptuary! I defy thee.—He who regards no law is as independent as he who is subject to no law. (Act V, Scene iv)—

is a courageous attempt at middle-class self-assertion but also an expression of his irrational temper. When, on an equally rash impulse, he kills his daughter instead of the Prince, he seems unable to carry his middle-class sentiments to the point of rebellion, as he does again when he gives himself up to trial by the Prince, whom he can only threaten with the uncertain prospect of divine retribution:

> I go to meet you as my judge: then I shall meet you in another world, before the Judge of all. (V, viii)

Emilia feels capable of defying the Prince's power; but although the very admission of her susceptibility to his physical attraction is a relatively bold move in moral and psychological terms, her preference of death to seduction is a spiritual escape into stoic self-sacrifice which denies the possibility of worldly resistance:

> I will see who can detain me—who can compel me. What human being can compel another? . . . To avoid no worse snares thousands have leapt into the waves, and now are saints. (V, vii)

Thus Lessing reveals not only the new self-respect of the middle classes but also their inhibitions, which may be seen as both resulting from—and contributing to—their political impotence.

If middle-class virtues are applauded despite reservations, the court is radically condemned. The chief villain is the Chamberlain Marinelli, whose murderous schemes embody the corruption of the high civil service, which was to remain a prime target of criticism in domestic drama. The Prince is weak rather than wilfully evil, but his irresponsibility makes him patently unfit to rule, as is borne out by the misdeeds he connives at in his pursuit of Emilia in the plot as a whole, and by his facile disposal of a man's life in one famous episode in particular:

> Sentence of death for your Highness's signature.
> With all my heart!—Where is it? Quick! (I, viii)

Throughout the dialogue the court is exposed as the home of treachery ('A curse on these court slaves! Their tales! their lies!', IV, iii), time-serving sycophancy ('To cringe—to fawn—to flatter', II, iv) and cynical adultery ('Goods which cannot be obtained in their primitive perfection, must be bought at second hand', I, vi) and the indictments culminate in the open accusation of the ruler:

The Prince is a murderer! (IV, v)

In spite of Lessing's disclaimer, therefore, the anti-absolutist inter-pretations of the play seem justified. Complementing the innovations of *Miss Sara Sampson* with the qualified commendation of middle-class worth set against the denunciation of the ruling classes, *Emilia Galotti* inaugurates the tradition of class-conflict in domestic tragedy, which rarely reaches the revolutionary pitch suggested by some critics, but which mirrors both the aspirations and the limitations of the German *Bürgertum* as a political entity.

Emilia Galotti was hailed by the *Sturm und Drang* generation as a model attack on absolutism and class-distinctions. The dramatists of the movement were further indebted to Louis Sébastien Mercier, a disciple of Diderot and Rousseau, and the author of one of many French versions of Lillo's *The London Merchant*. The influence of his own plays, which belong to the line of serious comedy, was sur-passed in Germany by that of his treatise *Du théâtre ou Nouvel essai sur l'art dramatique* (*The Theatre, or A New Essay on Dramatic Art*), which appeared in 1773 and was translated in 1776 by Heinrich Leopold Wagner.

In the treatise Mercier continues Diderot's advocacy of the inter-mediate genres by pleading for moral instruction through 'what is called a "drame"', or a kind of sentimental spectacle halfway between tragedy and comedy, which uses prose, strives for a degree of realism and, dispensing with 'old kings' and 'elegant noblemen', concentrates on the author's 'beloved contemporaries' and 'the portrayal of present manners' (Chapter I). As a result of this approach the 'drame' becomes 'the image of bourgeois life in all its situations' (XII). At the same time Mercier assumes a new political stance. Outraged by social and economic injustice, he supports the Third Estate—'these workmen, these artisans' (XI)—against their courtly exploiters, and he exalts 'the bourgeoisie, which is undeniably the most respectable class of the state' (VII). The poet, according to him, is 'the spokesman of the unfortunate, the champion of the oppressed' (XI); writers are 'the most useful citizens' because they fight for 'truth' and 'human rights':

> In sum, it is the men of letters who will necessarily dictate to statesmen and kings those lessons which must initiate public happiness. (I)

He exhorts the dramatist to expose the ruthless 'despotism' of the rulers as well as the servile 'cowardice' of their subjects (XXI), but he attributes the self-interest rife among all classes to the 'bad administration' (XI) of the aristocratic-absolutist régime, which deliberately divides the masses in order to safeguard its own privileges. Consequently, passing beyond the idea that both rulers and subjects should be characterized as ordinary human beings, he urges that tragedy show the former as callous autocrats responsible for the deprivations of the latter:

> Well then! if you want to depict kings, present their ambition as the source of the people's misery; present the monarch, whom you adorn with the most beautiful colours, as a tyrant who demands slaves... When tragedy is presented in this way, men will feel that they are the plaything of the ambitious, for whose crimes they are paying. (III)

Thus Mercier, who eventually took an active part in the 1789 Revolution, explicitly adapts domestic drama to middle-class political propaganda.

The *Stürmer und Dränger* were less revolutionary than Mercier. Nevertheless, their individualistic protests against artistic and social traditions greatly advanced both realism and middle-class liberalism. As Arnold Hauser points out (vol. 3, pp. 103–4): 'With the "Storm and Stress" movement, German literature becomes entirely middle-class, even though the young rebels are anything but lenient towards the bourgeoisie... The whole period of German culture which extends from the "Storm and Stress" to the romantic movement is borne by this class.' Class-distinctions and absolutist-aristocratic tyranny as well as middle-class conventions are criticized in the plays of Friedrich Maximilian Klinger, Johann Anton Leisewitz and Heinrich Leopold Wagner: Wagner's *Die Kindermörderin* (*The Infanticide*, 1776)—in which a butcher's daughter is seduced by an

officer and sentenced to death for killing her illegitimate child—
provides the outstanding example of a new and highly popular theme
in domestic tragedy.

Jakob Michael Reinhold Lenz, in his theoretical *Anmerkungen
über das Theater* (*Remarks on the Theatre*, 1774), which recalls
Lessing, Herder and the early Goethe, rejects Neo-Classicism,
eulogizes Shakespeare and calls for truth to life instead of beauty, but
makes no social comments. In his plays, however, he underlines the
determination of men by their social standing. In *Der Hofmeister*
(*The Tutor*, 1774) he modifies the familiar constellation by making
the middle-class title-hero the seducer and by allocating a large share
of the seduction to the heroine, who is the daughter of aristocratic
parents; the action, after the hero's self-castration, concludes with
three suitable marriages, but this ending has a bitterly parodistic
rather than happy flavour. In *Die Soldaten* (*The Soldiers*, 1776) the
petty-bourgeois heroine is ruined through her affairs with aristocratic
officers, and her chief seducer is murdered by her middle-class
fiancé, who then commits suicide. In both plays the denunciation of
the aristocrats' brutal treatment of their inferiors, which proves the
main cause of the misfortunes, continues the liberal evolution of
domestic drama, while the exposure of the snobbery, greed and
narrow-mindedness of middle-class characters carries the genre further
from pro-bourgeois towards anti-bourgeois positions. Both plays show
remarkably realistic devices of language and structure, but the elements
of irony, absurdity and grotesque tragicomedy place them outside
domestic tragedy in the strict sense.

The extraordinary appeal of the genre is obliquely reflected in the
works of Goethe, who was one of the most prominent *Sturm und
Drang* rebels in his youth but became one of the foremost 'Classicists'
in his maturity, and who, with his patrician background, belonged to
the upper middle class but was made a member of the ruling class by
his appointments in the Weimar Establishment. His main artistic
interests lay in different fields, as is best illustrated by the historical
subject matter of *Götz von Berlichingen* (1773) and *Egmont* (begun
in 1775, finished in 1788), the spiritually refined message and verse of
Iphigenie auf Tauris (1787) and *Torquato Tasso* (1790), the idealized
picture of upper-class conservatism in *Die natürliche Tochter* (*The
Natural Daughter*, 1803) complementing the satire on the French
Revolution in *Der Gross-Kophta* (*The Grand Cophta*, 1791) and

Der Bürgergeneral (*The Citizen General*, 1793), and the universal issues and infinitely varied poetic methods of *Faust* (completed in 1831). Nevertheless, most of his plays contain topics used by domestic dramatists. The clash of the treacherous court and the upright knight, who is aristocratic by title but bourgeois by personality, in *Götz*; the seduction of the simple maiden by the sophisticated scholar, and her eventual execution for infanticide, in the Gretchen episode (written in the mid-seventeen-seventies) of *Faust*; the sufferings of middle-class characters resulting from the middle-class hero's courtly ambitions in *Clavigo* (1774); the emotions of private individuals who solve their amorous difficulties by means of a 'ménage à trois' in the first version (and fail to do so in the second version) of *Stella* (1776); the homely love-idyll, destroyed by imperialist-absolutist politics, of the nobleman and his petty-bourgeois mistress, and the apotheosis of freedom, echoing middle-class liberalism despite the criticism of some middle-class cowards, in *Egmont*; the human integrity extolled in *Iphigenie*; the malaise of the poet-commoner at court in *Tasso*—all these features, dramatised in several cases with a great deal of realism, are more or less clearly related to domestic tragedy, which thus leaves its mark even on Goethe, who never fully accepted but seldom entirely ignored its concerns.

Schiller, like Goethe, began as a *Stürmer und Dränger* before he turned to Weimar Classicism. He had strong liberal feelings, which were shared by most middle-class intellectuals of his time. But his awareness of the 'real' compulsions of physical and social existence induced him increasingly to search for freedom in the 'ideal' realms of 'beauty', in which man's 'senses' or 'inclinations' are balanced by his 'reason' or 'duty', and of 'sublimity', in which the latter overcome the former, if necessary at the cost of life itself. In his essays, which are influenced by Rousseau, Goethe and chiefly Kant, he says little about politics. In *Über die ästhetische Erziehung des Menschen* (*On the Aesthetic Education of Man*, 1795), to mention only one of the greatest, he dreams of the utopian 'state of freedom' or 'moral state' (Letter IV) in which the conflicting material forces of the existing 'state of compulsion' or 'natural state' (III) would give way to the co-operation of liberated individuals in a just community guided by eternal ethical laws; but his notion that 'all political improvement shall proceed from the ennobling of character' by means of 'art' (IX) removes the argument, as always, to the level of aesthetics and metaphysics.

Schiller's plays are more political than his essays, and there are elements of domestic tragedy in all of them—the family conflicts, the rebellion against oppression and convention, and the final acceptance of law and order in *Die Räuber* (*The Robbers*, 1781); the republican uprising, betrayed by the leader's ambition, in *Die Verschwörung des Fiesco zu Genua* (*Fiesco, or The Genoese Conspiracy*, 1783); the private love-triangle of King, Queen and Prince, and the doomed but eloquent calls for a humane constitution, in *Don Carlos* (1787); the repudiation of power-politics and the exaltation of stoic spirituality in the *Wallenstein* trilogy (1798–9), *Maria Stuart* (1800) and *Die Jungfrau von Orleans* (*The Maid of Orleans*, 1801); the defeat of aristocratic tyrants by democratic farmers, highlighting Schiller's assent to the aims of the French Revolution, in *Wilhelm Tell* (1804). On the whole, however, the content and form of these works must be associated with heroic tragedy.

Kabale und Liebe (*Love and Intrigue*, 1784), on the other hand, was deliberately conceived as a domestic tragedy. Emulating *Emilia Galotti*, and showing the influence of the *Sturm und Drang* dramatists as well as of plays by Otto Heinrich v. Gemmingen, Gustav Friedrich Wilhelm Grossmann and Johann Christian Brandes, it combines Schiller's own preoccupations with the characteristics of the genre, of which it is the most admired example.

Set boldly in contemporary Germany, alluding unmistakably to Duke Karl Eugen of Württemberg and his minister Montmartin, the play denounces class-distinctions and absolutism with unique vigour. The undoing of the lovers by the cabal of politicians turns the entire action into an indictment of the court, which is accused of specific malpractices. The Gallic foppery of Baron von Kalb satirises precious courtly manners. The President's reported crimes and his readiness to prostitute his son Ferdinand for the sake of power illustrate the viciousness of courtly ambition. The perfidy of courtiers, whose greatest asset is their capacity for opportunistic calculation, is epitomized in the cynical knowledge of the President's secretary, Wurm, that an oath which he and his master would brush aside as a trifle will enforce the submission of the middle-class Luise to their iniquitous scheme :

An oath? Ridiculous! What restraint can an oath be?
None upon us my lord, but the most binding upon people of their stamp. (Act III, Scene i)

The aristocratic President and the renegade bourgeois Wurm represent corrupt officialdom. But Schiller, unlike most domestic dramatists, even attacks the monarch. Although he does not appear on stage, the Prince's evil presence is felt everywhere. It is he who, in historically authentic fashion, sells thousands of citizens for foreign military service to finance his luxuries; it is he who has made Lady Milford his mistress against her will; and it is with him in mind that she accuses the ruling class in general of destroying the supreme middle-class values— 'separating bridegroom and bride', 'tearing asunder even the holy bond of marriage', shattering 'the tranquil happiness of a whole family', and exposing 'a young and inexperienced heart' to the 'blighting pest' of lust (II, iii)—in the pursuit of lascivious desires. Thus the Prince and his henchmen are equally guilty of the economic, social and indeed physical oppression of their subjects, which Ferdinand castigates in a similar tirade, and to which he opposes his own private and emotional—or 'middle-class'—morality:

> Envy, terror, hatred are the melancholy mirrors in which the smiles of princes are reflected—Tears, curses, and the wailings of despair, the horrid banquet that feasts your supposed elect of fortune . . . My ideas of happiness teach me to look for its fountain in myself! All my wishes lie centred in my heart! (I, vii)

Writing drama rather than propaganda, Schiller includes two sympathetic characters among the aristocrats. Nevertheless, the noble-woman Lady Milford—who abandons her advantages at court in order to regain her virtue—hails from England, the country of middle-class freedom. And the nobleman Ferdinand—who interprets his defiance of the 'worldly prejudices' of his own class for the sake of his union with Luise, 'a maid of humble birth', as a battle between 'nature' and false 'conventions' (II, iii)—is basically a radical fighter for middle-class liberalism and egalitarianism raised to a divine level:

> True, I am a nobleman—but show me that my patent of nobility is older than the eternal laws of the universe—or my scutcheon more valid than the handwriting of Heaven in my Louisa's eyes? 'This woman is for this man?' (I, iv)

While the rulers are held up to execration, middle-class characters
are presented in a more appealing light; but they too are criticized.
Wurm has betrayed his origins by seeking advancement at court.
Miller's wife sees Ferdinand's love of her daughter as an opportunity
for social climbing. Miller, who is a musician but whose temperament
is that of an artisan rather than an artist, has enough spirit to repudiate
the promiscuity of the aristocracy and to try to defend his rights as a
private citizen against any unlawful infringement by the President:

> No offence, I hope—your excellency may have it all your own
> way in the Cabinet—but this is my house.—I'm your most obedient
> very humble servant when I wait upon you with a petition, but
> the rude, unmannerly intruder I have the right to bundle out—No
> offence, I hope! (II, vi)

But he is coarse, bumptious and easily intimidated. The pleasures and
refinements he blindly plans to lavish on himself and Luise, when
Ferdinand throws money at him before administering a truly domestic
glass of poisoned lemonade to her, paint a pathetic picture of middle-
class snobbery:

> I'll hold up my head with the best of them ... I'll give my lessons
> in the great concert room, and won't I smoke away at the best
> *puyke varinas*... And she shall learn to speak French like a born
> native, and to dance minuets, and to sing, so that people shall read
> of her in the newspapers... and the fiddler's daughter shall be
> talked of for twenty miles round. (V, v)

Luise's innocence, sincerity and dignity are beyond doubt. Her
'sublime' willingness to give up Ferdinand on earth, and her belief
that she will be his equal in another world where human goodness
overcomes the barriers of class and wealth, endow middle-class
sentiments with a religious significance:

> I renounce him for this life! But then, mother—then when the
> bounds of separation are removed—when the hated distinctions of
> rank no longer part us—when men will be only men ... O, then
> shall I be rich ... then shall I be noble! (I, iii)

When, in an act of Kantian duty, she sacrifices her love to save her
parents she may seem heroic; her alleged heroism, however, becomes

less plausible when she accepts the existing structure of the state as a symbol of the universal plan :

> Let me be the heroine of this moment . . . I will renounce a union which would sever the bonds by which society is held together, and overthrow the timeless general order. (III, iv)

Thus, unlike Ferdinand, who avoids the prejudices of his aristocratic circles, Luise proves a prisoner of her bourgeois mentality.

Kabale und Liebe functions on several levels. It is a typical domestic tragedy in its realistic depiction of characters determined by social conditions and speaking a lifelike albeit rhetorical prose; in its criticism of class-distinctions and absolutist misrule; in its qualified defence of middle-class attitudes. At the same time it demonstrates the philosophical proposition that the 'ideal' is inaccessible to the realm of 'reality', as true love falls victim to Machiavellian machinations; and that idealism may turn into fanaticism, as Ferdinand's worship of Luise yields to murderous jealousy. The play has revolutionary implications. Nevertheless, the notion that freedom and fulfilment are only achieved through self-denying spirituality can be understood as yet another expression of the political inefficacy of middle-class intellectuals in Schiller's day.

After *Kabale und Liebe* domestic drama underwent an artistic decline, although its popularity remained undiminished for many decades. The most celebrated practitioners during the last quarter of the 18th century were Friedrich Ludwig Schröder, August Wilhelm Iffland and Ferdinand v. Kotzebue; Charlotte Birch-Pfeiffer was extremely successful in the first half of the 19th century, and Eduard v. Bauernfeld and Friedrich v. Halm continued her efforts with much acclaim well into the second half. On the whole they, and numerous less accomplished writers, followed the tradition of preaching rationalist-sentimental homilies by means of recurrent themes, which are discussed, with reference to the early phases of the genre but with equal relevance to the later ones, in a survey by Wolfgang Schaer. Middle-class existence, according to Schaer, is shown in domestic drama to be based on 'the home and the family inhabiting it'; the centre of the family—and consequently of middle-class society—is 'the absolute authority of the father'; the belief in industry, frugality and probity is summed up in 'the concept of "duty" ' which, together with sexual self-control, produces a virtuous way of life and is often related to religious observance of a puritanical and utilitarian rather than mystical or transcendental kind, so that 'the dual concept of "religion and virtue" becomes one of the foundations of middle-class morality'. 'The family—and the middle-class community—may be threatened by the intrusion of aristocrats and high officials from courts which are marked by 'seduction, flattery, ambition and in-fighting' as well as by 'prodigality, ostentatiousness, insincerity and craving for prestige'; they may also be threatened from within by the attempts of middle-class characters 'to transgress against the bourgeois ethic of moderation and self-sufficiency' and 'to live in a style unwarranted by their social status' (p. 148, p. 117). The ambivalence of the writers, who combine the 'tendency towards middle-class emancipation' with 'polemics against the overstepping of limits' (p. 37), may correspond to the ambivalent position of the middle classes themselves. The portrayal, to quote Guthke, of 'the rigid conventionality, the passive acceptance of the evils of the class-structure' as well as 'the desire for social climbing'[7] seems characteristic of a bourgeoisie which sustained its economic and cultural rise throughout the 18th and 19th centuries but which, in Germany, never attained a complete political identity of its own.

Conservative acquiescence, then, is the lesson taught by the domestic dramas of the time, most of which, incidentally, are serious comedies rather than tragedies. Lessing, Schiller and the *Stürmer und Dränger* dream of revolutionary alternatives, but even they either derive their tragic dilemmas from the helplessness of the middle classes or suggest spiritual escape routes instead of political solutions. Raymond Williams's pointed comment on *The London Merchant* has wider applications: 'Humanitarianism, as an ideology, . . . expresses sympathy and pity between private persons, but tacitly excludes any positive conception of society, and thence any clear view of order or justice.'[7] It may be a symptom of the middle-class predicament that Goethe's and Schiller's 'Classical' works show little more social realism than the fantasies of the Romantics, that Grillparzer dramatizes legend and history in subtle verse, and that Heinrich von Kleist writes his poetic plays chiefly about eccentric epistemological, psycho-analytical and existential questions.

The first explicitly 'committed' political movement in German literature was that of *Das Junge Deutschland*, which emerged in the eighteen-thirties. Inspired by the 1789 and 1830 French revolutions, and recalling some *Sturm und Drang* features, the 'Young Germans' advocated realistic techniques and liberal reforms. Although Heinrich Laube, for one, wrote clever 'well-made' pieces, only Karl Gutzkow succeeded in producing a few plays of more lasting interest. In *Richard Savage* (first performed in 1839), *Werner* (1840) and *Ottfried* (1849) the heroes' efforts to rise from their middle-class status clash with the prejudices of the aristocracy in a still class-ridden world. Bourgeois self-sufficiency is once again made to overcome social ambition, although the tone is more radical than that of the domestic genre in general. While *Richard Savage*, with its unhappy ending, is close to domestic tragedy, the other plays end happily; they thus prove typical of most 'Young German' writing, which—reaching a new stage of hopeful middle-class propaganda—deserves more critical attention than it has received, but which contributed little to the development of domestic tragedy or of German drama as a whole.

Georg Büchner's contribution to German drama, on the other hand, cannot be overestimated, although he only left three plays when he died at the age of twenty-four. Loosely associated with the 'Young Germans', he far surpassed them in artistic ability and political radicalism. The period between the 1830 and 1848 revolutions saw what Arnold Hauser describes as the 'undoubted and undisputed ... victory of the middle class'; he thinks of France but intimates that in Germany too 'the victors form a thoroughly conservative and illiberal capitalist class adopting the administrative forms and methods of the old aristocracy', while adhering to an 'unaristocratic ... way of life'; and he adds that 'as soon as the emancipation of the middle class is accomplished, the struggle of the working class for its rights already begins' (vol. 4, pp. 2–3). The conflict of aristocracy and middle classes, then, gave way to the conflict of the upper middle class, allied to the surviving aristocracy, and the proletariat, with the lower middle class caught between them. Of those middle-class intellectuals who did not turn to conservatism as the 19th century progressed, some carried on the liberal bourgeois endeavours of earlier decades, whereas others moved towards socialism. Following such theorists as Saint-Simon and Enfantin, anticipating Marx and Engels by several years, Büchner —who organized conspiracies modelled on the French uprising of July 1830—was one of the first German writers to recognize the economic and class factors of modern society: as his correspondence and the pamphlet *Der hessische Landbote* (*The Hessian Messenger*,

1834) reveal, he hoped for a revolution of peasants and small craftsmen against their absolutist-capitalist exploiters. His other major
innovation was the uncompromising rejection of idealism in art for the
sake of a more advanced—and more complex—kind of realism than
had been known in Germany before him.

Despite his activism Büchner was primarily a grimly deterministic
and sceptical tragedian, whose concerns went beyond those of domestic drama. Nevertheless, some aspects of his plays are related to the
genre. The tragedy *Dantons Tod* (*Danton's Death*, 1835) exposes the
bloody futility of the 1789—and indeed any—revolution, but includes
significant allusions to the poverty of the oppressed masses as a revolutionary lever. The sad comedy *Leonce und Lena* (1836) occasionally satirizes absolutism in the small states of Germany. In the
tragic fragment *Woyzeck* (left unfinished in 1837) the obsessions
which drive the hero—or anti-hero—to murder and self-destruction
invoke existential suffering on a cosmic scale transcending the social
and psychological level; but the Doctor and the Captain, who combine callousness and brutality with unctuous moralizing, represent the
now powerful bourgeoisie, while the fact that Woyzeck himself—who
must perform humiliating menial services and submit to degrading
medical experiments in order to earn a pittance for his mistress and
his illegitimate child—is the earliest proletarian in the German theatre
may be considered as a further development of the introduction of
non-aristocratic protagonists in domestic tragedy. The use of symbolic,
surrealistic and proto-expressionistic devices in all three plays is not
incompatible with a realistic approach which Büchner has in common
with domestic dramatists.

The beginnings of socialism in Büchner were not followed up by
German playwrights till the advent of Naturalism. In the meantime,
however, Friedrich Hebbel produced what is held to be the fourth
great domestic tragedy in the language : *Maria Magdalene* (1843).

Among Hebbel's other plays, *Julia* and *Ein Trauerspiel in Sizilien*
(*A Sicilian Tragedy*, both completed in 1847) display various features
of domestic tragedy but are artistically negligible. His bias towards
near-Hegelian metaphysics and heroic characters, for instance in
Judith (1840), *Herodes und Mariamne* (*Herod and Mariamne*, 1849)
and *Gyges und sein Ring* (1855), echoes Classical drama, as does his
repeated employment of blank verse. *Agnes Bernauer* (1852) is written
in the prose characteristic of domestic tragedy and reiterates the

theme of love crossed by class-conflict and politics in that the heroine, a barber's daughter, is drowned on the order of the Duke when her unequal marriage to his son threatens to provoke a war of succession; but Hebbel's interest in historical personalities and events, and his concern to dramatise his philosophical notion that the individual, however pure, must be sacrified to the harmony of the universal, exceed the familiar everyday issues, while his demand for the citizen's total subordination to the state, voicing the conservatism of middle-class Germans after 1848, contradicts the liberal desires found in most examples of the genre.

Maria Magdalene, on the other hand, is entirely a domestic tragedy and, as Hebbel claims, a domestic tragedy of a new kind. The old domestic tragedy, he argues in his prefatory essay *Vorwort zur 'Maria Magdalena'* (1834), has 'fallen into disfavour' owing to its reliance on superficial class-conflicts rather than on conflicts arising from the inadequacies of the middle-class outlook as such:

> First and foremost, because it has not been constructed of those inner elements peculiar to itself: the uncompromising abruptness with which the individuals, incapable as they are of all dialectic, face one another in the narrowest possible sphere and the terrible one-sided cramping and confining of life resulting therefrom. Rather has it been patched together out of all kinds of externalities: for example, lack of money and surplus of hunger; above all, however, the conflict of the third estate with the first and second in love-affairs.

And, in his letter of December 11, 1843 to Auguste Stich-Crelinger, he praises his own domestic tragedy for its concentration on the intrinsic helplessness and bigotry of the bourgeoisie:

> If the play...has a partial merit, it probably lies in that the tragic impact here is derived not from the collision of the bourgeois world with the aristocratic...but quite simply from the bourgeois world itself, from its stubborn and self-motivated adherence to traditional patriarchal views and its inability to manage in complex situations.

It is debatable whether the prejudices of one class must of necessity appear more tragically inevitable than the clash of two classes. But it is true that the play itself, disregarding the aristocracy which had

indeed lost much of its significance to the middle classes, offers one of
the most devastating indictments of bourgeois attitudes ever encountered in the German theatre.

Avoiding, for once, all abstruse speculation, Hebbel succeeds in
making *Maria Magdalene*—which is partly autobiographical—a
masterpiece of Realism : the prose dialogue, despite its network of
claustrophobic images, accurately reproduces the spoken idiom; the
action is consistent with the characters, who are convincingly shaped
by social and professional conditions. Many themes of earlier domestic
tragedy recur, but they do so in fresh variations. The anguish of the
seduced girl is experienced again by Klara, the pregnant heroine.
The evils of snobbery are re-stated in the master-joiner Anton's snub-
bing of the bailiff, which leads to the wrongful arrest of his son Karl,
to the death of his wife, and, indirectly, to the suicide of his daughter;
social climbing is once more denounced through the unscrupulousness
of the clerk Leonhard, who abandons Klara after taking advantage
of her, in order to marry the prosperous mayor's niece and to promote
his career in the provincial civil service. The authority of the father
is maintained but shown up as a menace. Although Meister Anton is
said to be capable of generosity, his conduct is bitterly inhuman. Love,
for him, must yield to financial security; prayer must be accompanied
by life-denying gloom; sensitivity must hide behind aggression. His
tyrannical treatment of others—chiefly shown in his blackmailing
threats to kill himself if his daughter should disgrace him—may be a
reaction to a society which has subjected him to poverty and mortifica-
tion, but his own behaviour makes him an agent, as well as a victim,
of that society. His moral weakness is measured above all by his quest
for respectability. The Secretary, who owes a higher degree of penetra-
tion to his education, finally recognizes the hollowness of the code;
but, while Anton actually drove Klara to suicide through his fear
of the pharisees' disapproval, he too conformed when he failed to
reassure her of his love as a result of his preoccupation with the
apparent need to protect himself from the indignity of being associated
with her by the contemptible Leonhard :

When you suspected her misfortune, you thought of the tongues
that would hiss at it, but not of the worthlessness of the snakes
that own them. And I, instead of folding her in my arms, when she

opened her heart to me in nameless terror, thought of the knave
that might mock me . . . (Act III, Scene xi)

The play, then, not only repeats the criticism of middle-class frail-
ties found in domestic dramas preceeding it, but it totally reverses
most of the middle-class values which were formerly glorified in the
genre. Middle-class self-respect is turned into self-righteousness, duty
into pedantry and meaningless toil, virtue into hypocritical convention, religion into sterile routine :

. . . in this house we have twice ten commandments. 'Put your hat
on the third nail, not the fourth.' 'You must be sleepy at half past
nine.' 'You've no right to be chilly before Martinmas and no right
to sweat after it.' And that's on a level with 'Thou shalt fear God
and love Him.' . . . planing, sawing, and hammering, and then eat-
ing, drinking, and sleeping between-whiles to be able to go on
planing and sawing and hammering. And a-bending of the knee on
Sundays into the bargain : O God, I thank Thee for letting me
plane and saw and hammer. (III, vii, viii)

Karl may escape this environment as he goes to sea, and Klara may
rise above it in a spiritual sense, also suggested by the biblical title, as
she sacrifices herself for her father. But Anton and Leonhard never
understand their predicament; the Secretary's insight comes too late;
and Klara, a woman in a misguided male-dominated society, remains
utterly submissive. Although Hebbel is writing about the petty bourgeoisie, his views could apply to the German middle classes of the
mid-19th century in general : the power of middle-class morals over
the characters seems to reflect the social importance of the middle-
classes in reality, while the mutual destruction of middle-class characters on stage is arguably a sign of the real-life inability of the middle
classes to direct their energies outward to the attainment of political
supremacy.

Maria Magdalene marks a turning-point in German theatrical
history. Presenting man not as an 'autonomous individual' but as 'a
product of determining circumstances', to quote Elise Dosenheimer,
'Hebbel took a decisive step from the domestic tragedy of the 18th
century to the social drama of the 19th.'[8] It was in the second half of
the 19th century that the industrial revolution swept through Germany, providing entrepreneurs with unprecedented wealth and

furthering the ascendancy of the capitalist-imperialist Second Reich under Bismarck; while the misery of the proletariat grew, the middle classes prospered, readily obeying the conservative regime and often supporting its resistance to socialist reforms. Hauser may exaggerate in declaring that 'until about 1848 the intelligentsia is still the intellectual vanguard of the bourgeoisie, after 1848 it becomes, consciously or unconsciously, the champion of the working class' (vol. 4, p. 127). Nevertheless, it is correct that many writers sympathized with the workers and proved increasingly hostile to the middle classes.

The foremost movement in late 19th century drama was that of Naturalism. Aware of Darwinian science, the positivist philosophy of Auguste Comte, Hippolyte Taine and Ludwig Feuerbach, and the works of Dostoevsky and Tolstoy, German Naturalists were chiefly indebted to the novels and theories of Zola and the prose tragedies of Ibsen, most of which were written in the eighteen-seventies and eighties. Domestic tragedy was frequently dismissed in favour of broad social drama, whether of a left-wing or of an impartially objective kind. But the presentation of the sordid and painful existence of the poor, already found in Büchner, may be seen as a continuation of the descent from the aristocracy to the middle classes, and the repudiation of bourgeois exploiters as an intensification of the criticism of middle-class attitudes, in domestic tragedy; similarly the new 'slice-of-life' technique may be considered as a sequel to the realistic trends found in that genre. The survival of domestic tragedy itself in the Naturalist period is most evident in the family pieces of such writers as Arno Holz and Johannes Schlaf, Hermann Sudermann and, above all, Gerhart Hauptmann, who is in fact the only dramatist of the movement with a claim to lasting fame.

Hauptmann was an uneven as he was prolific. His poetic plays on mystical subjects are unsuccessful; his autobiographical studies and theoretical notes show limited intelligence. Some of his Naturalist dramas, however, are extremely impressive.

In the present context his masterpiece, *Die Weber* (*The Weavers*, 1893), the first and greatest working-class mass-drama in the language, must be remembered as a brilliant example of the proletarian modification of domestic tragedy and as a hard-hitting denuciation of bourgeois capitalism, embodied in the rich manufacturer, whose manipulations are aided and abetted by representatives of state and church; while his first play, *Vor Sonnenaufgang* (*Before Dawn*, 1889), which signalled the sensational arrival of Naturalism on the German stage, recalls domestic tragedy in those episodes which deal with the private betrayal of the loving heroine by the fanatical reformer, and in those which again expose bourgeois capitalism through the disingenuous civil engineer and speculator.

Das Friedensfest (*Reconciliation*, 1890) and *Einsame Menschen* (*Lonely Lives*, 1891) are closer to the plays of Ibsen as well as to traditional domestic tragedy. In the former the Naturalist invocation of heredity and environment through the quarrels of ill-matched parents and maladjusted children stresses private suffering in the manner of the early phases of the genre, whereas the unveiling of the hateful reality behind the respectable façade of the middle-class family, which is typical of the later phases, remains in the background. In the latter both aspects are prominent. The hero, a youngish scholar, dreams of improving the world by modern scientific thought and of finding happiness with the emancipated girl-student. As his research is hampered and his romance shattered by the demands of his commonplace wife and his puritanical parents, the middle-class family, which was once exalted as the foundation of a progressive society, is shown up as an obstacle to personal fulfilment and to communal liberation. When, unable either to accept or to break his ties, he commits suicide, the private catastrophe reveals the full pernicious force of the conventions which moulded the conduct of the bourgeoisie towards the turn of the century. *Fuhrmann Henschel* (*Drayman Henschel*, 1898) and *Rose Bernd* (1903) are also primarily domestic tragedies, above all owing to the petty-bourgeois responses of their rural Silesian characters. While *Fuhrmann Henschel*, where the elevation of the small-time transport contractor to the stature of a tragic hero is in line with domestic tragedy as a whole, seems largely devoid of the social criticism of late domestic tragedy, *Rose Bernd* contains social criticism as well as the raising of a socially inferior person to tragic dignity. The affair of the peasant's daughter with the landowner conjures up the theme of love across the class-barrier, seen in *Emilia Galotti*, *Kabale und Liebe* and other domestic tragedies. The plight of the unmarried mother who kills her child is similar to that of *Sturm und Drang* domestic heroines. The villain is the brutal seducer—a mechanic whose ominous threshing machine perhaps suggests the dangers of industrialization—but the sharpest accusations are levelled against that mentality which is mainly represented, as it

was in *Maria Magdalene*, by the pregnant girl's father : his greed, his
narrow-mindedness, his effete pietism and his self-defeating search for
respectability indicate the extent to which former middle-class values
are now regarded as vices; despite some instances of Christian charity,
the inhuman conventions triumph, causing the suicide of the heroine,
whose own assent—again echoing earlier domestic tragedy—is borne
out by her misplaced sense of shame. Profoundly moving in its mani-
festation of private grief, rousing in its demasking of false public
morality, the play is both a memorable example of its kind and a
distinguished individual work of art.

Although Hauptmann continued to write till the nineteen-forties,
it may be argued that his last completely satisfactory play was *Die
Ratten* (*The Rats*, 1911). As a tragi-comedy it goes back to the inter-
mediate genres of the 18th century, while its tragic plot belongs to
domestic tragedy.

The juxtaposition of various ranks of the community in the de-
crepit tenement building—which has been interpreted as a symbol of
the doomed Wilhelmine Reich—recalls the class-distinctions of earlier
domestic drama. The theatre manager Hassenreuter, a superbly comic
charlatan, provides a caricature of upper middle-class political conservatism, and the cruelty of the nobility is illustrated through Frau
Knobbe, who was abandoned to prostitution and drugs by her aristocratic family after a sexual faux-pas. But once again the criticism is
mainly directed against the moral code of the middle classes, personi-
fied by the elder Spitta. This hypocritical clergyman, who secretly
lusts after the dissipations he reviles in public, who decries his son's
social and artistic efforts in the name of a specious respectability, and
who, instead of practising the benevolence he preaches, pushed his
daughter to suicide when—like many other girls in domestic tragedy
—she became pregnant, is a pillar of the bourgeoisie. The travesty of
Christianity perpetrated by his class—a position also adopted by the
foreman-mason John, who is best located between the petty bourgeois
and the worker, and who, with similar obduracy, rebuffs his wife's
plea for help in her distress—is most forcefully condemned by the
younger Spitta, who appears as a slightly absurd but sympathetic
champion of genuine humanity :

O these Christians! . . . O thou good Shepherd, how have your
words been perverted! How have your eternal truths been falsified

into their exact contrary...the poor outcast and her terrible accusation shall never die in my soul! And into this flame of our souls we must cast all the wretchedness, all the lamentations of the oppressed and the disinherited! Thus shall my sister stay truly alive, Walburga, and effect noble ends before the face of God through the ethical impulse that lends wings to my soul, and that will be more powerful than all the evil, heartless parson's morality in the world. (Act IV)

The action centres on Frau John. As the authorities unfeelingly deprive her of the child she has bought from the chambermaid Piperkarcka—yet another unmarried mother subjected to undeserved hardship and disgrace—Hauptmann adds more criticism of the dominant bourgeois order to his keen observation of proletarian misery. The strongest impact, however, is made by his compassionate portrayal of Frau John as one lonely female, whose mother-instinct, frustrated by unfortunate circumstances, entangles her in deceit, crime and despair, from which she can only escape into suicide.

It is interesting to note how the play combines theoretical discussion with practical demonstration. The young Spitta not only rebels against conservative bourgeois conventions in his fight for humanity, but he also advocates a new type of drama. While Hassenreuter praises both the Bismarckian empire and the Classical heroic theatre, Spitta attacks injustice in society as well as what he calls the 'Goethe-Schiller-Weimar school of idealistic artifice' (I) on stage. Rejecting histrionic declamation, bombastic dialogues, contrived intrigues and false poetic justice, he claims, linking social and aesthetic considerations, that members of any class are capable of tragic greatness, and that drama must be artistic but truthful. Citing Diderot and Lessing as well as Schiller and Goethe in their *Sturm und Drang* period, he associates a large share of his Naturalist views with the domestic form:

Before art as before the law all men are equal... In believing this I probably find myself at variance with Schiller and Gustav Freytag, but not at all with Lessing and Diderot... And if the German stage is ever to recuperate it must go back to the young Schiller, the young Goethe ... and ever again to Gotthold Ephraim Lessing! There you will find set down principles of dramatic art which are adapted to the rich complexity of life in all its fullness, and which are potent to cope with Nature itself! (III)

And the plot as a whole, in which the undoing of an ordinary char-woman is recorded with realistic accuracy and tragic power, proves him right, as even Hassenreuter, with magnificent inconsistency, finally admits:

Tragedy is not confined to any class of society. I always told you that!(V)

Die Ratten thus supplies conclusive evidence of the continuity of domestic drama from the Enlightenment to Naturalism. Even while Hauptmann was writing the last outstanding examples of the genre—which is still recognized in the 'kitchen-sink' mode of today—such innovators as Wedekind and Sternheim, soon to be followed by the Expressionists, were turning to different styles. But for a century and a half domestic drama, above all in its tragic variant, represented one of the most vital strands in the evolution of the German theatre.

NOTES

1. Arnold Hauser, *The Social History of Art*, translated in collaboration with the Author by Stanley Godman, London 1962, vol, 3, pp. 92, 82.
2. Georg Lukács, *Zur Soziologie des modernen Dramas* (1914), in: Georg Lukács, *Schriften zur Literatursoziologie*, ed. Peter Ludz, Neuwied 1961, p. 277.
3. Lothar Pikulik, *'Bürgerliches Trauerspiel' und Empfindsamkeit*, Cologne-Graz 1966, pp. 170, 152.
4. Karl S. Guthke, *Das deutsche bürgerliche Trauerspiel*, Stuttgart 1972, p. 11.
5. Peter Szondi, *Die Theorie des bürgerlichen Trauerspiels im 18. Jahrhundert*, Frankfurt 1973, pp. 72, 167.
6. Wolfgang Schaer, *Die Gesellschaft im deutschen bürgerlichen Drama des 18. Jahrhunderts*, Bonn 1963, pp. 35, 85, 50, 48.
7. Raymond Williams, *Modern Tragedy*, London 1966, p. 92.
8. Elise Dosenheimer, *Das deutsche soziale Drama von Lessing bis Sternheim*, Constance 1949, p. 90.

4

John Osborne: ANTI-ARISTOTELIAN DRAMA FROM LENZ
TO WEDEKIND

In a commentary on his adaptation of Lenz's *Die Soldaten* (*The Soldiers*) Heinar Kipphardt writes: 'The author regards *Die Soldaten* by J. M. R. Lenz as one of the key works in the history of the German theatre. Its influence can be traced through Büchner, Grabbe, Wedekind, Brecht, Horvath, up to the contemporary German drama.' In choosing *Die Soldaten* as a work worth adapting, Kipphardt is directly following the example of Brecht, who considered Lenz's *Der Hofmeister* (*The Tutor*) to be a standard work in the tradition of the bourgeois social drama, and who adapted it for performance by the *Berliner Ensemble* in 1950. At the same time Kipphardt is appealing to a continuous tradition within the history of the German drama which, in the last decade or so, has acquired a certain respectability, even orthodoxy, but whose exponents, in their respective historical contexts, had a uniformly oppositional role, and whose names recurrently figure in a variety of investigations into literary-historical phenomena which stand aside from the mainstream: the grotesque (Wolfgang Kayser), tragi-comedy (Karl S. Guthke), the Bohème (Helmut Kreuzer), 'open form' (Volker Klotz), 'Brecht's tradition' (Max Spalter), 'epic theatre' (Reinhold Grimm).

Lenz, Büchner, the Hauptmann of the Naturalist period, and Wedekind are four dramatists who have made significant contributions to this particular tradition, and who have consciously built on the achievements of their predecessors. They are united in their rejection of the Aristotelian canon as an authoritarian norm, and are even disposed to see in it a symbol of political oppression; they exploit the possibilities of the 'open form' in the conviction that such a form is necessary to do justice to the subject matter which, for them, constitutes 'reality', and which is explicitly excluded by the rigorously classical theories of the mature Schiller, who writes in the preface to

Die Braut von Messina (*The Bride of Messina*): 'The introduction of the chorus would be the final, the decisive step . . . it should be a living wall, within which tragedy encloses itself in order to cut itself off entirely from the real world and preserve its ideal basis, its poetic freedom'.

In contrast to this ideal world, firmly enclosed by a surrounding wall, the anti-Aristotelian dramatists set a world with open windows, through which external reality can penetrate; and they tend to choose their characters from among those individuals in whom the sense of exposure to the forces from the world outside is at its greatest: unheroic, average mortals, with an inadequate understanding of their predicament. They anticipate Brecht in relating the fate of their characters to the socio-political situations in which they are placed, and in questioning the absolute necessity of these situations; but they are by no means certain that the wretchedness of the human condition, and the exposure of the individual are entirely explicable in economic terms; and they are by no means optimistic about the possibility of change.

The model to whom the dramatists of this anti-classical opposition have constantly appealed has been Shakespeare. The oppositional role is already most provocatively taken up by an 'Aristotelian', Lessing, in the famous *17. Literaturbrief* (1759). During the subsequent decade and a half the emancipatory impulse underlying Lessing's response to Shakespeare is amplified and deepened. In the writings of Hamann and Gerstenberg the concept of the individual *Genie* as a quasi-divine creator comes to occupy a decisive place, and so the doctrine of the imitation of nature undergoes a radical revision; and in Herder's Shakespeare essay the idea of historical relativism in aesthetics receives its classic formulation, clearing the way for an appreciation of Shakespeare on his own terms—whereas Lessing had been content to assert that his work measured up to the absolute demands of the ancients: 'Even when judged by the standards of the ancients, Shakespeare is a far greater tragic poet than Corneille'.

In these years there is little attempt to analyse the form of Shakespearian drama, or to devise a programmatic Shakespearian dramaturgy. Lessing does little to substantiate the claims he makes for Shakespeare's orthodoxy; nor is Herder's attempt to explain

Elizabethan drama in terms of its historical origins anything like as precise as his examination of the sources of Greek drama, and he soon abandons the task, to indulge in that rhapsodic praise of—and intense personal identification with—Shakespeare which is characteristic of much of the writing of the early seventeen-seventies. In Goethe's Shakespeare essay of 1771 (*Zum Schäkespears Tag*) and in Lenz's *Anmerkungen übers Theater* (*Remarks on the Theatre*) we encounter this same tendency to use Shakespeare as an oppositional watchword; and a tendency to seek—and find—in his work precisely those themes which preoccupy the two young writers at this particular time. Thus Goethe, who was shortly to dramatize, in *Götz von Berlichingen*, the conflict of the individual and his age, writes of Shakespeare : 'his plays all revolve around the secret centre which no philosopher has yet seen or defined : at which our most individual peculiarity, our claim to freedom of the will, clashes with the necessary course of the world'; and Lenz, whose own personal struggle for emancipation (his departure from his Livonian home, and his efforts to assert himself as a writer) brought him inevitably into conflict with an authoritarian father, and whose own works are centred obsessively on the theme of the Prodigal Son, concentrates in his analyses of dramas such as *Romeo and Juliet* and *Julius Caesar*, and in his subsequent adaptation of *Coriolanus*, on the disruption of family relationships.

In *Götz von Berlichingen* Goethe wrote the first major drama of the anti-Aristotelian tradition; but his importance in this tradition is exceeded by that of Lenz. The reasons for this do not lie so much in the relative quality of their literary work, as in the fact that the two writers provide a ready-made contrast. After a close friendship in the early seventeen-seventies, and a serious and definitive break in 1776, their fortunes proceeded in totally different directions. Whereas Goethe became the greatest exponent of the classical style, and returned, with such dramas as *Torquato Tasso* and *Iphigenie auf Tauris* to Aristotelian norms, Lenz suffered a mental breakdown, and came to a wretched end, having written no drama of consequence subsequent to *Die Soldaten*. Goethe's unfriendly characterization of Lenz in his autobiography, *Dichtung und Wahrheit* (*Poetry and Truth*), emphasized this contrast and, in a negative way, has no doubt helped to contribute to the mythologization of Lenz as the fountain-head of the anti-Aristotelian tradition in German drama.

Götz von Berlichingen, however, dates from the time when Lenz
was an admirer of Goethe, and he commended the play to his friends
in the Strasbourg Philosophical and Literary Society without reserva-
tion. His enthusiastic essay on *Götz von Berlichingen* begins with a
vision of the human condition which is at once a lament and a
protest:

> We are born—our parents give us food and clothing—our teachers
> impress into our brain words, language, science—some nice girl
> impresses into our heart the desire to possess her, to enclose her in
> our arms as our own, if indeed some animal need does not play a
> role—there is a vacancy in society into which we fit—our friends,
> relations, patrons set to and push us happily into it—for a while we
> revolve in this place like the other cogs, and push and drive—until
> we are worn out and finally have to make way for a new cog—
> that, gentleman, without boasting, is the story of our life—and
> what, then, is Man but an excellent, artificial little machine, which
> fits, more or less well, into the great machine which we call the
> world, world-events, the course of the world.
>
> No wonder philosophers philosophize like this, if people live
> like this. But can this be called living? can this be called feeling
> one's existence, the divine spark? Ah, it must lie elsewhere, the
> charm of life: for to be a plaything of others is a gloomy and
> depressing thought.

The desire to be free from this oppressive determinism is one of the
underlying factors in Lenz's most extensive dramaturgical essay, the
Anmerkungen übers Theater, and it is at the root of his insistence on
the primacy of character over action. Following Herder, Lenz
relativizes the Aristotelian principles by referring them to their
origins; he argues that in the context of the religious ethos of the
Greeks actions had to be motivated by an external fate, and not by
individual character, for the purpose of the drama was to instil in the
audience fear of the gods. In protest against this irrational and, for
him, blasphemous attitude, Lenz advances a theory of tragedy in
which the central position is occupied by a great and titanic figure,
who is the master of his own destiny:

> I am speaking of characters who create their own events, who
> independently and consistently turn the whole great machine

themselves, without having any need for the gods up in the clouds except—if they so wish—as spectators; not of painted images or puppets—but of men.

Lenz's attempt to write this drama of the emancipated individual remained fragmentary; nor were his contemporaries among the *Stürmer-und-Dränger* any more successful. Where they bring such characters on to the stage—Klinger in *Die Zwillinge* (*The Twins*), Schiller in *Die Räuber* (*The Robbers*), Lenz himself in *Der neue Menoza* (*The New Menoza*)—they show them failing to overcome those inner and outer constraints against which Lenz protests.[1] In his dramaturgical writings Lenz also reveals a sense that the time was not ripe for the ideal tragedy he envisaged; and in his theory of comedy he begins to outline an alternative form. In comedy action takes precedence over character, for it does not arise from the depths of the individual personality or the individual will, but from a specific social-historical situation. Comedy, he argues in his own review of *Der neue Menoza,* gives a picture of the conditions of society; and in *Pandämonium Germanicum* he suggests that comedy liberates by satire, so preparing the way for a new society and a new drama: 'what used once to terrify us, ought now to make us smile . . . for us the sufferings of Greek heroes are middle-class phenomena'. In his essay on the theatre as a moral institution the young Schiller writes in much the same spirit : 'If we wanted to evaluate comedy and tragedy according to the degree of effectiveness, then experience would perhaps favour the former. Mockery and scorn wound a man's pride more sharply than abhorrence tortures his conscience.'[2]

Lenz's reputation as a dramatist rests on two plays, *Der Hofmeister* and *Die Soldaten*, which stand much closer to comedy, as he himself defines it. It would, however, be wrong to see in his dramaturgical writings a practically-orientated poetic comparable to Brecht's. The formal implications of Lenz's advocacy of a dramatic style in which the individual is seen as the product of a deterministic system are considerable; and he shows himself strikingly aware of these implications in an essay dedicated to his contemporary, Heinrich Leopold Wagner, by his use of a metaphor which anticipates Wölfflin's categories of 'closed' and 'open form', which have been used with such signal success to vindicate the originality of Lenz and his successors :

There are two kinds of garden, one which can be surveyed entirely at the first glance, the other in which, as in nature, one proceeds step by step, from one variation to another. There are also two kinds of drama ... in the one everything is connected up and is presented at once, and so is easier to grasp, in the other it is necessary to climb up and down, as in nature.[3]

In practice, however, Lenz's bold use of open form is to some extent undermined by the simultaneous use of an enclosing didactic framework. In the first act of the drama a specific problem is explicitly identified, in *Der Hofmeister* the problem of private or public education, in *Die Soldaten* the law which forbade soldiers to marry; and in the final scene of each play, after a series of complex and loosely connected actions, the moral of the respective story is drawn : namely that children should not be educated by private tutors, but in public institutions, and that an official brothel should be set up by the monarch to cater for the sexual needs of the soldiers, and so to safeguard the wives and daughters of honest citizens. In both cases, however, this didactic framework is curiously isolated from the realities of the action which it encloses; just as in Brecht's *Der kaukasische Kreidekreis* (*The Caucasian Chalk Circle*) the rational Utopia of the young woman tractor-driver is isolated from the realities of the world of Grusche Vachnadze. We read Lenz—as we read Brecht—not for such easy solutions, but for his illumination of the world in which the struggle takes place, in which the individual must fight to assert himself, or be reduced to the level of a marionette, whose movements are dictated by his milieu.

An analysis of the initial stages of the action of *Die Soldaten* will illustrate the way Lenz proceeds. The central figure in the play, Mariane Wesener, is introduced in the opening scene as an attractive but immature girl, the favourite of her father, and very much reliant on him as a moral authority. Her future within her own social sphere would seem to be secure, for she has a bourgeois suitor, Stolzius, whose devotion to her is beyond question. However, the aristocratic officer, Desportes, presents a serious threat to this future, in that he offers an exciting alternative to the constriction of the bourgeois household within which Mariane suffers. A willing victim of the flattery of Desportes, Mariane is readily persuaded to disobey her father and accompany the officer to the theatre. The profound effect of this glimpse into a different world, and her need, within her family situation, for her father's approval, are such that Mariane cannot conceal her deceit. The immediate response of Wesener is a conditioned reflex rather than the result of serious thought, but in a world where class barriers are firmly drawn, and where people behave predictably, it is correct : he assumes that Desportes' intentions are dishonourable, and sends his daughter to her room in disgrace. The scene ends with Wesener sunk in thought, that is falling out of his role as the stern father, the instinctive upholder of middle-class morality.

The sixth scene takes place in Mariane's room, and opens with her seated on her bed, a gift from Desportes in her hand, lost in reverie : confined by the moral authority of her father to a room in a middle-class household, her thoughts are elsewhere. But in the course of the scene it becomes clear that the confining moral authority is by no means as firm as at first appeared. Wesener's weakness is his social ambition, his fond hope that at this time of social change, and growing confidence among the middle classes, his pretty daughter may be able to cross hitherto unsurmountable barriers, and secure for herself the title of 'gnädige Frau'. At the same time Wesener is aware of the risks; he advises his daughter to create the impression that her affair with Desportes does not meet with her father's approval, and to hang on to her bourgeois suitor, Stolzius, as a kind of insurance. Throughout these scenes father and daughter have an essentially passive role; they respond impulsively when they feel they can see a way out of their present situation; but both, in subtly differentiated ways, are held back by the class morality they are betraying : Wesener encourages the relationship of Mariane with Desportes, but attempts to keep up appearances by insisting on a chaperone, by forbidding his daughter to accept presents, and by feigning disapproval; Mariane thinks of the effect her adventure will have on Stolzius. This conflict is carried out in an environment which is by no means neutral : as we have seen, the constriction of the bourgeois interior is contrasted with the gaiety of the world outside; but with the moral reversal of Act I, scene 6 this contrast is inverted. In the window-scene, with which the first act ends, the forces which would restrain Mariane's own desires, the social norms and their reflection in her bourgeois conscience, are now outside, threatening to break in. Mariane cannot overcome these forces; the most she can do is to try and forget them, shut them out of the—now corrupted, but more attractive—interior, and hope that she will not have to pay the penalty :

> MARIANE (. . . *heaves a deep sigh and goes to the window, unlacing her bodice.*) I feel so miserable. I think there's going to be a storm tonight. What if it struck—(*Looks up to the sky, striking herself above the breast with her hands.*) But what have I done wrong?— Stolzius—I do still love you—but if I can do better for myself— and Papa himself advises me to. (*Draws the curtain.*) If it strikes me, then it strikes me, I don't care if I die. (*Puts out her light.*)

Such a scene shows the character confronted by an alive and active environment, forced inwards or outwards according to the direction from which the pressures come, but not fully able to comprehend these pressures as part of an ordered system, and not independent or self-confident enough to attempt to impose his own will, his own order upon them. The dramas of the young Schiller have many formal characteristics in common with the open dramas of Lenz and his successors, but the relationship between man and nature is totally different. Act III, scene 2 of Schiller's *Die Verschwörung des Fiesko zu Genua* shows the hero standing at a window overlooking the city of Genoa. This is the scene in which Fiesko reaches his decision to make himself Duke of Genoa, and from beginning to end it consists of a single, extended outward movement: it begins in twilight, the window is opened, the sun rises over the city—but these natural manifestations do not *cause*, they *reflect* the inner state of the hero. His action of opening the window is not an escape, but an act of assertion, dictated by his own dreams and ambitions. Like Mariane Wesener he is inhibited by a moral conscience; but he displays a sovereign intellectual detachment towards this. Whereas Mariane's thoughts turn to a real individual, Stolzius, whom she is aware of hurting by her actions, Fiesko has no sense of the suffering he will bring upon the people of Genoa; Fiesko's 'Virtue' is an abstraction which melts to nothing before his assertive will :

> but I shall be acting unvirtuously. (*Stands motionless.*) Virtue?— the sublime spirit is open to other temptations than is the base— ought he to share the same virtue? The harness which binds the

puny body of the pigmy—should *that* have to fit the frame of a giant?

(*The sun rises over Genoa.*)

The masterful subjectivity of Fiesko does not bring him success any more than the clumsy opportunism of Wesener and his daughter; but the nature of their respective downfalls emphasizes still further the essential differences between their respective creators. The Weseners' 'tragedy' is enacted within a totally immanent sequence of events; underlying Schiller's play is a pattern of justice in which nemesis overtakes a hero who has asserted himself beyond the measure to which he is entitled. *Fiesko* already points to those later dramas of Schiller where we encounter tragic heroes who begin to measure up to the demands made in the *Anmerkungen übers Theater*, and who are, in a very special Schillerian sense, 'creators of their own events', who understand and affirm the system within which they meet their end.

The brief contrast between closed and open form which Lenz made in an analogy with the contrasting—French and English —styles in landscape gardening, has a counterpart in Büchner's *Novelle, Lenz.* Again the contrast is made with reference to a neighbouring art form, painting; but where the real Lenz was concerned simply to justify one style alongside another, the fictitious Lenz— and in this he can be said to be speaking for his creator—makes a radical attack on the classical style itself, by inverting the judgment of Winckelmann as to the relative merits of classic art and the realistic works of the Dutch genre-painters. In his interpretation of Raphael's *Sistine Madonna* (*On the Imitation of Greek Works of Painting and Sculpture*) Winckelmann had seen a central figure, radiating peacefulness and saintliness, reflected and affirmed by the gestures of the subordinate figures, arranged symmetrically within the picture to either side of the Madonna. Against this enclosed totality Büchner sets a Dutch interior, full of every-day detail, and composed in such a way as to refer outwards to a reality which is not contained within the arbitrary frame of the picture :

A woman is sitting in her room, a prayer-book in her hand. It has been tidied up for Sunday, sand has been strewn, it is so homely, clean, and warm. The woman was not able to go to church, and she is saying her prayers at home, the window is open, she is seated facing it, and it is as if, across the flat, open landscape, the sound of bells from the village and the singing of the congregation are echoing in through the window, and the woman is following the text in her prayer-book.

The dramas of Büchner contain a number of scenes which correspond to this interior, but invariably the idyllic quality is absent. Act II, scene 5 of *Dantons Tod* shows Danton, like Fiesko, looking down from his window over the city of Paris, the field of his political exploits; but unlike Fiesko he cannot regard the city as so much raw material over which he can extend his will; no more can Marie, as she dances with the drum-major in the inn-scene in *Woyzeck*, and fails to notice Woyzeck looking in at the window. For Danton and Marie, as for Mariane Wesener, the world outside the window is a world in which they belong by virtue of their relationships with others. The failure of their respective attempts to escape into indifference serves to illustrate the power of this social reality.

Büchner's sense of the exposure of man to forces outside himself and beyond his control is similar to, but more radical than that expressed by Lenz in his essay on *Götz von Berlichingen*; and in a celebrated letter to his fiancée he expresses more clearly the sense of an underlying existential exposure :

> I studied the history of the Revolution. I felt somehow annihilated beneath the cruel fatalism of history. In human nature I find a dreadful uniformity, in human institutions an inavertable force, bestowed on all and on none. The individual no more than foam on the wave, greatness a mere accident, the rule of genius a puppet-play, a ridiculous struggle against an iron law; the highest achievement : to recognise this law; to control it—an impossibility.

Starting from this despairing nihilism, Büchner vigorously attacks a doctrine which proclaims the superiority of mind over matter. The stoicism which was practised by the noble heroes of Racine, Corneille, Schiller and Goethe, and which the 'democratic' Lessing had claimed for his middle-class heroes, is denied as a value by Büchner: the Virginia-story, which Lessing adapted in *Emilia Galotti*, is held up to ridicule in *Dantons Tod* (Act I, scene 2). Büchner turns decisively away from heroes who, like Fiesko, stand above the common norms of virtue, to characters like Woyzeck, who stand far below :

we ordinary people, we've no virtue, only nature, but if I were a gentleman, with a hat and a watch and a frockcoat and could talk finely, I would be virtuous all right. There must be something beautiful about virtue, captain. But I am a poor man.

The ideal of heroic resistance to suffering gives way to the conviction that suffering, without promise of redemption, is the only guarantee of reality. From its deliberately prosaic title, to its conclusion in the impulsive and absurd self-sacrifice of the insane Lucile, with the words: 'Long live the King!', everything in *Dantons Tod* runs counter to the assumptions underlying the traditional five-act tragedy, with its tautly organized and purposeful structure, and its climax in the meaningful death of the hero. Here death is simply biological decay; in death, as in life, man is worn away by alien forces, whose overall purpose he cannot comprehend: 'There is no hope in death, it is just a more simple form of decay, whereas life is a more complex, more organised form of decay, that is all the difference!' Critical though they are of social conditions and the exploitation of the under-privileged, there is no room in Büchner's dramas for optimistic, practical proposals for social reform. In their attempts to assert their individual freedom both the 'makers of history', the articulate, intelligent (and therefore cynical and passive) Danton, and the downtrodden, inarticulate Woyzeck are revealed equally as victims, without any significant room for manoeuvre. At the conclusion of Büchner's dramas the curtain falls on unresolved problems.

In the mid-19th century, when the theory of drama was orientated on the closed form of the classical Schiller, the works of Lenz and Büchner found little echo. Freytag's *Technik des Dramas* (*Technique of the Drama*), with its static image of the drama as a pyramid, and its exclusion of revolutionary social content; Hebbel's view of tragedy, in which conflicting social-historical forces are hypostatized into symbols of an existential dichotomy; Hettner's demands for a revival of classicism; all these are characteristic of an age which had become reconciled to political resignation, and had turned its back on disruption and opposition: 'What I want is basically no different from what all writers have been wanting since the *Sturm und Drang* and the Romantic period: more calmness and simplicity, a reaction against the haste and breadth and turbulence of *Götz von Berlichingen*', wrote Hettner in a letter to Gottfried Keller.[4]

Nevertheless, developments in the philosophy and in the social and natural sciences, together with the social and political changes which accompanied the industrialization of Germany, began to create a climate which was favourable to a different kind of drama. Signs of this change are already evident in the contradiction between the formal demands of Hettner and his simultaneous recognition of the importance of social *content* for the drama of the future. The success of the Meiningen Court Theatre in the eighteen-seventies is another significant pointer. Although offering a traditional repertoire—predominantly Schiller, Shakespeare, and Kleist—and owing much of their popularity to contemporary taste for spectacularly decorative historicism, its productions decisively shifted the emphasis away from the star-performer to the background against which the events took place. The company's production methods were taken over and applied to different material by the three great directors of the Naturalist period, all of whom witnessed their productions in the eighteen-eighties: Otto Brahm, André Antoine, and Stanislavsky.

Apart from two isolated performances of Ibsen's *Ghosts*, the Meiningen Company did not itself produce any modern works in which the deterministic theories of the latter part of the 19th century were in any way exploited in the drama. To this extent they remain a transitional phenomenon, whose literary influence was less important than their influence in the development of the modern theatre. The discovery of the dramas of Lenz and Büchner required the deeper literary concern and the more consciously oppositional attitude of the young writers of the Naturalist generation. In Hauptmann's autobiography one can recognize that same sense of identification with a neglected predecessor which we encountered in the provocative writings of the *Stürmer-und-Dränger* on Shakespeare:

> George Büchner's work, on which I gave a talk in the *Durch*-Society, had made a profound impression on me. The incomparable monument which he had left after a life of only twenty-three years, the *Novelle*, *Lenz*, the *Woyzeck*-fragments, were for me great discoveries. . . . The spirit of George Büchner now lived with us, in us, over us. And whoever is familiar with him, this poetic spirit thrown up like glowing lava from the depths of the earth, can well imagine that, for all his uniqueness, he was our kin.[5]

The scientific theories of the Naturalists do not posit an ideally ordered world in which man occupies a central position. Reality for the Naturalists consists of the discovered facts of the positive sciences. Their world is a world without a teleology, in which all—even man's spiritual activity—is governed by a relentless mechanical causality.

Such theoretical convictions demanded a revolution in the drama: the development of an anti-heroic milieu drama, in which man more or less disappears in his environment. Characters in such a drama would be victims, incapable of responsibility, and incapable of incurring tragic guilt. Inter-personal conflicts, expressed fully and completely in a dialogue form, would give way before the extra-personal forces embodied in the activated milieu, whose overall purpose the dramatist does not feel able to explain adequately, and which therefore resist containment in the symbolic framework of the classical drama. If the audience is to understand that the dramatic conflict is not brought about by an active exercise of will, an *epic* manner is required: through a profusion of stage-directions an implied narrator can tell us that his characters are the product of a certain set of circumstances, which have their own independent existence in the empirical world; even more frequently than in the works of Lenz and Büchner the set in Hauptmann's early dramas opens up, through doors and windows, on to this outside world and its activities. The drama of Naturalism comes to resemble a sequence of tableaux, which reveal milieu and character, but without relating to any ideal purpose, or archetypal plot-structure; the drama contains no complete, rounded action, but tends to remain open, at both beginning and end; Hauptmann speaks for many of his contemporaries with the rhetorical question: 'In cases where we cannot adapt life to the dramatic form—ought we not adapt this form to life?'[6]

In practice, however, German Naturalism itself remained a transitional phenomenon; such a consistently realist drama as that outlined above was not developed in the eighteen-nineties. It is characteristic of the inconsistencies within the Naturalist movement that whereas Hauptmann should champion Büchner, the theorist and dramatist Bleibtreu should—like the Naturalists' Marxist critic, Franz Mehring —condemn the 'shapelessness' of his work, and (like the writers of the preceding generation, whom the Naturalists so furiously attacked) regret the absence of 'a rounded, real [sic] conclusion' in Ibsen's *A Doll's House*. Indeed Bleibtreu's essay, 'Ibsen and the modern drama of the future', betrays a continued adherence to the conception of closed form of drama: 'If a dramatist slams the door in our faces, and sends us home shaking our heads discontentedly, we are perfectly entitled to reject such riddles, since they offend against all the rules of drama, the most closed of all art-forms.'

Even Hauptmann, who argues as firmly as any of his contemporaries against the Aristotelian primacy of plot, frequently brings the action of his dramas to a decisive conclusion with the death of the protagonist, and the strong final curtain of the *pièce bien faite*.

Despite this ambiguity Hauptmann stands, with his best-known works, *Die Weber* and *Der Biberpelz* (*The Beaver Coat*), firmly within the traditions of the social drama and the open form; and it is by no means coincidental that these are the works which have had most resonance among dramatists of the 20th century, such as Toller and Brecht.[7] From the outset *Die Weber* was regarded as a drama without a hero. Each of its five acts has a different setting, and in each the attention of the audience is focused on a different group of people. These several tableaux combine to throw light on the situation of the weavers from differing points of view, to show the various pressures to which they are subject, and the various ways in which they respond to these pressures. There is no single representative figure; Old Hilse, the solitary weaver who, in Act V, resists the urge to revolt, belongs just as much within this unified structure as his friend, Baumert, who allows himself to be carried forward, and the younger men, Bäcker and Jäger, who—for different reasons—assume the active role of agitators. The dramatic tension of the work arises from the outbreak of the revolt, the gradual formation of the individual weavers into a violent and destructive mob. The reasons for this are fairly clear—one has only to observe the set, or read the stage-directions—but the actual process itself begins outside the drama, before the first act, and it ends after the final curtain with the crushing of the revolt by government troops.

This final curtain falls shortly after the death of Hilse, who is hit by a stray bullet as he sits at his loom before an open window, continuing his work, and faithfully adhering to a religious belief which sees protest as sinful. It would probably be correct—and it would be consistent with the rest of the play—to see this final scene in more or less Marxist terms, and regard Hilse as the dupe of his oppressors, a victim, who has been fobbed off with the promise of an afterlife which will compensate for the deprivation of his life on earth. Nevertheless, the religious tone of Hilse's words, and the exceptional position he holds in this last act have caused some commentators to see him as introducing a new, metaphysical dimension, which brings the play nearer to the closed form, with its meaningful conclusion in the death of the hero. Even if the certainty of salvation (and vengeance) which Hilse proclaims shortly before his death, is intended to be no more than a personal illusion, the scene in its entirety does point to a tendency in Hauptmann's subsequent dramas, such as *Hanneles Himmelfahrt* (*The Apotheosis of Hannele*), *Florian Geyer*, and *Michael Kramer*, to absolutize this subjective certainty, and to construct around it a drama which harks back to the classical tradition.

In our interpretation *Die Weber* is a social drama which presents unsolved (but not necessarily insoluble) problems. The interest in the causal patterns of the immanent world implies a conviction similar to that of Zola: that the Naturalists' purpose in understanding phenomena is to master them; and it links up with the optimism of Lenz, the pupil of the Enlightenment, for whom the social drama was a means of political emancipation. Naturalism, at least in its early stages, was a predominantly rationalist tendency, which cultivated open form for the sake of its truth to life. The Naturalists admired in Lenz a writer who turned away from great men and grandiose ideas to the weak and the humble; they admired the Büchner who put into the mouth of his fictitious Lenz the following words:

Everywhere I demand life, the possibility of existence, and then it is good; we do not then need to ask whether it is beautiful or ugly, the feeling that what has been created has life is superior, and is the only criterion in aesthetic matters.

There is, however, as we have observed, another, pessimistic side to Büchner: the disillusioned revolutionary, whose sense of existential isolation is expressed in the metaphorical language of Woyzeck, in his sense of the hollowness of the very ground on which he stands. This aspect of the tradition is not neglected by the Naturalists, if one thinks, for instance, of Hauptmann's *Die Ratten* (*The Rats*), but the dramatist who is most prominent in taking it up and amplifying it is their contemporary, Frank Wedekind.

Up to a point the dramas of Wedekind can be seen in terms of the theory of *tragedy* outlined by Lenz in his *Anmerkungen übers Theater*, that is to say tragedy as character-drama, in which the hero is an emancipated individual, who shapes his own destiny. But whereas Lenz

—in this an idealist—envisages tragic heroes who are free from both
outer, social forces and inner 'animal' needs, Wedekind, in an aggressively anti-idealist way, glorifies the vital animal forces which bring
his heroes into conflict with an inhibiting society. With the Schillerian
values ironically reversed,[8] the following lines from *Wallenstein* stand
programmatically at the head of *Erdgeist* (*Earth-Spirit*), the first
of Wedekind's two Lulu-dramas :

> Mich schuf aus gröberm Stoffe die Natur,
> Und zu der Erde zieht mich die Begierde.
> Dem bösen Geist gehört die Erde, nicht
> Dem guten. Was die Göttlichen uns senden
> Von oben, sind nur allgemeine Güter;
> Ihr Licht erfreut, doch macht es keinen reich,
> In ihrem Staat erringt sich kein Besitz.
> Den Edelstein, das allgeschätzte Gold
> Muß man den falschen Mächten abgewinnen,
> Die unterm Tage schlimmgeartet hausen.
> Nicht ohne Opfer macht man sie geneigt,
> Und keiner lebt, der aus ihrem Dienst
> Die Seele hätte rein zurückgezogen.

(Nature fashioned me out of coarser stuff, and my desires draw
me earthwards. The earth is the territory of the evil spirits, not
the good. What the gods bestow on us from above are but general
bounties; their light brings joy, but makes none wealthy; in their
realm their are no conquests to be made. The precious stone, the
treasured gold, have to be wrested from the false powers who lurk
wickedly beyond the light of day. They are not to be won over
without sacrifices, and there is none alive who left their service
with his soul untainted.)

Frühlings Erwachen (*Spring Awakening*), one of Wedekind's earliest
dramas, and possibly his finest, remains fairly close to Naturalism.
The problems of its characters are largely comprehensible in rational,
social terms : the young Wendla Bergmann becomes pregnant through
ignorance, a result of the pathetic inadequacy of her mother's attempts
at sex-education; her death, as a result of an abortion, is a further
symptom of the sense of shame which, in her society, represses the
life-giving impulses. The fate of Moritz Stiefel provides a parallel

case : at a time when he is occupied intensely by his awakening sexual feelings, a rigid and authoritarian educational system makes excessive demands on him, and causes his suicide.

Like the schoolmaster, Wenzeslaus, in Lenz's *Der Hofmeister*, the repressive and repressed schoolmasters of Wedekind's drama are cut off from life by the closed window of their stuffy conference room; whereas the children, so long as they are permitted, are—like Fritz von Berg in the student scenes of *Der Hofmeister*—totally open to the impressions of the wider world. In Act II, scene 1, as Melchior Gabor and Moritz Stiefel sit in Melchior's study, the living forces of the world outside pour in directly upon them through the open window :

How the garden stretches out in the moonlight, so still, so deep, as if it reached out into infinity.—Beneath the bushes mysterious figures step out, flit across the clearings in breathless activity and disappear in the twilight. It seems as if a council meeting is going to take place under the chestnut-tree——Shall we go down there, Melchior?

It is into this vaguely apprehended, but uncorrupted nature that Melchior flees at the conclusion of the drama, when he escapes from the institution to which he has been confined, and following the 'masked gentleman' opts for life rather than the suicide chosen by his friend Moritz.

The conclusion of *Frühlings Erwachen* has another important feature in common with the dramas of Lenz : it is clearly separated off, by its anti-realistic style, from the rest of the play which, apart from some satirical exaggeration, is composed in a decidedly realistic manner. The success of Melchior Gabor—heralded by some contemporaries as a break with the deterministic pessimism of the Naturalists —is not achieved in the real world. For Wedekind, too, the time is not ripe for such a hero; and Melchior remains something of an exception in his work. In dramas such as *Erdgeist*, *Die Büchse der Pandora* (*Pandora's Box*), *Der Marquis von Keith*, and *König Nicolo* (*King Nicolo*), Wedekind introduces heroes of tragic proportions, in so far as they all possess an intense will to self-assertion, and places them in comic situations, where their energy is relentlessly sapped, thwarted, or frustrated in a senselessly repetitive cycle of events, which are most adequately described in the imagery of the circus or the fairground : 'Life is a helter-skelter . . .', concludes the Marquis von

Keith. This gulf between the powerful will to life, and the dreadful reality of existence produces, in *Musik*, a nihilism which harks back to that of Büchner's Danton :

> up there above us there is no god! I have learnt that beyond all doubt. Unless he is a monster, in whose ears the pathetic cries of my poor abandoned child are music! ... It is beyond the power of human understanding to grasp that there are such tortures! I stand in the pillory! Strangulation is impossible! No suicide. Laughter above me! Laughter beneath me! Laughter! Laughter!

*   *   *

Even in the 19th century the anti-Aristotelian drama has a much wider and more varied tradition than it has been possible to indicate here; and its heirs in the 20th century have increased this range and variety immensely. In the German theatre, the work of Brecht no doubt represents the most productive continuation of the anti-Aristotelian tradition, and the foregoing discussion has constantly looked towards the culmination of the tradition in his work. It is perhaps permissible, however, to conclude with a glance towards the opposite end of the spectrum, and draw attention to the inspiration which modern opera composers have derived from the work of Büchner, Wedekind, and Lenz: to Alban Berg's *Wozzeck* and *Lulu*, and to Bernd Alois Zimmermann's *Die Soldaten*.

NOTES

1. The heir to this particular aspect of the anti-Aristotelian tradition is Grabbe, with plays such as *Napoleon* and *Hannibal*.
2. For Brecht's views on the close relationship of epic theatre and comedy see *Bertolt Brechts Dreigroschenbuch. Texte, Materialien, Dokumente*, S. Unseld, Frankfurt/M. 1960, p. 134.
3. Lenz's contrast also clearly corresponds to Brecht's schematic opposition of 'dramatic form' and 'epic form' in the notes to *Aufstieg und Fall der Stadt Mahagonny* (*Rise and Fall of the City of Mahagonny*), Cf. also 'Verfremdungseffekt in den erzählenden Bildern des älteren Breughel', *Schriften zur Literatur und Kunst*, Frankfurt/M. 1967, pp. 88 ff.
4. *Der Briefwechsel zwischen Gottfried Keller und Hermann Hettner*, J. Jahn, Berlin and Weimar, 1964, pp. 26 f. See also Helmut Schanze, 'Die Anschauung vom hohen Rang des Dramas in der zweiten Hälfte des 19. Jahrhunderts und seine tatsächliche "Schwäche" ', *Beiträge zur Theorie der Künste im 19. Jahrhundert*, I, Helmut Koopmann u. J. Adolf Schmoll gen.

Eisenwerth, Frankfurt/M. 1971, pp. 91 ff. And cf. Hebbel's criticism of Lenz's *Die Soldaten* in his diaries (entry no. 1471).

5. Gerhart Hauptmann, *Das Abenteuer meiner Jugend, Sämtl. Werke*, Hans-Egon Haß, Frankfurt/M. 1962–74, VII, 1061. Cf. Max Halbe's essay on Lenz, *Die Gesellschaft*, VII (1892), (i), pp. 568–82. The first performance of a play by Büchner (*Leonce und Lena*) was staged in Munich in 1895 by a group of young writers closely associated with the Naturalist movement. The role of Leonce was taken by Halbe.

6. *Die Kunst des Dramas*, zusammengestellt von Martin Machatzke, Frankfurt/M and Berlin 1963, p. 183.

7. See Ernst Toller, *Die Maschinenstürmer* (*The Luddites*), Leipzig 1922; and 'Biberpelz und roter Hahn von Gerhart Hauptmann in der Bearbeitung des Berliner Ensembles', *Theaterarbeit. 6 Aufführungen des Berliner Ensembles*, Berliner Ensemble, Helene Weigel, Dresden 1952, pp. 171–226.

8. Cf. the numerous inversions of the meaning of Schillerian lines and situations in the work of Brecht; most notably in the play *Die heilige Johanna der Schlachthöfe* (*St. Joan of the Stockyards*).

5

Nicholas Hern: EXPRESSIONISM

First Station: In the trenches, our young hero, called simply Man, experiences the full horror of war and the shattering of his faith in God and the Fatherland. Second Station: Back in his middle-class home, Man confronts his loving but uncomprehending Mother and his autocratic industrialist Father, whose unstinting endorsement of the capitalist status quo brings Man near to parricide. He leaves home. Third Station: Becoming a worker in a vast highly mechanized factory, Man's eyes are opened to the imprisonment and near-annihilation of the soul of man under such inhuman conditions. He meets a Girl, and fortified by her faith in him he sets out to liberate man's soul. Stations 4–7: Now he journeys through a succession of establishments representing different facets of contemporary life and encounters the grotesque caricatures that inhabit them—a Night Club with its Prostitutes, Gamblers, Alcoholics and down-trodden Waiters; a Bank with its greasy Manager, robot-like Cashiers, and bloated or bejewelled Clientele; a Hospital for the War-Wounded staffed by callous Doctors; and a Tenement Slum where a whole family is dying of poverty, starvation and disease, while a Priest piously promises them eternal life to come. In between these episodes, Man soliloquises his growing awareness of the urgent need for universal spiritual rebirth and regeneration. Station 8: He meets the Girl again and returns with her to the factory, where a mass meeting is in progress, at which the Workers' leader is agitating for violent revolution. Man takes the stand and pleads for non-violence and the need for spiritual renewal instead of physical destruction. But the incensed mob stone him to death. Before he dies, however, he bids the Girl to forgive them because they don't yet understand; she in her turn removes the pain of death by revealing that she is carrying his Child who will carry on his work for future generations.

This pastiche of a German Expressionist play serves if for nothing else to emphasize the intense homogeneity of the genre, since this one scenario is in fact composed of recurrent elements from well over a dozen plays written around the end of the Great War, with further importations from the pre-war period. This is not to say that *all* German Expressionist drama conforms to this pattern, but so strong are the similarities amongst a certain group of plays that there *is* a temptation to use the common denominators as a yardstick of orthodoxy and dismiss those that do not conform as mere 'plays with expressionist tendencies', rather than fully-fledged Expressionist dramas. The problem of definition is further complicated by the multiple meanings ascribed to the term 'expressionism', but it is a multiplicity which has been helpfully codified by John Willett:

Expressionism is normally
   1. a family characteristic of modern Germanic art, literature, music and theatre, from the turn of the century to the present day.
   2. a particular modern German movement which lasted roughly between 1910 and 1922.
   3. a quality of expressive emphasis and distortion which may be found in works of art of any people or period.

At least it is clear that our concern here is with the second meaning, and then only as it affects drama and the theatre (and Willett's convention of distinguishing this kind of Expressionism with a capital E will also be adopted here). Accepting that the pastiche scenario exhibits many of the typical characteristics of 'this particular modern movement', German Expressionist drama, we can ask where these characteristics originated, how they were affected by concurrent theatrical practice, and what changes they underwent as the movement developed and dispersed. We might also wonder what influence they in turn have had on the subsequent development of drama.

It has become a critical commonplace to designate certain plays by Büchner, Wedekind, Strindberg and (less frequently) Sternheim as foreshadowing aspects of Expressionist drama. Though widely diverse in age and nationality, all four have in common that the first sustained recognition of their work came in Germany in the first years of this century—just as the Expressionist movement was getting under way and was therefore most susceptible to their influence. Büchner's *Woyzeck* (written 1836; staged 1913), one of the most celebrated cases of delayed reaction in the history of drama, has been claimed to be an anticipation of Naturalism and Brechtian Epic Theatre as well as of Expressionism. Brecht himself thought it a masterpiece, and it is certainly of far greater interest than merely as a storehouse of expressionist techniques, though it may well have been recognition of these and their relevance to the climate of 1913 which prompted the first staging of the play in Munich. *Woyzeck*'s contribution to Expressionism was in fact both thematic and stylistic. Thematically, the play shows an ordinary man crushed and victimized by a hierarchical society from which he can see no escape. Conventional religion is little comfort: 'If we ever get to Heaven, I think we'd have to help with the thundering', says Woyzeck gloomily, and his only relief is his concern for his girl. Her betrayal of him is the last straw. Woyzeck also suffers hallucinations, and although these are probably the result of an exclusive diet of peas, they do suggest a visionary quality in the man, which might have been creative if it hadn't been so inhumanly perverted. Spalter points to Woyzeck's 'powerful inner life' in contrast to the emptiness of those who surround him. More important, Expressionism is foreshadowed stylistically in the short episodic scenes built around the central character, in the tendency to reduce certain unsympathetic characters to caricatured and nameless types (The Captain, the Doctor, the Drum-Major), and in the compressed, elliptical, often exclamatory language and its lurid imagery—Woyzeck, says Spalter, 'mutters, babbles, screams, bellows and howls his way through the play'. Finally, the play's very spareness promotes ambivalence of interpretation: where the Naturalist sees the beginnings of social determinism in the depiction of Woyzeck's environment, the Expressionist is equally justified in viewing Woyzeck as the subjective centre of a play which offers only a phantasmagoric image of the world around him, as if seen exclusively through his tormented eyes.

Many of the proto-Expressionist techniques employed by Büchner are re-used by Wedekind in his notorious *Frühlings Erwachen* (1891; staged 1906, Berlin). Here again is an episodic structure—of nineteen short scenes—designed to show the conflict between the adolescent protagonists and their social environment; here, in the staff-room scene, is blatant caricaturing of the schoolmasters with their Jonsonian names and monomanias; and here too is dialogue which can reach heights of exclamatory ejaculation. But it is in his contempt for Ibsen and the German Naturalists for merely scratching the surface of life that Wedekind really anticipates the Expressionists. He sets his three young protagonists on a voyage of sexual self-discovery which, because of the perverting repression and hypocrisy practised by the older generation, ends in the death of all but one. In the final scene, the survivor, Melchior, confronts both Death and Life in the persons of his dead friend, Moritz, and of a mysterious Masked Man. In choosing the Life Force, Melchior proves himself the ancestor of the Expressionist New Man, who will also experience a species of spiritual awakening.

The device of incarnating an abstract quality in a living character (much used by Expressionist playwrights) was worked more thoroughly by Wedekind in *Erdgeist* (*Earth Spirit*, 1895; staged 1898, Leipzig) and *Die Büchse der Pandora* (*Pandora's Box*, 1904; staged 1904, Nuremberg), which trace the fortunes of Lulu, the luscious and amoral embodiment of the Sexual Instinct. That she eventually comes to a sticky end does not mean, as some have thought, that Wedekind is thereby condemning sexual freedom, but rather that, as in *Frühlings Erwachen*, he is demonstrating the perversions to which it is subjected by contemporary society. In the Lulu plays, that society is represented by a gallery of Bohemians, criminals and aristocratic perverts whose grotesquery already far outdoes the most lurid of Expressionist creations. Wedekind also gives them a condensed, mechanical, depersonalized dialogue deliberately devoid of warm human intonation, which is the more effective the more violently emotional their actions. Furthermore, although written in five and three acts respectively, the plays seem nonetheless episodic as Lulu passes from husband to lover to ponce in a reverse spiritual progression, a negative example by which Wedekind wishes to point to the inverted moral values of the world—just as the Expressionists were to do in their more direct, more preachy plays.

Wedekind's accessibility to the Expressionist generation is unquestionable. Throughout the formative and climactic years of the movement, his plays were hardly ever off the stage; so, one of the most potent influences was virtually on tap for all to draw.[1] But it was really Strindberg who was the strongest single influence on the growing movement. His work too was well disseminated in Germany during the crucial period : already by 1906 some thirty of his works had been translated into German, while the years 1913–16 saw over 1,000 performances of his plays in some sixty German theatres. Rühle says that

Reinhardt alone produced seventeen Strindbergs, though not all these were relevant to Expressionism.[2]

It is the post-Inferno plays such as the metaphysical *To Damascus* (three parts: 1898–1904), *A Dream Play* (1901) and *The Great Highway* (1909), and even the most realistic *Crime and Crime* (1899) and *Easter* (1900), which are important here. The last two are interesting enough with their theme of spiritual redemption symbolized in Christian imagery yet contained within conventional sets, characters and structures—a hybrid that was imitated by several subsequent Expressionist playwrights. But it is in the first three plays that Strindberg achieved his most influential innovation: struggling to express in dramatic terms the full intensity of the religious experience of his Inferno years, he found that existing dramatic structures and conventions simply could not hold all he wanted to say. The resulting explosion can be seen in the first part of *To Damascus*, which, as one critic says, 're-enacts his conversion in a universalised symbolic form and inaugurates an enlarged idea of a theatre *in which conscious and subconscious elements may co-exist'*. Add to this a nameless subjective protagonist in restless search of spiritual satisfaction who, like a dreamer, is both in control of and controlled by the action, an unnamed lady (christened Eve by the hero) whose faith leads him onwards, an abundance of Christian symbolism (title included), and a rigorously symmetrical structure of seventeen 'stations'—add all this up, and one has indeed what Willett calls a 'virtually' Expressionist drama. It would be cheating, however, to rope in the succession of unnamed characters (The Beggar, The Doctor, An Old Man etc.) and unidentified locations (Street Corner, By the Sea, On the Road) as further proof of Expressionism in this and other Strindberg plays, since they are not generalized features of contemporary life (as the Expressionists would use them), but rather anonymous versions of very specific people and places from Strindberg's private life. It is indeed the strength of this autobiographical element which really prevents Strindberg from being wholly Expressionist. He never achieves the totally depersonalized universality which was the Expressionists' aim, and which tends too often to make their plays magniloquent and turgid. For it is as well to remember at this point that the three dramatists so far cited as foreshadowing Expressionism more accurately *over*shadow the movement, being all of far greater stature than any playwright of the Expressionist generation.

By way of illustration: in *The Great Highway*, subtitled 'A Way-faring Drama with Seven Stations', Strindberg makes a greater effort to generalize the autobiographical ingredients and place the drama on a purely abstract plane. The Hunter is clearly the author, but the nameless characters he meets, and who embody various abstract qualities, are largely acceptable as such and do not seem in need of a key to unlock their private associations. Yet the play is ultimately far less palatable (or highly regarded) than *A Dream Play*, riddled as it is with specific autobiographical references and personal obsessions. These are threaded through the universal parable of the descent of the Daughter of Indra to earth to share in man's sufferings. It is, as the title suggests, like looking at someone else's dream—partly comprehensible in general terms, partly mysterious, yet with a strong surface fascination. As Strindberg writes in the preface:

> In this dream play, as in his former dream play, *To Damascus*, the Author has sought to reproduce this disconnected but apparently logical form of a dream... The characters split, double and multiply; they evaporate, crystallise, scatter and converge. But a single consciousness holds sway over them all—that of the dreamer.

It is this mixture of subjectivity of approach with universality of subject matter that is to be most useful to the Expressionists.

To move from Strindberg to Sternheim is to realize how compara-tively unjustifiable it is to rank the latter among the Expressionists. Certainly his chief period of creativity exactly coincides with the Ex-pressionist era, and a number of his plays suffered the same fate of being banned from performance for the durafion of the war: e.g. *Die Hose* (*The Bloomers*, 1911: staged 1911, Berlin), *Die Kassette* (*The Strongbox*, 1912: staged 1911, Berlin), *1913* (1915; staged 1919, Frankfurt). But Sternheim's real contact with the movement is at two points only: his merciless caricaturing of the arriviste bourgeoisie and of the society they inhabit, and secondly the artificially contrived language he gives them to speak, compounded, as Garten says, of 'deliberate bathos, spurious romanticism, misquotations from Wag-nerian opera and student songs, and clichés from newspaper leaders'—a language which especially in *Bürger Schippel* (1913; staged 1913, Berlin), can also verge on the telegraphese of later Expressionists:

SCHIPPEL : Morning, Hicketier old man!

HICKETIER : How dare you—what do you think you're ...

SCHIPPEL : Mustn't be so gross. Understand. Keep my distance.
HICKETIER : Manners! Behave! Or else . . .
SCHIPPEL : Enough. I'll sing. With a voice like an angel. Mind's made up.

It might, however, be argued that Sternheim, like Wedekind, paints a negative picture in order that a positive might be implied, and that his odious if vital protagonists embody the antithesis of all the values a healthful society should uphold. Certainly the careers of Schippel and the Maskes, father and son, seem like grotesque inversions of the spiritual searchings of the Expressionist New Man. But in the end Sternheim is too cynical, too satirical, and too funny, whereas the Expressionists mitigate cynicism and satire with positive idealism, and are never very strong on humour. Even when Sternheim does introduce a positive New Man in *Das Fossil* (*The Fossil*, 1923, staged 1923 Hamburg), the last of his hexalogy on *The Heroic Life of the Bourgeoisie*, it is to deal with him ironically and discreditably—murdered behind a curtain in the arms of a scion of the aristocracy. Sternheim compared himself with Molière; others have compared him with Wedekind, Labiche and even Noël Coward. His voice finds its strongest echo, however, in his coeval, Heinrich Mann (e.g. in *Man of Straw*, 1918), and is to be heard again in Bertolt Brecht, rather than in Kaiser and Toller.

So much for the established pantheon of 'forefathers of Expressionism', all of whom were present, in spirit at least, at the birth of the new generation. But other forces, deeper seated in the German literary and dramatic consciousness, were also at work—forces which had been ignored by those dramatists intent on the illusion of reality as their theatrical goal.

Mention of Strindberg has already revealed the extent to which he re-introduced man's search for spiritual salvation as a subject fit for treatment as episodic drama. But the original of this genre is surely the medieval morality play, the most famous and longest-lived example of which is *Everyman*, known in Germany in various versions from at least 1529 onwards. Significantly, it was revived by Reinhardt as *Jedermann* in 1911, and repeated almost every season up to its regular incorporation in the Salzburg Festival in 1920. Subjecting *Everyman* to the same criteria as for other pre-expressionist plays, we find a single unnamed protagonist representing mankind, who is awakened to the spiritual emptiness of his life and sets out on a journey in the course of which he encounters a succession of nameless incarnations of abstract qualities (Fellowship, Good Deeds, Beauty, etc.), and at the end of which he achieves spiritual calm in face of Death (a further incarnation). The structure is episodic and punctuated by Everyman's soliloquies; Christian imagery is integral; and the homiletic element essential. Conclusion : in all but a few respects (most notably language), *Everyman* is an expressionist play.

The link between the Christian morality play and 20th century Expressionism is to be found in those great 'soul-searching' plays like *Faust* and *Brand,* where the individual man tests the outer limits of his individuality vis-à-vis God and his fellow men. In order to contain such a theme, the structure breaks up into episodes and the characters tend to become generalized. But although such plays were read and revered at the end of the 19th century, their potential as *theatrical* models had been submerged in the prevailing trend towards smaller scale social and psychological realism. It needed the promptings of Strindberg, of the omnivorous Reinhardt (whose repertoire included both parts of *Faust* by 1911), and, it must also be said, of Nietzsche, before the Expressionists rediscovered the dramatic power in the conflict of such 'supermen' with the world around them. *Faust II* especially, according to Willett, 'influenced a number of Expressionist dramas by Unruh, Werfel, Kornfeld and other young writers'.

If this line of development clearly issues in Expressionism, one must be more wary of another apparent relationship with earlier dramatic modes. The dramatists of *Sturm und Drang* are in many ways similar to those of Expressionism, but are different in as many other ways. The *Stürmer und Dränger,* like countless other artistic rebels, were in passionate revolt against contemporary society, but they were more specifically like the Expressionists in dramatizing their revolt in terms of son clashing with father and, in Lenz's case at least, by means of caricaturing the opposition. Aesthetically they rejected the pseudo-Aristotelion 'rules' for dramatic composition and looked instead to the character-centred plays of Shakespeare. Some, notably Klinger, indulged in extravagant language, unfinished sentences and wild ejaculations expressive of emotions constantly at fever pitch. So far, so similar. But, on the other hand, they were able to admit the faults in their heroes, and their reason for adopting episodic structure was its greater scope for encompassing social and psychological reality. In short, there is a historical objectivity in the best of *Sturm und Drang* which is quite foreign to the subjective orientation of Expressionist drama. Nevertheless, Reinhardt's 1916 season of rarely revived plays by Lenz and Klinger as well as of Schiller's early *Kabale and Liebe* (1784) and Büchner's Shakespearean *Dantons Tod* (1835; staged 1902, Berlin) must have come as a further reminder to the Expressionists of the usefulness of unconventional construction for unconventional material.

Multifarious as all these influences may seem, together they point to one of the chief reasons for the Expressionist *Revolution* being so called. For in their anxiety to communicate in dramatic terms their vision of the need for the renewal of the soul of man, the Expressionists threw over one of the basic precepts governing dramatic art since Hamlet asked the Players 'to hold, as 'twere, the mirror up to nature'. Now, following 300 years of dedication to this concept of realism in the theatre (refined by each succeeding age), the Expressionists turned their back on mirror images both of the external world and of individual human psyches.[3] For they were interested in the world as cosmos[4] and in the human figure as a member of mankind. And for this revolutionary concept, a revolutionary de-individualized, anti-realistic method of dramatic presentation was required. Similarly, the pseudo-Aristotelian unities, resuscitated in large measure by the Naturalist playwrights, were also rejected, just as in Expressionist painting, music and poetry, the conventions governing pictorial representation, tonality, and syntax and vocabulary were swept away.

One further feature of the climate prevailing at the birth of Expressionism must finally be mentioned: the parallel anti-realistic revolution that design and production techniques underwent at the turn of the century. Briefly, two major trends are discernible, which might be called the painterly and the monumental abstract. The first resulted from the impact of Cubism and Expressionism in painting on stage decoration, costume design, make-up and even acting style. It is now best known from the film, *The Cabinet of Dr Caligari* (1919; dir: Robert Wiene; des: Hermann Warm, Walter Reimann, Walter Röhrig), which is anyway very theatrical with its motionless camera often apparently placed in the middle of the stalls so as to take in the whole of the set. Here are the walls, windows and chimneys painted 'out of plumb' and patterned with jagged patches of light and shadow, and here (at least in the case of Caligari and Cesare, his tame somnambulist) are the eccentric costumes, extravagant make-up and exaggerated gait, gesture and expression—all features which occur again and again in contemporary stage productions and other films.[5] This technique was particularly well geared to the intensely subjective type of Expressionist play or film, since the physical distortions forced the audience to share the protagonist's vision of the grotesqueness of the world around him.

The importation of ideas from the visual arts into the theatre is standard practice, but the innovations of Appia and Craig were really revolutionary, bringing about a monumental, abstract, truly three-dimensional stage which was the complete reverse of realism and more like a return to the Graeco-Roman theatre, by which both men had been inspired. Though Swiss and English respectively, Appia and Craig both had their greatest immediate influence in Germany.

Appia's fundamental theoretical work, *La musique et la mise en scène*, including eighteen important illustrations was published in German first in 1899. In it he called for flexible, atmospheric lighting (thus foreseeing the then unexploited potential of directional spotlighting), for three-dimensional settings to replace flat painted scenery (thus complementing and liberating the three-dimensional actor), for breaking up the stage floor into various levels, and for a despotic director to co-ordinate the whole production! Thereafter, reviews and exhibitions of his work appeared sporadically in Germany until 1912, when his liaison with Emile Jaques-Dalcroze and their joint realization of a studio theatre at Hellerau near Dresden made possible a production of part of a Gluck opera in Appia's settings, which caused a sensation in Europe and America. By this time Appia had abandoned all trace of representationalism, and the sets consisted solely of steps, ramps, platforms, and directional lighting. It is no exaggeration to say that this was the birth of the modern stage.

Significantly, Craig's first influential theoretical work, *The Art of the Theatre*, was also published in German first (in 1905)—not the only coincidence between him and Appia. For though apparently unknown to each other until 1911, their ideas are remarkably similar. Craig's designs possibly show more versatility and less practicability than Appia's, but Craig too strips away all inessential detail, offering sets similarly composed of abstract geometrical elements and dramatic lighting—sets which can dominate the human figure or throw it into gigantic relief. In either case, the effect (of much interest to the Expressionists) is to rob it of personal characteristics, making it anonymously insignificant or hieratically larger than life. By the end of 1905, Craig was already well known in German theatrical circles, having had a public row with Otto Brahm over the lack of realistic detail in Craig's designs for a Berlin production of *Venice Preserv'd* in 1904, and exhibitions of his work in five German cities in 1905. Also that year he did some unrealized but highly influential designs for Hofmannsthal's adaptation of *Electra* and was (unsuccessfully) invited by Reinhardt to stage a number of plays. The invitation was repeated in 1908 but again came to nothing, although on both occasions Craig produced a large number of sketches, which were to influence Reinhardt immeasurably, particularly in his 1908 *Lear*, his 1910 *Oedipus Rex*, and his 1911 *Oresteia* (all projects originally offered to Craig).

These last two were produced in the Schumann Circus, Berlin (later Reinhardt's Grosses Schauspielhaus) on an arena stage backed by a broad flight of steps topped with huge columns. They are among the most powerful realizations of Craig's (and Appia's) ideas and point once again to Reinhardt's towering importance as a theatrical catalyst, even for those (like the Expressionists) with whom he was basically out of sympathy.[6] In these two much-repeated productions, the striking polarity between the single elevated figure on the steps and the clustered mass of the Chorus in the arena provided the Expressionist playwrights and directors with a potent theatrical image for the opposition of Protagonist with Mob which bulks so large in their work.

The most obvious heir to this legacy was to be the director Leopold Jessner and his designer Emil Pirchan, whose Expressionist productions of *Wilhelm Tell* (Berlin, 1919) and *Richard III* (Berlin, 1920) were both largely mounted on a single flight of steps raked back from the front of the stage.[7] That these productions were indeed Expressionist and not simply classically austere is clear not only from the arbitrarily expressive use of lighting and colour (Gloucester, his minions, *and* the steps in blood-red; Richmond and his followers in purest white), but also from the adoption of a grotesque acting style—an element derived less from Appia, Craig and Reinhardt than from painterly Expressionism. Which only goes to show that once Expressionism is in full spate, it is fruitless to maintain rigid distinctions between the two styles, since *every* impactful theatrical technique was likely to be pressed into service regardless of its origins.[8]

This indeed was precisely the case with the myriad technical innovations introduced mainly in Germany to the early 20th century stage in the interests of heightened realism. For instance, the various new methods of changing solid naturalistic sets, such as the revolving stage,[9] the sinking stage, and the use of stage wagons,[10] were seized on by post-war Expressionist directors to solve the problems of shifting their equally solid abstract settings. The other main area of technical progress was in stage-lighting, where again Germany led the world in the practical extension of Appia's ideas, made possible by the adoption for stage use of the recently invented high wattage incandescent lamp. This lamp, incorporated into a whole range of floods and spotlights, equipped with variable colour screens or gels, and all controlled from a single, newly perfected dimmer-board, provided both superbly realistic lighting for the conventional stage and endless expressive possibilities for the non-realistic. Further, thanks to the experiments of Mariano Fortuny, who had worked with Appia in Paris in 1903, the rear of the stage no longer needed a painted backdrop but could give the impression of infinite space or variable skyscapes by means of a lit cyclorama. Finally, the combination of both inventions made possible the projection of painted or photographic slides (diapositivies) on to the cyc in place of scenery, and again this device was capable of realistic or (more successfully) non-realistic application. So, with all this technical paraphernalia at its disposal, the stage was really set for Expressionism.

But, as is usually the case with innovatory artistic movements, one of the last media to respond to Expressionism was in fact the theatre. Although expressionist tendencies were occasionally discernible in some pre-war productions of Wedekind, Strindberg and Sternheim, only one fully Expressionist play had been staged by 1916,[11] even though over a dozen had been published, and many more were available in manuscript. So the standard critical view of two phases of Expressionist drama—one up to and one after 1916—can only apply to written plays, not to their staging. This view sees the first phase as predominantly concerned with individual man's search for *personal* spiritual satisfaction, while in the second phase, having himself undergone spiritual renewal, he urges moral regeneration on the *society* around him.

The shift of emphasis from individual to society coincides with the turning-point in the playwrights' attitude to the war. Prior to 1914, there seemed to be a yearning amongst most young German writers and artists for some unspecified but preferably violent upheaval—a yearning most startlingly depicted in the prophetically apocalyptic landscapes of Ludwig Meidner and the uneasy poems of Georg Heym. When war was declared, it was greeted with enthusiasm by all but a few of the Expressionist generation: here was the necessary demolition of the old, the rotten, the decayed; here was the crisis which would promote the wished-for spiritual awareness. By 1916 their expectations had been cruelly shattered, and those who survived the trenches began to call for universal brotherhood and an end to the carnage, and for the building of a new concept of humanity on the ruins of the old—sentiments which eventually found their political counterpart in the overthrow of the Kaiser and the establishment of the Republic, and, more radically, in the sporadic outbursts of violent revolutionary activity in 1918–19, though the calls for Revolution resounding from Expressionist drama of that period were uniformly non-specific and politically naive in the extreme. But the prevailing Utopianism was short-lived. Continuing strife between militant factions from the left and the right combined with a fast-failing economy to turn even the most euphoric playwright into a pessimist or at least into a forlorn prophet of better times in ages yet to come. So a third and final phase of Expressionist drama set in about 1921, hall-marked by a high fatality rate among protagonists, and fading out in 1924 as Expressionism lost its identity and sense of purpose in the cynical matter-of-factness of the *Neue Sachlichkeit* (New Objectivity).

The plays of the first phase are notable for the extent to which the playwrights are gate-crashers from other art forms, and for the extremes to which they take their experimentation, coloured as it is by the dramatist's original medium. So the painter Oskar Kokoschka's play, *Mörder, Hoffnung der Frauen* (*Murderer Hope of Womankind* 1910; staged 1908, Vienna), resolves into a succession of dynamic, colour-strewn tableaux depicting the violent clash of Man and his chorus of Warriors with Woman and her Maidens, in a kind of mythic abstraction of a Strindberg sex play. The language is disjointed and exclamatory, the characters archetypally anonymous, the contrast between Individual and Chorus clearly pointed, and there are intimations of the arrogant New Man as the hero slays the mediocre minions and strides off into the dawn through a gulley of flames

—yet for all this, the play is closer to Artaud than to Expressionism in its instinctive understanding of the totality of the theatrical experience, something which the Expressionists rarely got right, for all their insistent emotionalism. In a different direction, the poet August Stramm imported into *Erwachen* (*Awakening* 1915; staged 1929, Dresden) and other short plays the extreme telegraphic style of his poetry:

SHE : What was that? What was that?
HE : Thunder!
SHE : Where am I?
HE : Here!
SHE : (whimpers and listens): Roaring of the river.
HE : Roaring of the rabble.
SHE : That's water! Water! The river! We've crossed the river! Oh! So black! So black in the evening sun.

And in other respects too the play is a positive compendium of Expressionist motifs with its Superman hero, faithful Girl, Christian symbolism, and chorus of money-grubbing bourgeois hypocrites. It is less easy, however, to see the immediate connection between Ernst Barlach's sculptures and his first play, *Der tote Tag* (*The Dead Day* 1912; staged 1919, Leipzig), about a Son's yearning for his unknown Father and his Mother's slaying of the magic horse sent to carry him away; but Garten sees both Barlach's plays and sculptures as 'blending a heavy and earth-bound realism with a mystical, religious ecstasy'. Barlach was certainly the first to expose the quasi-religious nature of the Expressionist impulse.

The importance of Reinhard Sorge's *Der Bettler* (*The Beggar* 1912; staged 1917, Berlin), Walter Hasenclever's *Der Sohn* (*The Son* 1914; staged 1916, Prague), and Paul Kornfeld's *Die Verführung* (*The Seduction* 1916; staged 1917, Frankfurt), all first plays by new writers, lies chiefly in their essential similarity. For, quite spontaneously, the same pattern, strongly influenced by Strindberg and Wedekind, underlies all three: the ego-hero—virtually the playwright himself—wakes up to the soul-destroying effect of established society (epitomized in the bourgeois family), rises in revolt and murders—or almost murders—a representative of that society. Two of the heroes enjoy the faithful allegiance of a young woman, and two enjoy final ecstatic visions of the future. Here was evidence of more than experimentation: the Expressionists were gaining a consolidated purpose and identity, both of which grew stronger with successive stage productions of the plays after 1916.[12]

The status of Georg Kaiser was also to be confirmed by successful performances of his first important plays, *Von Morgens bis Mitternachts* (*From Morning to Midnight* written 1912; published 1916; staged 1917, Munich) and *Die Bürger von Calais* (*The Burghers of Calais* written 1913; published 1914; staged 1917, Frankfurt). They mark the transition from the first to the second phase, the shift from individual to social regeneration. For while *Von Morgens bis Mitternachts* concerns the abortive attempts of a bank-clerk Everyman to find personal spiritual fulfilment by indulging in the worthless pleasures of a modern money-based society, *Die Bürger von Calais* tells how the New Man (so called for the first time) instils a new set of values in his fellow-citizens, so that they accept self-sacrifice for the greater good of mankind. An unusual sense of authorial aloofness evidenced in the calculatedness of both plays—in their deadening structural symmetry, their overstressed Christian symbolism, and their highly artificial language (telegraphic in one, impossibly heightened in the other)—makes them more than a little preposterous now, though Kaiser's predictive abilities cannot be denied as both plays had to wait for national sentiment to catch up with them before being published and performed.

Die Bürger von Calais was preaching pacifism before the war began, but it was not till 1917 that specifically anti-war Expressionist plays began to appear.[13] Hasenclever's *Antigone* (1917; staged 1917, Leipzig; then banned and re-staged 1919, Frankfurt) and Fritz von Unruh's *Ein Geschlecht* (*A Generation* 1917; staged 1918, Frankfurt) are still non-specific insofar as they remove the battlefield to ancient Thebes and a timeless war-cemetery respectively, whereas Reinhard Goering's *Seeschlacht* (*Naval Encounter* 1917; staged 1918, Dresden) takes place before and during the Battle of Jutland, though even so the sailors and the action are clearly abstracts of reality. The momentum of all three is the same, however, and closely parallels the wartime experience of their authors: as a result of the horrors of war, the protagonist is 'converted' to a new realization of the need for human brotherhood and attempts to convince his fellow-men. In other words, the New Man is now born out of actual devastation and destruction, or, strictly, the New Woman is, since in the first two plays the chief protagonist is female.

By 1917 Kaiser had already moved on to the problems confronting a society whose industrial technology had undergone rapid advancement during the war years. In his most Shavian play, *Die Koralle* (*The Coral* 1917; staged 1917, Frankfurt and Munich), and its sequels, *Gas I* (1918; staged 1918, Düsseldorf and Frankfurt) and *Gas II* (1920; staged 1920, Brünn), Kaiser projects this society into the future, becoming more pessimistic with each episode. The New Man, who in the first play acquires a social conscience and strong disapproval from his millionaire industrialist father, emerges as a Utopian socialist in the second, where he tries to convince the workers in his mighty Gas Plant that the quality of life is more important than serving the demands of an accelerating technology. He fails, and in the third play, with the factory geared now to total warfare, his grandson takes up the call for universal brotherhood. But he too goes unheeded, and the play ends in hideous holocaust. Interestingly, as the pessimism deepens, so does the Expressionism. But this time Kaiser's favourite devices, above all the striking geometrical symmetry of settings, characters and action, are well suited to embodying his hellish vision of a super-technological society of the not-too-distant future—a vision apparently much drawn upon for the film *Metropolis* a few years later (1926).

Kaiser's Gas-trilogy rather overshadows not only his own contemporary plays—for instance, the sub-Damascan *Hölle Weg Erde* (*Hell, Road Earth* 1919; staged 1919, Berlin and Frankfurt) with its untypical and unconvincing optimistic ending—but also Unruh's attempt at a similar trilogy based on his *Generation*. The second part, called *Platz* (*Square* 1920; staged 1920, Frankfurt), deals with an abortive attempt at revolution by the New Man who had emerged in the first play. But the third part, *Dietrich*, in which the revolution was to be accomplished by a later generation, was, significantly, never published —it would have been badly out of step with the times.

The only dramatist of these immediate post-war years to match Kaiser's stature was Ernst Toller. He knew all about revolution, having played a leading part in the Bavarian Soviet Republic of 1919, for which he was gaoled for five years. And his first four plays were actually written in prison. Yet for all this, they are little more concerned with the precise political objectives of revolution than are the plays of Kaiser and Unruh. The idea of using theatre for that kind of specific propaganda simply did not occur to the Expressionists, even though Piscator was already moving towards agit-prop in 1920 with his Berlin-based Proletarisches Theater. True, Toller tells of attending strike meetings in 1918 and reading 'scraps of speeches' from his first play, *Die Wandlung* (*Transfiguration* 1919; staged 1919, Berlin), 'with the purpose of arousing the apathetic, of prompting the reluctant to march,'[14] but the call for (non-violent) revolution at the end of the play is euphoric rather than agitational:

> Brothers, stretch out your tortured hands
> With cries of radiant, ringing joy!
> Stride freely through our liberated land
> With cries of Revolution, Revolution!

Which is a pity, since the first four of the six 'Stations' needed to complete the hero's spiritual transfiguration are fired with a bitterly impressive anger against the obscenities of war. One nightmare scene is set is a military hospital:

ARMLESS SOLDIER: Can no-one hear me? . . .
    Just a little necessary service . . .
    It's so horrible having to lie in one's own dung.
SOLDIER WITH SHATTERED SPINE:
    What's a little bit of dung?
    I'm used to it by now.
    I hardly know whether I'm still a man
    Or just a living latrine.

A succession of such horrors,[15] effectively portrayed in dream sequences which interlace the scenes of the hero's real life, bring him near to the brink of suicide. But he is saved just in time by his visionary sister setting him on the right road, 'the road to humanity'.

Toller's subsequent protagonists are less lucky and their fates more convincing. In both *Masse-Mensch* (*Masses and Man*, 1921; staged 1920, Nuremberg) and *Die Maschinenstürmer* (*The Machine-Wreckers*, 1922; staged 1922, Berlin), where Toller comes nearer than any other Expressionist to facing the real problems of the industrial working-class, his protagonists both die for their belief in passive resistance rather than violent strike action or machine-breaking. The first play carries on from *Transfiguration* in its use of interpolated dream scenes, in which the real characters can re-appear in different guises, but *The Machine-Wreckers* drifts much closer to conventional historical realism in its treatment of the Luddites, even though the depiction of the monstrous Machine and the raving Engineer are more in the spirit of *Gas* and *Metropolis*. Despite being in prison, Toller seems to have sensed that concrete social problems (and Germany had plenty) needed a more concrete dramatic treatment. Even so, he himself could not forsake Expressionism overnight, and the fevered atmosphere of his *Hinkemann* (1923; staged 1923, Leipzig) contrasts unfavourably with the cool cynicism of Bertolt Brecht's *Trommeln in der Nacht* (*Drums in the Night*, 1922), staged in Munich the year before. Both plays use the same device of the soldier returning after the war (the *Heimkehrer*) to point up the grotesque discrepancy between the ideal society the soldier thought he was fighting for and the putrefaction which in fact he finds. But while Toller's Woyzeck-like emasculated hero, finding his wife turning from him, takes a job as a fairground freak, before driving her and himself to suicide, Brecht's Kragler decides not to join the Spartacist rebellion but to settle instead for home, bed, and his second-hand fiancée. Yet it would be surprising if the play, which Brecht originally wrote in 1919 during the early days of Toller's Bavarian Soviet, were totally devoid of Expressionist devices,[16] such as its obsessive images, particularly the red moon that glows every time Kragler appears, its sometimes raving, often staccato dialogue, its episodic structure, and its caricatured subsidiary figures. On the other hand, there is a new timbre discernible in the play's consistently anti-romantic stance and anti-theatrical trickery:

> KRAGLER [at the end of the play]: I'm fed up to here. It's just play-acting. Boards and a paper moon and the butchery off-stage, which is the only real part of it ... (*he staggers around, throws the drum at the moon, which was a lantern, and drum and moon together fall into the river, which is without water*).

The Expressionists would never permit themselves such a change of gear and especially not at the end of a play. It is when one wonders about the audience's attitude to such a 'hero' that Brecht's essential departure from Expressionism becomes clear. The Expressionists tried to ensure identification and sympathy with their heroes by means of a bludgeoning subjectivity. Brecht creates a morally reprehensible hero whose refusal to join the revolution or preach moral regeneration, or at least commit suicide, is a direct critique of the Expressionist protagonist.[17] And if the audience are shocked by Kragler's cynicism, the answer is clear: they should think about the social conditions that make his cynicism the only sensible attitude. At heart the 'message' is the same as was the Expressionists': true human values cannot survive in a corrupt society. But their solutions were different: change mankind, preached the Expressionists; change society, said Brecht.

Four years later, two further plays by Brecht and Toller were sharply illustrative of the utter decay of the Expressionist ideal. *Mann ist Mann* (*A Man's a Man*, 1926; staged 1927, Darmstadt) is the cynical reversal of the Expressionist belief in Man's capacity for spiritual growth. Far from being transformed into a fuller human being, Galy Gay is converted in the other direction and moulded into a vicious, unthinking automaton. Toller's *Hoppla, wir leben!* (*Hoppla! Such is Life!*, 1927; staged 1927, Hamburg and Berlin) takes the New Man—gaoled for revolutionary activity eight years earlier—on a last, disillusioning voyage of discovery through the society of the mid-twenties. Making a last desperate attempt at a meaningful political act, and failing, the hero commits suicide, as Toller did himself in 1939.

But he and most Expressionist writers lived to see the rise of Nazism, however, and with it a hideously distorted revival of their ideals. They too had felt and expressed the need for a new beginning, had pictured the sickness of post-war society, had exploited the power of emotional language and subjective imagery, had understood the dynamism of the single visionary calling the masses to action; but when the New Age dawned on January 30, 1933, it had the wrong ideals.[18] The real legacy of Expressionist drama was never likely to be its simplistic content and its naive ideals. Far more important for the future were their anti-realist techniques and their re-discovery of a dramatic tradition older than the Renaissance yet better equipped to express the complexities of modern life. Brecht and subsequent writers for the epic and documentary theatre were reminded by the Expressionists of the advantages of episodic structure, of blatant caricature, and of the ability to range wide over society in pursuit of one's theme. Dramatists of the theatre of the absurd learned from the Expressionists, the first post-Freudian generation, how to portray dreams, fantasies, and subjective visions in the theatre, how to construct a play from inside the hero's head, and how to dramatize the inner workings of a mind at odds with the outside world. The conventional realistic play did not die with coming of Expressionism; but after the Expressionists and their championship of Büchner, Strindberg and Wedekind, there was at least a viable alternative to realism.

NOTES

(Dates: except where stated otherwise, the date immediately following a play title is that of publication, and the date and location of staging are always for the première production.)

1. For example, *Frühlings Erwachen* remained unstaged until Reinhardt directed it in 1906, whereupon it kept its place in the repertoire till 1925, by which time it had been given an astonishing 661 performances. Similarly, *Erdgeist* (in successive productions by Reinhardt and by Wedekind himself) was rarely out of Reinhardt's Berlin theatres between 1902 and 1916, while *Die Büchse der Pandora*, though rarely given in public before the end of censorship in 1918, was thereafter constantly in Reinhardt's repertoire till 1925. Other 'pre-expressionist' Wedekinds, such as *Der Marquis von Keith* (1900; staged 1901, Berlin), *Hidalla* (1904; staged 1905, Munich), and *Franziska* (1912; staged 1912, Munich), were also regularly seen in Berlin before and during the war, and the situation in the capital was paralleled in other theatre centres like Dresden, Frankfurt and Munich. The Wedekind boom was further augmented by Wedekind himself, who from 1905 repeatedly toured the country in batches of his own plays, directed by and starring himself.

2. Though even *The Father* (1887), *Miss Julie* (1888), and *Dance of Death* (1900) have a degree of subjectivity and an obsessive use of images and objects which give the lie to their surface realism.

3. In the epilogue to his play, *Die Verführung* (*The Seduction* written 1913), Paul Kornfeld gives this un-Hamlet-like advice to his actors: 'Let not the actor in this play behave as though the thoughts and words he has to express have only arisen in him at the very moment in which he recites them. If he has to die on the stage, let him not pay a visit to the hospital beforehand in order to learn how to die; or go into a bar to see how people act when they are drunk. Let him dare to stretch his arms out wide and with a sense of soaring speak as he has never spoken in life; let him not be an imitator or seek his models in a world alien to the actor. In short, let him not be ashamed of the fact that he is acting. Let him not deny the theatre or try to feign reality.' (The whole essay is reprinted in English translation in Sokel's anthology).

4. Kaiser, for instance, planned to write a drama to be called simply *Die Erneuerung* (*Regeneration*), where according to Kaiser 'confinement within a limited space is at an end; everything that happens is communicated to the totality of the cosmos...'

5. For instance, in such stage productions as: *Transfiguration* (dir: Karlheinz Martin; des: Robert Neppach, Berlin 1919), *A Generation* (dir: Gustav

Hartung; des: August Babberger, Frankfurt 1918), and *Hell, Road, Earth* dir: Viktor Barnowsky; des: César Klein, Berlin 1920); and in such films as *The Golem* (dir: Paul Wegener/Henrik Galeen; des: Hans Poelzig; 1920), *From Morn to Midnight* (dir: Martin; des: Neppach; 1920), *Genuine* (dir: Wiene; des: Klein; 1920), and *Raskolnikov* (dir: Wiene; des: Andrei Andreyev; 1923).

6. Nevertheless, between 1917 and 1919 Reinhardt mounted two seasons of Expressionist plays in his Berlin theatres, under the group title *Das junge Deutschland*. These included *The Beggar* and *Naval Encounter*, which Reinhardt directed himself, and *The Son, A Generation*, and plays by Kokoschka, Franz Werfel and Else Lasker-Schüler. Kaiser's *Coral* and *From Morn to Midnight* were also seen then, as were revivals of plays by Lenz, Büchner, Wedenkind and Strindberg.

7. Jessner's production style was in fact much more versatile than the coinage 'Jessnertreppe' (Jessner-steps) might imply, as can be seen from photographs of his *Marquis von Keith* (Berlin 1920) and *Othello* (Berlin 1921), which are nonetheless clearly in the 'monumental abstract' tradition. In the cinema, this tradition most notably affected the geometrical designs evident in Fritz Lang's two-part *Die Nibelungen* (1922–24) and *Metropolis* (1926), all designed by Otto Hunte, Erich Kettelhut, and Karl Vollbrecht.

8. A good example is Jürgen Fehling's production of *Masses and Man*, designed by Hans Strohbach (Berlin 1921), where scenes with steps, drapes, spotlights, and a choreographed mob alternated with more grotesque images such as crookedly leaning prison walls and a cell the size of a large bird-cage. A full and enthusiastic eye-witness account in English of this production (and of Jessner's *Richard III* and *Othello*)—with sketches by Robert Edmond Jones—appears in: Kenneth Macgowan, *Continental Stagecraft*, New York: Harcourt Brace, 1922.

9. The revolving stage, invented by Karl Lautenschläger and first installed in the Residenztheater, Munich, in 1896, was also increasingly exploited by Reinhardt in productions at the Deutsches Theater, Berlin, from 1905 onwards.

10. The new Dresden Schauspielhaus of 1914, for instance, had an amazing combination of tri-sectional sinking and sliding stages, designed by Adolf Linnebach.

11. This was Kokoschka's *Murderer Hope of Womankind* (dir: Ernst Reinhold, who also played the main part), staged in connection with an art exhibition, the Vienna Kunstschau, in July 1908, and therefore something of a 'fringe' production.

12. Both *Der Bettler* and *Der Sohn* were important in this respect: *Der Bettler* because the script itself specified sophisticated lighting and scene changes within composite sets, in order to facilitate the interpolation of semi-phantasmagoric scenes indicative of the central character's state of mind and outlook; *Der Sohn* because in his 1918 Mannheim production, the director Richard Weichert used his spotlight for the first time as a kind of persecutor, throwing the characters into vivid relief against the surrounding blackness of the minimal set (designed by Ludwig Sievert)— free-standing door and window frames set in black drapes.

13. Hasenclever's one-acter, *Der Retter* (*The Saviour*, 1915; staged 1919, Berlin), is an insignificant exception.

14. From a letter to Kasimir Edschmid in October 1920. This and other relevant material appears in English translation in: Nicholas Hern, 'The Theatre of Ernst Toller', *Theatre Quarterly* II, No. 5 (Jan.–Mar. 1972), pp. 72–92.

15. The tone, particularly in the scene quoted, is strikingly similar to Brecht's ballad, 'The Legend of the Dead Soldier', also written round about 1918 (first publ. 1922 as an appendix to *Trommeln in der Nacht*).

16. Indeed, its 1922 Munich première (dir: Otto Falckenberg; des: Otto Reigbert) was given the full Expressionist treatment with Caligari-esque sets and an angular and eccentric acting style to match.

17. As also was the hero of Brecht's first play, *Baal* (written 1918; publ. 1922; staged 1923, Leipzig), which was a kind of counter-play to Hanns Johst's Expressionist *Der Einsame* (*The Lonely One:* 1917; staged 1917, Düsseldorf), an apotheosis of the dissolute poet, Grabbe. Spalter neatly suggests that 'a fair judgment would be that the early Brecht was expressionist and anti-expressionist at the same time, sharing the spirit of revolt permeating the movement but not its naive idealism nor its highly emotional frame of reference.'

18. It is also possible to see unfortunate and unintentional foreshadowings of aspects of Nazi ideology in certain Expressionist films—a point which Siegfried Kracauer tediously hammers into the ground in his book *From Caligari to Hitler—A Psychological History of the German Film*, Princeton University Press, 1947.

Stuart Parkes: WEST GERMAN DRAMA SINCE THE WAR

The leading West German theatrical magazine *Theater heute* preceded its review of Martin Walser's first play *Der Abstecher* (*The
Detour*; staged 1961, Munich) with the headline 'Hope for the
German drama'. Walser himself, already well known for his novels
Ehen in Philippsburg (*The Gadarene Club*) and *Halbzeit* (*Half Time*),
described the play as a first try at writing drama, something he was
moved to attempt because of the dearth of plays by German writers.
Today the most interesting feature about *Der Abstecher* is Walser's
stated motives for writing it and the reaction of *Theater heute*. Before
the nineteen-sixties, there were few West German plays of any value
and hardly any at all that dealt satisfactorily with the social and
political problems of the day: the legacy of the Nazi past and the
society of the 'economic miracle'.

Those that did had mostly been written immediately after the
war, one by an already well-known dramatist Carl Zuckmayer: *Des
Teufels General* (*The Devil's General*: staged 1946, Zürich) and
another by a newcomer Wolfgang Borchert, who died shortly after
the premiere of his only play: *Draußen vor der Tür* (*The Man
Outside*: staged 1947, Hamburg). Borchert's play was immediately
successful. It recounts what happens when a soldier, Beckmann,
returns home from Siberia to find the whole basis of his existence
destroyed; his wife is with another man, his parents have committed
suicide. Beckmann's situation was immediately felt to be akin to that
of thousands of others and he became almost a symbol for a whole
generation. Although this generation of outsiders has since been integrated into society, the play is more than a period piece. Beckmann
himself is the eternal outsider. Rather than a world in chaos, *Draußen
vor der Tür* presents an individual at odds with bourgeois society. It
can be argued that bourgeois society can hardly have existed in

Germany in 1947 but the power of the play lies not least in its language and its use of symbols: for instance, Beckmann's wartime spectacles are a sign of how the past still dominates his view of the present. Elsewhere, the play is strongly marked by Expressionistic elements.

While the form of Borchert's play partly looks back to Expressionism, *Des Teufels General* has much of the traditional tragedy about it. The hero Harras is a Luftwaffe general, whose aristocratic swashbuckling individualism leads him to hold the vulgar Nazis in utter contempt. His 'tragic guilt' lies in his having allowed his passion for flying to be put at their service. Against him, Zuckmayer puts forward the ideal of a resistance, in which all shades of religious and political opinion unite. This is propounded, albeit in a dramatically unconvincing way, in the final scene by an engineer Oldenbruch, who suddenly changes from a colourless figure into a passionate moral crusader. Zuckmayer is also faced with one of the major dramatic problems of the post-war period: how to portray Nazis on stage. He presents a fanatical and cold propagandist Dr Schmidt-Lausitz and a daemonic Circe-like temptress Pützchen, who tries to lure Harras into acceptance of Nazi ideas by appealing to his manliness. The title itself shows the connection Zuckmayer makes between Nazism and the diabolic.

After these plays there are few attempts to deal with similar themes. One possible exception is Leopold Ahlsen's *Philemon und Baucis* (staged 1956, Munich). This shows what happens to an elderly Greek couple caught between the occupying German forces and local partisans. Their simple humanity is contrasted with the roughness of the partisans and the self-interest of the Germans, who enjoyed themselves throughout Europe during the good times but are now sick of war. The play, however, does not come to life because of the inadequate dialogue, which is a mixture of slang and stilted grammatical language. It was not until the sixties that new writers began to deal successfully with this kind of German theme.

By the middle of the nineteen-sixties the West German theatre had put behind it the aridity of the fifties. In general, two types of play began to appear; those that were largely realistic and those that used techniques related to the theatre of the absurd. The distinction cannot be clear-cut; few realistic plays confine themselves to straightforward realism, tending rather to symbols and parables, whilst many 'absurd' plays aim to throw light on social reality. The plays that can be called realistic though are distinguished by a concern for contemporary social and political questions. In addition, they are aware of the legacy of Brecht, which means not only technical aspects of his 'epic theatre' but also his challenge to western dramatists in 1955 that the world had to be presented on the stage as capable of change. By contrast, in the non-realistic 'absurd' plays, the aesthetic techniques appear to be the dominant factor.

One major attempt in the sixties to respond to the vital social and political questions of the day was by means of 'documentary theatre'. This term, too, is difficult to define. Every dramatist, whose plays aim in some way to reflect historical fact, has presumably used documentary evidence to support his conception. A closer definition is possible by saying that true documentary theatre will generally incorporate factual material, be it the speeches of a historical figure or transcripts of a court hearing. This technique is not particularly new; Georg Büchner incorporated many of the historical Danton's speeches into his *Dantons Tod*. The other main point about documentary theatre is that any documentary material is used for a specific purpose. In other words, documentary theatre is committed. Facts may be left to speak for themselves, if the aim is simply to bring something to light that a certain section of society prefers to suppress. Elsewhere, the material may be much more clearly ordered for a specific purpose. Documentary theatre may be thought to exist in its purest form where the ordering hand of the dramatist is least visible, as in those plays like Hans Magnus Enzensberger's *Das Verhör von Habana* (*The Havana Hearing*: staged 1970, Essen) that have some kind of courtroom setting and reproduce actual proceedings. But here, too, the demands of the stage compel the dramatist to be selective. Documentary theatre remains theatre and it is inconsistent when Enzensberger says his work is not a theatre play and then speaks of it being played on the stage or on television. By contrast, Peter Weiss accepts documentary theatre as an art form. What is more, both by its commitment and the technical means it uses, it is in the tradition of the Brechtian theatre. To state their message, documentary plays make use of alienation techniques: they may include film material or narrators or have the material spoken by a number of actors, who do not represent any one individual character. Here, the debt is not only to Brecht; the 'political theatre' of Erwin Piscator in the nineteen-twenties had used film to support the political content of the plays. It is significant that Piscator was the first director of Rolf Hochhuth's *Der Stellvertreter* (*The Representative* : staged 1963, Berlin) and Heinar Kipphardt's *In der Sache J. Robert Oppenheimer* (*In the Matter of J. Robert Oppenheimer*; staged 1964, Berlin and Munich).

If these factors are taken to be the major characteristics of documentary theatre, there are several West German dramatists whose works are marked by documentary and connected techniques. The most significant is Peter Weiss, who, although living in Sweden, has his works published in West Germany. His *Die Ermittlung* (*The Investigation* : staged 1965, Berlin) reproduces in documentary form the evidence at the trial of people involved with Auschwitz held in Frankfurt in 1965. The emphasis of the play is on the relationship between past and present, Weiss saying specifically that it is impossible to portray what Auschwitz was like on the stage. His stated aim is to show that Auschwitz was a product of capitalism, and, as one of the witnesses says, that the camp in its organization was an extreme form of capitalism. It is noticeable how Weiss stresses the continuity between Auschwitz and the Federal Republic; for instance, certain witnesses, Germans on the fringe of Auschwitz and now said to hold prominent positions in the Federal Republic, are shown to be little better than the accused. Despite these attempts to relate Fascism with the present, *Die Ermittlung* does not come over principally as an attack on capitalism. The horror of the descriptions of the camp remains the strongest factor despite the use of alienation techniques; free verse, the division of the play into cantos in the manner of Dante and the condensing of the great number of actual witnesses into the anonymous witnesses one to nineteen, who represent a certain type— witness 1, for example, always being one of the Germans on the fringe of the camp.

Weiss's plays written before *Die Ermittlung* show his movement towards Marxism and his greater use of documentary techniques. His first play *Der Turm* (*The Tower* written in Swedish, 1948, first staged in German 1967, Vienna) is largely existential. An individual attains freedom by breaking with traditional forces, symbolized by the tower; the conception is thus reminiscent of Sartre's *The Flies*. Weiss's best play to date *Die Verfolgung und Ermordung Jean Paul Marats dargestellt durch die Schauspielgruppe des Hospizes zu Charenton unter Anleitung des Herrn de Sade* (*The Persecution and Assassination of Marat as performed by the Inmates of the Asylum of Charenton under the direction of the Marquis de Sade*: staged 1964, Berlin) shows the development of his dramatic technique and political thinking. The aim of the play is to contrast the social-revolutionary doctrines of Marat with the extreme individualism of de Sade. Since the first appearance of the play Weiss has been at pains to identify himself with the views of Marat. The ending has been amended a number of times in an attempt to underline this point. Nevertheless everything still ends with Sade triumphantly presiding over a scene of complete chaos, whilst throughout the play the difficulty of all revolution because of man's physical and sexual urges is stressed. It cannot, therefore, be accepted as a clear revolutionary statement. In its form *Marat/Sade* shows a marvellous complexity of techniques and styles. Although there is a documentary element in the incorporation of Marat's actual speeches, the play is anything but simply documentary. The full title shows in itself the complexity of the dramatic situation. The setting, an asylum in the post-revolutionary Napoleonic era, the acting of the murder by mental patients whose diseases are connected with the characters they play—Marat, for instance, is played by a paranoiac—the connections made between figures in the revolution and those responsible for the asylum—for instance, the head of the asylum Coulmier in the framework action and the authoritarian Duperret in the Marat play—are all factors, which mean that the themes of the play, revolution, individualism, physical desire, are illuminated from a variety of angles. Together with the use of verse this differentiation of level alienates Marat's revolutionary doctrines further; despite the statements of its author, *Marat/Sade* is less a revolutionary play than a brilliant exposure of the disjunction between man's individual nature and political action.

There can be no such doubts about the political message of the two plays that followed *Die Ermittlung*. *Gesang vom lusitanischen Popanz* (*The Song of the Lusitanian Bogeyman*: staged 1967, Stockholm) is an attack on Portuguese colonialism in Africa, and *Viet Nam Diskurs*[1] (*Viet Nam Discourse*: staged 1968, Frankfurt) is a history of Vietnam with particular emphasis on what is seen as the struggle against American imperialism. Both plays use documentary techniques. Historical and documentary material is presented by a group of actors, who play a variety of roles. The danger of this method is that complicated events are simplified—the Vietnam play seeks to deal with hundreds of years of history within the framework of a single work.

More recently Weiss has moved from strict documentary theatre to historical themes and characters, first to Trotsky in *Trotzki im Exil* (*Trotsky in Exile*: staged 1969, Düsseldorf). His most recent play *Hölderlin* (staged 1971, Stuttgart) presents the German poet as a sensitive revolutionary, largely misunderstood by his contemporaries. Hegel, Schelling, Fichte, Goethe and Schiller all appear on stage and are all shown to be out of sympathy to some degree with Hölderlin. Only when Marx appears briefly at the end—a meeting not based upon historical fact—does Hölderlin find any kind of kindred spirit. Whatever the validity of the interpretation of Hölderlin, the dramatic means employed are hardly acceptable. Weiss alienates the action by the use of verse and archaic language. The result is that everything appears over-simplified; complicated issues are reduced to a very basic level. It is arguable that it would have been preferable to use traditional dramatic techniques, as Weiss's aim is to present Hölderlin in a sympathetic light. Weiss has not yet improved on the great achievement of his Marat/Sade play.

Heinar Kipphardt, who moved to the west from East Germany in the nineteen-fifties, is another leading writer of documentary plays. The techniques he uses, though, are frequently different from those of Weiss. In particular, he insists much more on individual psychological realism. Each character is individualised, there being no question of one actor playing several anonymous roles. The stage directions of *In der Sache J. Robert Oppenheimer* demand that the actor playing Oppenheimer imitates his actual way of walking. Secondly, Kipphardt is not as clearly committed to a particular political standpoint. His plays seek to question courses of events rather than to give clear answers to general social and political questions. He does, however, use alienation techniques: Oppenheimer acts as narrator introducing the play about himself, the characters address the audience directly, whilst both this play and *Der Hund des Generals* (*The General's Dog*: written 1957, staged 1962, Munich) use film. This latter is a kind of documentary drama without documents, the action being entirely fictitious. A tribunal investigates the case of a general on the Eastern front, who apparently sent some soldiers to certain death because one of them killed his dog. The courtroom setting, so typical of documentary theatre, is not used, however, solely in the usual way as a forum for argument. It provides a framework for the recreation of the events of the past, forming a kind of play within a play. By contrast, *In der Sache J. Robert Oppenheimer* stays within the court-room. The play reproduces the hearing at the height of the McCarthy era, as a result of which the nuclear physicist Oppenheimer was refused security clearance. The issues come into the open during the courtroom debate, Kipphardt's aim being to discredit the official verdict. The tautness of the play shows again that the courtroom is an ideal setting for documentary drama.

Closely connected with documentary theatre, although perhaps not fully admissible examples of the genre, are the controversial plays of Rolf Hochhuth. His use of documentary material is visible not so much in the texts of the plays, which resemble traditional dramas, as in the mass of material he usually appends to the printed editions. This illustrative material, together with the length of the plays them-selves, gives Hochhuth's writing an encyclopaedic element. He is never loth to display his knowledge in the texts of the plays, with references to Rudi Dutschke and Che Guevara in *Die Guerillas* (*The Guerillas*: staged 1970, Stuttgart), and even in the comedy *Die Hebamme* (*The Midwife*: staged 1972, Munich and Zürich) managing to refer to such diverse subjects as the politician Franz Josef Strauss and the tree-planting programme of the GLC.

It is not this somewhat irritating pedantry that has made Hoch-huth's plays controversial but his choice of subject-matter. At the same time, his views on writing plays have not endeared him to the majority of German critics. The first play *Der Stellvertreter* has probably the most controversial subject. It raises the question of the Pope's attitude to the extermination of the Jews, criticizing his silence on the matter. The second play *Die Soldaten* (*The Soldiers*: staged 1967, Berlin) suggests that Churchill was responsible for the death of General Sikorski, the head of the exiled Polish government in London, and it also attacks the indiscriminate bombing of civilian targets from the air. Even if the methods of these two plays are not entirely those of the documentary theatre, the themes are very similar to those of many documentary plays. Since these first plays, Hochhuth has turned away from historical subjects. *Die Guerillas* is a piece of political fiction, examining the possibility of a coup in the United States, aimed prin-cipally at the evil influence of the CIA. Recently Hochhuth has written two comedies, *Die Hebamme* and *Lysistrate und die NATO* (*Lysistrata and NATO* : staged 1974, Essen).

Hochhuth's dramatic methods are so traditional that he has been described as a latter-day Schiller, especially in view of his use of free verse and his belief that a play must be centred around powerful individuals cast in a traditional dramatic mould. This led in 1967 to a controversy with the philosopher Theodor W. Adorno, who accused Hochhuth of ignoring the impersonal forces that hold sway in the modern world. The playwright, however, has not changed his attitude. In *Der Stellvertreter*, Father Riccardo chooses a martyr's death in Auschwitz as a protest against the Pope, whilst *Die Soldaten* centres around conflicts between Churchill and Sikorski, and Churchill and the Bishop of Chichester, an opponent of indiscriminate bombing. In *Die Guerillas*, Senator Nicholson attempts a coup, and in *Die Hebamme*, Sister Sophie takes the law into her own hands by burning down the insanitary accommodation of the homeless. It is easy to see that Hochhuth's attitude to history and society is a little naive. His attempts to show Auschwitz on stage and to personify Nazism through a devilish SS man are complete failures. On the other hand, his choice of subject is unswervingly accurate, his themes vital. Thus he is one of the most popular German dramatists; his comedy, *Die Hebamme*, perhaps underlines why. He uses all the stock comic devices : regional accents, a speech impediment, dirty jokes, plays on words, not to mention corrupt local politicians to create a play it is impossible not to laugh at.

The development of Hochhuth and Weiss away from documentary drama may suggest that the genre has lost its appeal. This is not the case. In addition to Enzensberger's play about the abortive Bay of Pigs invasion of Cuba, a young writer has recently shown by his play *Martin Luther und Thomas Münzer oder Die Einführung der Buchhaltung* (*Martin Luther and Thomas Münzer or The Introduction of Book-keeping*; staged 1970, Basle) that the documentary form is still capable of development. Documentary material is used to contrast the revolutionary Münzer with Luther, whose support for the princes in the Peasants' War of 1525, it is suggested, was partly based on mercenary motives. Forte develops his theme against the background of the rise of capitalism. The early capitalist methods of the banker Fugger are amusingly contrasted with the financial incompetence of the Emperor Maximilian and the backwardness of the Elector of

Saxony, who bases his financial dealings on the security offered by holy relics. Such a play indicates that documentary and related plays may continue to play as significant a part in German drama as they have in the last ten years or so.

The dramatist who has possibly been most aware of the legacy of Brecht is Martin Walser—at least in his early plays. Parallel with these plays, he evolved a theory of the theatre, which was a clear response to Brecht. Whilst respecting Brecht's achievement, he no longer considered Brecht's methods as suitable for portraying the changed social and political situation, pointing out, for instance, that *Mother Courage* would probably not offend most armaments manufacturers. Walser formulated what he called 'Realismus X', a realism that would avoid Brechtian parables without just being a reproduction of external reality. A mixture of symbolism and realism would reveal what lay hidden beneath the surface of reality. After *Der Abstecher*, which tends towards the theatre of the absurd, Walser sought to apply his theories in what he called a German chronicle, of which, however, only two of the three planned parts were completed.

The first play *Eiche und Angora* (*The Rabbit Race* : staged 1962, Berlin) seeks to compare different reactions to the changes in German society that took place between 1945 and 1960. Gorbach, a middle-class Vicar of Bray figure, is able to change from Nazi in 1945 to pacifist in 1950 to anti-communist businessman in 1960, whereas the working-class Alois fails to keep pace with these changes and keeps finding himself in trouble with the authorities. It is through these events that Walser seeks to show the development of German society, in particular the continuing power of the bourgeoisie. He is also at pains to show that character is largely a product of circumstance, that adaptability is a prime human quality. The Nazi is no longer a daemonic figure but, in many ways, similar to the majority of other people. This is the originality of Walser's conception, different as it is from those of Zuckmayer and Hochhuth. Unfortunately the play suffers a little from repetitiveness and from an uncomfortable mixture of tragic and comic elements, particularly in the presentation of the permanent victim of social change, Alois, through whom Walser seeks to show the passivity of the German working class.

The second play in the planned trilogy *Der Schwarze Schwan* (*The Black Swan* : staged 1964, Stuttgart) extends Walser's view of Nazism. If the Nazi is often little different from the rest, it follows that not being involved in Nazi crimes may often be more a matter of circumstance than of character. This is what plagues Rudi Goothein, a boy too young to have been involved with Nazism, especially when he learns of his father's crimes. As he tries to confront his father with the past, he cannot escape the question of what he would have done in the same circumstances. Since the play also specifically questions society's attitude to the whole Nazi past, in particular its refusal to accept any responsibility, it is a most uncomfortable work. It is only regrettable that the *Hamlet*-like plot—Rudi finally commits suicide—rather disintregrates before the end of the play.

Walser's most interesting attempts to write a new kind of socially relevant play cannot, therefore, be judged as entirely successful. More recently he has formulated a new idea of the theatre, plays which should concentrate not on plot but on revealing individual consciousness. After *Die Zimmerschlacht* (*Home Front*: staged 1967, Munich), often compared with *Who's Afraid of Virginia Woolf?*, whose private theme appears a reaction against the political nature of the previous plays, he attempted this in *Ein Kinderspiel* (*Child's Play*: staged 1971, Stuttgart). The play shows a brother and sister seeking to come to terms with the influence of their capitalist father. Their success gives the play a political element; it reflects Walser's enthusiasm for the student rebellion of the late sixties. It is too soon to say, though, whether he has found a new outlet for his considerable talents.

Despite their failings, Walser's plays dealing with the question of the Nazi past are far ahead of many others. The play by Siegfried Lenz, now much better known as a novelist, *Zeit der Schuldlosen* (*Time of the Guiltless*: staged 1961, Hamburg) is a far too obvious parable of Nazism. A group of people are shown firstly in a totalitarian state and then after liberation. The second part abounds with such passages as: 'He who fails to act is still in no way free from guilt. Nobody preserves his purity by indifference. Guilt is something as total as an eclipse; it affects everyone.' Lenz descends to preaching through endless aphorisms. This kind of political parable is perhaps more a feature of East than of West German drama. Only Hartmut Lange, who lives in the west, has used it recently with any success. As he, however, only moved to the west in the middle sixties and as his themes have remained dominantly those of a socialist playwright, he is, regardless of his dramatic skill, only a western writer to a limited degree. His latest play *Die Ermordung des Aias* (*The Murder of*

Ajax : staged 1973, Berlin) is a good example both of his themes and of the dramatic parable. The play centres around a conflict between Ajax and Odysseus about the future conduct of the Trojan War after the death of Achilles. Ajax wants to continue with the same tactics, whereas Odysseus is building the wooden horse. It becomes clear that Achilles signifies Lenin, Ajax Trotsky and Odysseus Stalin. The horse symbolizes Stalin's industrialization programme. The play also raises the question of the relationship between lies and truth in propaganda. Such a choice of themes confirms that Lange is primarily an East German in exile.

The first faint stirrings in the West German theatre in the nineteen-fifties were mainly in plays which showed some connection with the theatre of the absurd. This term, however, requires some clarification when used in connection with German playwrights. A number of critics have made the point that German dramatists have seemed to take over the techniques of the French theatre of the absurd without having statements of comparable intensity to make. A number of differences are immediately noticeable; the petty bourgeois setting, the sense of the author's involvement found in French absurd plays are often missing. By contrast, German absurd plays often come closer to direct parable, indeed the leading German dramatist of the absurd, Wolfgang Hildesheimer, has said that every absurd play is a parable. His theatre stands, therefore, somewhere between the French theatre of the absurd and Brecht. This parabolic element is particularly clear in *Pastorale* (staged 1958, Munich), where a strange quartet of singers assemble in the open air and talk a mixture of business and artistic jargon. As summer turns to winter and two of them die, the connection between bourgeois business and cultural life and death and decay is shown. The message is stressed by the title Hildesheimer gave to the cycle of plays to which *Pastorale* belongs : *Spiele in denen es dunkel wird* (*Plays in Which Darkness Falls*). The difference between the Brechtian parable and Hildesheimer's plays is that the latter suggest no solution to human problems. Hildesheimer's contention is that the whole world is absurd. This seems to be the idea behind the play *Die Verspätung* (*The Delay* : staged 1961, Düsseldorf). A professor comes to an almost depopulated village in an attempt to discover a bird, from which he claims man is descended. At the end of the play, he thinks he does sight it, but it is an illusion. He sinks down dead. Hildesheimer points to the futility of all human efforts to find any

meaning in life, whilst stressing the 'absurdity' of existence through
the setting of the play. What lies behind Hildesheimer's conception of
life becomes clearer in *Nachtstück* (*Night Play*: staged 1963, Düsseldorf). It is the sense of having been born too late, of having no new
outlet because everything has already been done. The chief figure
in the play, simply called a Man, lies unable to sleep in a room full
of pictures. These, together with the grotesque visions he has of march-
ing cardinals and civil servants, represent the burden of cultural and
social traditions.

The absurd plays of Günter Grass lay themselves open to the charge
of lack of depth. *Die bösen Köche* (*The Wicked Cooks*: staged 1961,
Berlin) shows a number of cooks pursuing the Count for the recipe of
a delicious soup he has made. Finally, he shoots himself. Any symbolic
significance the soup may have never becomes clear. As for the fate
of the Count, it bears some analogy with the Passion of Christ—there
is a feet-washing ceremony shortly before his death—but in the Berlin
production the actor wore a mask with the features of Grass himself.
By contrast, *Noch zehn Minuten bis Buffalo* (*Only Ten Minutes to
Buffalo*: staged 1959, Berlin) is more acceptable because of its brevity,
its intentional humour and the use of visual effects—a rusting loco-
motive stands in a field of cows. Grass's theatre has recently moved
away from the absurd. *Die Plebejer proben den Aufstand* (*The
Plebeians Rehearse the Uprising*: staged 1966, Berlin) turns to the
problems of the writer in society and the need for the kind of commitment Grass himself has aimed at in his support for the Social Democratic Party in West Germany. The play shows Brecht's failure to
respond to the workers' uprising in East Berlin on June 17, 1953.
This intention is clear, although Brecht is only called 'The Boss' in
the play. Despite the relevance of the theme, the play never approaches
the quality of Grass's best novels.

In the late nineteen-fifties and early sixties, a number of plays were
written, which cannot be classed as absurd but seem more connected
with that kind of theatre than with social realism. Peter Hirche's
Die Söhne des Herrn Proteus (*The Sons of Mr Proteus*: staged 1962,
Stuttgart) has a theme very similar to that of Hildesheimer's plays. It
shows the utter domination of the sons by the father, who lives up to
his name. Like Hildesheimer, Hirche aims to show that the modern
world presents no opportunities for anything new.

Somewhat differently, Konrad Wünsche aims at a theatre where there is no social comment of any kind. He speaks of 'abstract theatre', which will concentrate solely on the formal elements of drama. His ideas are visible in *Der Unbelehrbare* (*The Unteachable One* : staged 1963, Darmstadt). The situation of the play is an intentional travesty of *Hamlet*. A son is told by his dead father, who has been poisoned by his wife, to take revenge. Eventually he commits suicide but this does not appear to be a tragedy. All he has done is join the other characters, who in their egoism were 'dead' all the time. This might seem like social comment but Wünsche chose to set his play in 1860.

Where there is social comment in many plays of this period, it does not reflect the kind of commitment found in the plays of Weiss or Walser but rather a certain aloofness from society. This, in turn, may be a sign of the position of the writer in the first years of the Federal Republic : isolated from a world dominated by the pursuit of the material gains afforded by the 'economic miracle'. In addition, there is the point, often made by Professor Ralf Dahrendorf, that the society of the Federal Republic has lacked the coherence of other societies, has been a society without leaders and without direction. In this way, it is extremely difficult to portray on the stage. Thus it is not surprising that Herbert Asmodi sets his comedy *Nachsaison* (*Late Season* : staged 1959, Nurenmberg) in Austria among the aristrocracy, which in reality no longer plays any important social role in any German-speaking state. The result is an amusing play without deep significance. The aristocracy also plays a substantial part in Richard Hey's *Der Fisch mit dem goldenen Dolch* (*The Fish with the Golden Dagger* : staged 1958, Stuttgart). Set in an unnamed divided country, it concentrates on the fate of Sergei Rival, who has been hounded on both sides of the demarcation line. In *Weh dem, der nicht lügt*[2] (*Woe Betide Him Who Does Not Lie* : staged 1962, Stuttgart) the hero is an aristocrat out of tune with the modern world, whose nature is alluded to in the title and which is represented in the play by the film industry. Unfortunately the portrayal of this industry, especially the figure of the fat bald domineering director surrounded by unintelligent girls, never rises above the most banal caricature. It is this distance to society, reflected in the use of allegory and the choice of hero that has won this kind of play the title 'poetic theatre'.

The initial distinction made between plays that tend more towards realism and those with absurd elements cannot be regarded as all-inclusive. It would be difficult to include two important playwrights,

Tankred Dorst and Hans Günter Michelsen, in either category. Dorst has formulated the idea of a play where any social comment is explicable in terms of the aesthetic demands of the play itself rather than the personal attitude of the author. This is how he seeks to explain *Große Schmährede an der Stadtmauer* (*Great Denunciation by the City Wall*: staged 1961, Lübeck), which is reminiscent of certain plays by Brecht not merely in its Chinese setting but principally in the denunciation of the Emperor and his system by the woman who has lost her husband. Rather than identifying himself with her views or considering them applicable to any modern society, Dorst says they must be regarded only in the context of the play. His goal of what might be called a self-contained play can also be seen in *Die Kurve* (*The Bend*: staged 1960, Lübeck) which contains elements of the theatre of the absurd. Two brothers live by salvaging the wrecks from car accidents that frequently occur at a dangerous bend. To appease their consciences, they also frequently protest to the ministry about the state of the road. When a ministerial official appears and speaks of doing something about the situation, the brothers take the logical step of murdering him. In two of his later plays, *Toller* (staged 1968, Stuttgart) and *Eiszeit* (*Ice Age*: staged 1973, Bochum), Dorst chooses political themes but again does not show any clear kind of political commitment. *Toller* is critical of the Expressionist playwright Ernst Toller, who was at the head of the short-lived Soviet Republic declared in Munich in 1919, whilst *Eiszeit* shows most sympathy for the character called Old Man, who is based on the Norwegian writer Knut Hamsun, who collaborated with the Nazis and then, as the play shows, was subjected to psychiatric examination after the war. Dorst's plays do not endear him to left-wing critics; they are, however, successful theatrically. By using a revue technique in *Toller*, he is able to show the whole complexity of the situation, for instance the role of the Communists, of intellectuals, of right-wing students and of the central government in Berlin. At the same time, he hits on the real tragedy of the episode, the harsh death sentences passed on workers involved in the rebellion as opposed to the lenient sentence of five years' imprisonment given to the intellectual Toller.

Michelsen's plays centre around the questions of memory and repetition, often in connection with petty bourgeois life. Sometimes these themes are treated existentially; in other plays in connection with a historical situation. *Drei Akte* (*Three Acts*: staged 1965, Ulm) consists of three connected playlets, in each one of which a character in trying to break with the past and with the continuing monotony of his or her existence. Only in one case does there seem to be any hope of success. *Frau L.* (staged 1967, Frankfurt) contains what appears to be one of Michelsen's basic beliefs : 'It is always the same . . . always and ever. Even if it was different.' In the play an old woman gives shelter to a tramp and is reminded of an adventure in her youth with another tramp. A young neighbour appears; it becomes clear that the same thing will happen between this tramp and her and that the interlude will be as the one was for the old woman, a respite in her dull bourgeois existence. By contrast, *Helm* (staged 1965, Frankfurt) has a clear historical setting. Five ex-soldiers are confronted with their past in the shape of a cook Helm, who was sent for court martial over a triviality and suffered dreadfully in consequence. Similarly *Planspiel* (*Planned Play* : staged 1969, Bremerhaven) shows, from the perspective of his funeral, the disastrous influence a general has had on other people's lives. These plays with a more obvious social reference add a further dimension to the already uncomfortable atmosphere of all Michelsen's works.

The middle of the nineteen-sixties might well be thought of as a caesura in the development of the German theatre and of German literature in general.[3] In the case of the drama, the self-doubts of Martin Walser and the first plays of the Austrian Peter Handke with their challenging of traditional theatrical forms are signs of this. Discontent about traditional forms and about the state of the highly subsidised West German theatre grow. A most amusing 'play' on the subject is *So ein Theater* (*What a Performance* : staged 1971, Frankfurt). Performed at one of the 'Experimenta' festivals, which are a feature of this period, it shows a number of people discussing the state of the theatre. The discussion was so realistic that several members of the audience joined in. In this way, the barrier between actors and audience, something Handke is very aware of, was broken.[4] In general, however, there have been very few good avant-garde plays. All that Wolf Wondratschek could think of for the 1971 Experimenta was to invite a weight-lifter to attempt a record on the stage. Unfortunately, the weight-lifters' federation refused permission for the event. Not all attempts to achieve something new on the stage have ended so disastrously. Botho Strauss' *Die Hypochonder* (*The Hypochondriacs* : staged 1972, Hamburg) uses a mixture of non-realistic techniques, elements of the absurd and the grotesque, parodies of detective and horror stories, to illustrate the impossibility of communication in a bourgeois capitalist society. The title refers to the state of people in such a society. This is a far more satisfactory play than, for example, Alf Poss' *Wie ein Auto funktionierte* (*How a Car Worked*: staged 1971, Ulm), a futuristic play in which the actors declaim about the horrors of the motor-car age.

The middle and late sixties also saw numerous attempts to extend the range of the theatre to the working class. This, like experimental theatre, was a reaction against established institutions, which were felt to be excessively isolated. In the wake of the students' rebellion when intellectuals sought contact with workers, street theatre groups sprang up, performing topical political plays in the manner of the agitprop groups of the Weimar Republic. Within the theatre, a connected development led to the re-emergence of the *Volksstück* (folkplay), one of the oldest theatrical forms. Simultaneously the plays of Ödön von Horváth, the last exponent of the genre in the Weimar Republic period, were rediscovered and held in some quarters to be as great as those of Brecht. The recent *Volksstück*, like its predecessors, is usually tied to a specific region and to lower-class characters. In common with Horváth's plays, it is frequently marked by strong social criticism. Thus, in Martin Sperr's Bavarian trilogy, the first play *Jagdszenen aus Niederbayern* (*Hunting Scenes from Lower Bavaria*: staged 1966, Bremen) shows discrimination practised against homosexuals in provincial Bavaria.

Frank Xaver Kroetz, too, sets his plays in his native Bavaria. His particular innovation has been to use people from the very bottom of the social scale as dramatic subjects. He is especially concerned with showing the difficulties such people face in communicating; the time it should take to play a scene consisting of largely incoherent utterances becomes an important stage direction. One play of this kind is *Heimarbeit* (*Homeworker*: staged 1971, Munich). Willy, the father, has to work at home after an accident. His wife is pregnant by another man. After they try to abort it with a knitting needle, the baby is born with lumps on its head and cries all the time. Willy finally murders it. Despite the horror in this and other plays, Kroetz, a member of the Communist party, is at pains to show sympathy with this class of people. This is not the case in *Maria Magdalena* (staged 1973, Heidelberg), where Kroetz chooses a middle-class subject. He is in fact trying to write a modern version of Friedrich Hebbel's 19th century tragedy of the same name but is not very successful, because middle class morality is hardly a contemporary theme. He has to eschew blood, whilst Hebbel's duel between the girl's two suitors becomes, albeit amusingly, an argument about who has the better connections among local dignitaries to help him achieve his aims.

Many of the plays of Rainer Werner Fassbinder, also a well-known film director, have a Bavarian setting. He tries to combine the *Volksstück* with a questioning of traditional theatrical forms—a group he worked with in Munich was significantly called '*anti-teater*'. *Blut am Hals der Katze* (*Blood on the Cat's Neck*: staged 1971, Nuremberg) shows a visitor from space, Phoebe Zeitgeist (spirit of the age), learning the language of society. The play is, therefore, not only a picture of society in the manner of the 'Volksstück' but also, like some of Peter Handke's plays, an investigation of the phenomenon of language. The treatment of this theme is not, however, particularly deep. The same can be said of the theme of women's rights in *Bremer Freiheit* (*Bremen Coffee*: staged 1971, Bremen). In general, Fassbinder's plays are marked more by emotional identification with his characters than by critical social questioning.

Not all *Volksstücke* have a Bavarian setting. Wolfgang Deichsel's *Bleiwe lasse* (*Leave It Be*: written 1965, staged 1971, Darmstadt) consists of a number of scenes showing life in Hesse. Fortunately Deichsel's view of petty-bourgeois society as ultra-conservative, does not affect the amusing realism of the play itself. Jochen Ziem's plays are not tied to a specific region at all. His *Nachrichten aus der Provinz* (*News from the Provinces*: staged 1967, Berlin) consists of eleven scenes set in different parts of Germany which seek to show narrow provincial attitudes. Thus two women in Stuttgart giggle over having almost recommended a doctor who was involved in Nazi experiments to the mother of a deformed child. This play, like most of Ziem's, suffers from its somewhat arid language; he does not try to localize his plays by using any form of regional speech. Nevertheless the *Volksstück* has been a revitalizing factor in German theatrical life in the last few years.

If any kind of common factor can be found among the diverse developments of post-war German theatre, it might be said to lie in the search for an adequate relationship with reality. This would include not only external reality, an area further complicated by the enormities of the Nazi past, but also the reality represented by the theatre itself. The search for a relationship with external reality is visible in the early plays of Walser, in the documentary theatre and in the rebirth of the *Volksstück*. Here one sees the search for a post-Brechtian form, which would be adequate for the treatment of social and political themes. Opposed to this, there are the doubts about external reality and the reality of the theatre. These doubts are reflected in the theatre of the absurd and in recent radical questioning of the theatre as an institution. It might be held that any attempt at definition that embraces such different plays is far too wide and furthermore that all plays are an attempt to deal with reality. Yet, there does seem to be a difference between English and German theatre in this respect. While a number of English playwrights still feel able to use traditional forms, to accept the possibility of portraying external reality through theatrical illusion, most German writers harbour grave doubts about their subject matter and the medium they use. Such an attitude may appear to be excessively introspective and, in theatrical terms, doomed to failure, but then how far is a complacent acceptance of traditional dramatic forms and techniques suitable for any attempt to produce effective theatre about the problems of the late 20th century?

NOTES

1. The full title of the play is significant: *Diskurs über die Vorgeschichte und den Verlauf des lang andauernden Befreiungskrieges in Viet Nam als Beispiel für die Notwendigkeit des bewaffneten Kampfes der Unterdrückten gegen ihre Unterdrücker sowie über Versuche der Vereinigten Staaten von Amerika die Grundlagen der Revolution zu vernichten. (Discourse on the Background and the Course of the Long-lasting War of Liberation in Viet Nam as an Example of the Necessity of Armed Struggle by the Oppressed against Their Oppressors as well as on Attempts of the United States of America to destroy the bases of revolution.)*

2. The title alludes to the 19th century comedy by Franz Grillparzer *Weh dem, der lügt (Woe Betide Him Who Lies).*

3. Factors that influenced intellectual life at this period included the students' rebellion, the Vietnam war and the entry of the Social Democratic party into government in 1966. This latter fact, coupled with the formation of a Social Democrat government in 1969, necessitated a reconsideration of the attitude of opposition most intellectuals had assumed in the era of Konrad Adenauer and the 'economic miracle'.

4. Attempts to involve the audience had already been made. Paul Pörtner's *Scherenschnitt (Scissors Cut;* staged 1963, Ulm) is described by the author

as a *Mitspiel* (play to participate in). After a conventional detective story plot, the audience is asked to discuss what has happened and to vote on which of the three suspects it considers guilty. As the play has three alternative endings so that the audience's verdict can always be 'correct', in reality the audience has hardly participated but been the victim of a clever gag.

II

EUROPEAN CROSS-CURRENTS

Hilde Spiel: THE AUSTRIAN CONTRIBUTION

'It takes a great deal of history to produce a little literature,' said
Henry James. In Austria, for a long time, an excess of history failed
to produce literature or even prevented it altogether. Until 150 years
ago, Austria's contribution to the world of letters was slight; moreover one could reasonably have asked what language was used by her
writers. For this state, having emerged from the dark ages as a small
country on the Danube, grew to be the heart of an Empire of many
tongues and nations in which, at its most glorious moment, the sun
never set. From 1806, when the Holy Roman crown was doffed by
the Emperor Francis I, until the First World War, it still contained a
dozen peoples and many more languages and dialects. Its rulers sometimes spoke Spanish, often French and always German with a soft
and languid Viennese inflexion. But throughout the ages, loyal toasts
as well as lyrical praise and epic eulogies were addressed to, and
understood by them, in widely different idioms of Latin, Slav,
Teutonic or Magyar origin. Still, it is commonly accepted that
Austrian literature is that written in Austria in German, or more
often than not in a language as akin to German as English is to
American.

It is in Austria that German writing began. On the banks of the
Danube the Nibelungen saga was first recorded. In the Tyrol, or in
Lower Austria, the greatest of all minnesingers, Walther von der
Vogelweide, was born. From another Tyrolese valley, two centuries
later, came the last of these troubadours, Oswalt von Wolkenstein. He
was a great poet and a widely travelled nobleman who at the age of
17, during the reign of Richard II, visited England. Yet some time
before him, there lived in Vienna another writer who seemed more
truly Austrian than either of these two medieval bards. A chronicler
by the name of Jans der Enenkel—John the grandson—he wrote a
Book of Princes and a history of Austria up to his own, the 13th

century. In him a quality can be detected which ever since has distinguished his compatriots from their German cousins : a soured view of the present and a nostalgic longing for the past.

Jans lived in an epoch of splendour and perpetual aggrandisement. His city and country, under Duke Frederick the Militant, flourished as never before. Yet to Jans, the golden age was irretrievably lost in the vaults of history. Reality held no hope for him, and not the slightest promise. In this he resembles most later Austrian men of letters who, to this day, have preferred a world of their imagination to the world of fact. Though they were rarely attracted or even fascinated by death, as were so many German writers from the Romantic movement onward, they were attracted and fascinated by the unreal. In whatever they drank and ate, they tasted a drop of gall and a grain of wormwood. Yet, for all their profound conviction that life, even at its most beautiful moments, left much to be desired, they were always eager to enjoy its fleeting pleasures in a melancholy but highly sensuous way.

The roots of Austrian literature went deep, but the tree took a long time to grow. After Jans and the minnesingers, for a period of nearly four centuries, the making of history seems to have left the Austrians no time to sit down and record it, while in England Stuarts followed Tudors, Hanoverians the House of Orange, while Valois, Orléans and Bourbon fought for the throne of France, Austria was busy ruling Europe under its single dynasty, the Habsburgs. Her energy was spent in warding off the Turks and the Plague. Her creative impulse was consumed in architecture and in music. Whatever this people had to say was not expressed in words. It was said by Mozart, by the master-builders Fischer von Erlach and Lukas von Hildebrandt, the painter Michael Rottmayr and the sculptor Raphael Donner. Not even the *grand siècle*, so rich in eminent Austrian soldiers, artists and composers, gave the nation a writer of distinction. As in earlier days there had been no Ronsard or Shakespeare, no Racine or Milton, so now there was no Rousseau or Richardson, no Alexander Pope or Voltaire. However, at that time the first crude attempts were made to hold the mirror up to nature, and it was from the heart of the people, not within the precincts of the court, that Austrian drama arose.

The theatre, around 1730, lived on Jesuit plays, taken from Greek mythology, mixed with Christian allegory, and presented with all the pomp and splendour of baroque spectacles, aided by the magic wonders of a naive, but carefully contrived machinery. These were loved by the Emperor and his guests, but neither meant for, nor to the taste of the man in the street—that is the streets of Vienna. There a great reservoir of natural wit, acting ability and urge for self-expression led to impromptu performances in public places, on open squares or small stages first on the fringe of the city, later in theatres nearer the centre of town. No author was needed for this Austrian *Commedia dell'Arte*. It was devised, on the lines of Punch and Judy shows, by the chief performer, invariably a dyed-in-the-wool comedian. While in Germany the theatre, born in a similarly popular way, soon took on a more scholarly and didactic character, the Viennese wanted to go on laughing. And there were many actors able to make them laugh, among them Prehauser, Kurz-Bernardon, Laroche, Hasenhut and Josef Stranitzky. This last, son of a lackey, the main representative of the *Hanswurstkomödie* later disdained and driven out by the high-minded courtier Joseph von Sonnenfels, was in fact Austria's first theatrical genius, a forerunner of Raimund and Nestroy in his sceptical humour and malicious wit.

In 1752 a decree was issued by the Imperial Court that every play had to be submitted, in a definitive written text, to the Censor's Office. This spelt the end to impromptu comedy and the beginning of both serious drama and the Vienna *Volkskomödie*. At this moment, which marks the actual birth of dramatic literature in Austria, the duality sets in which has characterized its writing for the stage ever since. For this development along two different paths, a simile may be used from the libretto of *The Magic Flute*, which was written by an entrepreneur and comedian of Stranitzky's ilk, Emmanuel Schikaneder. Just as Tamino, a man of high birth in search of morality and wisdom, is initiated into the higher rites of Sarastro's temple, so some of the Austrian playwrights emulated—and were admitted to—the school of German neo-classicist and neo-romantic writing. Others, like Papageno, bent on earthly pleasures and diversions, unwilling to leave the warmth and companionship of the simple folk for the lonely pursuit of spiritual elevation, went on writing popular comedy. The foremost writer to do so, Philipp Hafner (1735–64), had many successors, among them Gleich, Meisl and Bäuerle, who between them produced the hundreds of farces and burlesques linking Stranitzky's theatre with the great comedy-authors of the Biedermeier. For its first serious dramatist, Grillparzer, Austria had to wait another few decades.

Meanwhile in 1776 the 'Hof- und Nationaltheater' had been founded by the Emperor Joseph II. Without this institution, still alive today under the name of 'Burgtheater', much of Austria's serious literature would not have been written—though its outstanding playwrights, like the great prose-writers, made their way more easily with the help of German audiences and readers, German publishing houses and the German stage. At first even the Hoftheater, designed as a 'school of morals' by one of its apostles, Sonnenfels, had to stage light farce of local origin or tragedies imported from Germany. Austrian literature as a whole can be said to have begun in earnest only around 1820 or 1830, when five writers, all born at the turn of the century, emerged into the public eye. They were Franz Grillparzer (1791–1872), dramatist, poet and prose-writer, as important to his country as Schiller is to Germany and Corneille to France; Ferdinand Raimund (1790–1836), very much Stranitzky's heir, yet also influenced by the magic spectacles of the baroque, a popular playwright of great poetic charm with a highly ethical, if homespun, philosophy; Johann Nestroy (1801–62), like Raimund a comedy-writer, whose satire however probed deeply into social conditions and human predicaments; finally the lyrical poet Nikolaus Lenau (1802–50), an Austrian Byron from the Hungarian marshland, and Adalbert Stifter (1805–68), a writer of noble and polished prose. Of these five, two— Raimund and Stifter—ended in suicide. One, Lenau, went insane. The fourth, Grillparzer—whose brother took his own life—died a disgruntled old bachelor. And even Nestroy, the actor-playwright whose boundless wit made audiences roar with laughter night after night, was a hardened, disillusioned cynic at the end of a life spent in constant domestic crises and inadequate success.

It was customary in earlier days to bracket Nestroy with Raimund, though the latter did not attain his mastery of language nor his mordant wit. A true son of the people, Raimund believed in the simple virtues, domestic bliss, contentment and inner serenity. Once, in his *Der Alpenkönig und der Menschenfeind* (*King of the Alps and Enemy of Mankind*), he showed uncanny, pre-Freudian understanding of the hidden motives of a schizophrenic mind. Despite his lovely flights of fancy, he never rose to the height of those 'educated' poets he caricatured in his satire *Die gefesselte Phantasie* (*Fancy in Fetters*). Nestroy however was as great in his way, if not greater, than Grillparzer, of whose large oeuvre only two or three plays deserve to rank with the

German 'classical' drama he tried to emulate. Karl Kraus, Austria's
Aretino (1874–1936), the most severe critic of his time, has maintained Nestroy's pre-eminence as a master of wordplay and judge
of human nature. But these comedies, written in the wealth and
welter of Viennese vernacular, which abounds in words borrowed
from the Italian, the Czech and Hungarian languages, and deriving
their scurrilous types from the people they were meant to amuse, are
practically untranslatable. They are as exclusively Austrian as Restoration comedy is English, and couched in a language akin to Cockney,
with linguistic mysteries as impenetrable to outsiders as rhyming
slang. Round a usually primitive plot, more often than not lifted from
some obscure and long-forgotten French farce, Nestroy creates stock
characters of Viennese everyday life whose main preoccupation is to
reason, abundantly and magnificently, with each other and with their
own existence. His own extraordinary insight into human weaknesses
is echoed by some thoughtful cobbler or caretaker, a humble raison-
neur played, in his time, by the author himself. To this day his plays
are performed in Vienna with a historical precision guaranteed by the
basic unchangeability of its people.

   Einen Jux will er sich machen (*He's Out for a Lark*), the only
Nestroy play which made its way onto the English-speaking stage
through Thornton Wilder's adaptation, *The Matchmaker*, or, in musical form, *Hello Dolly*, bears a curious likeness to one of Grillparzer's
dramas. In the comedy, two young shop-assistants venture out into
the world by leaving their provincial town for the capital, go through
a series of imbroglios and get back in the nick of time, glad to have
escaped the vicissitudes of metropolitan life. Grillparzer's *Der Traum
ein Leben* (*The Dream as Life*), a dramatic poem inspired by Calderon's *La Vida es Sueño*, allows his hero to undertake similar adven-
tures merely in his somnolent imagination. In the course of one night
a young man goes through the experiences of a lifetime. He falls in
love with a beautiful princess, he fights a glorious battle and becomes
involved in intrigues which end in his being convicted for murder. At
the right moment, however, he awakens, cured for ever of his longing
to enter the great world, and content to remain in the idyllic seclusion
of his home. 'For,' it is said in this play, 'there is danger in greatness,
and fame is but an idle game.'

   This sentence may be taken as a motto of Grillparzer's own existence, which was beset by fears and scruples, by a definite reluctance to

commit himself in any way. He wrote classicist verse plays about Greek and Austrian history, the best of which, *Ein Bruderzwist in Habsburg*, concerned the fight between the two Emperors Rudolph II and Matthias. He also wrote, as he might not have done without Stranitzky, at least one light-hearted comedy, *Weh dem der lügt*. Yet, on the whole, he lacked humour and was a moody, crusty man, a civil servant by profession and temperament. And although he may not have known it, his life and his career were far more of an Austrian tragedy than his own drama of the two hostile Habsburg brothers. For he was himself the prototype of a peculiar kind of Austrian, not the best-known, the easy-going, voluble, extrovert kind, but one made of finer stuff and therefore all the more defenceless. He might have been the first in a long line of characters portrayed by later Austrian writers like Musil and Hofmannsthal—men of talent, of genius even, who are unable to face reality, unable to declare themselves to a woman, unable to stand up to their superiors, unable to utter the right word at the suitable time, although they might have hit on it sooner than anyone else.

If Grillparzer was the only Austrian dramatist to rank with his great German contemporaries, Friedrich Hebbel (1813–63) could claim admission to their Parnassus by virtue of his origin. In fact, it is doubtful whether he should be mentioned in the context of Austrian drama at all. Yet, having been born and bred in Hamburg, he chose to spend most of his life in Vienna, where he not only married an actress of the *Hofburgtheater*, but furnished that noble institution with a great number of plays. It may be argued that, like Beethoven or his own townsman Brahms, he was sufficiently assimilated by his surroundings to have shed his German characteristics, though he might not have grown to be a genuine Austrian. This is not the case. That deceptive lightness absorbed by their music, as in the second movement of Beethoven's 7th symphony, which so gracefully veils the depths of sadness, never entered his work. Hebbel remained a forceful, sincere and realistic German writer, whether in his Biblical and mythological drama, in his *Nibelungen*-trilogy, or in his domestic tragedy *Maria Magdalena*, a forerunner of naturalism. He was a man of great psychological insight, at times a volcano of feeling. The otherworldliness, the doubt, the constant temptation to withdraw from reality which were inherent in the Austrian character and still increased by Spanish influence—as Grillparzer was influenced by Calderon and

Lope de Vega—were not for him. As he had no ancestor in Austrian literature, so he had no successor. His heir was Gerhart Hauptmann, in faraway Silesia.

Grillparzer survived him. He died in 1872, ten years after the birth of Schnitzler, nine years after that of Hermann Bahr, two years before Hofmannsthal was born. Thus, this belated classic, whose collected works now rest on the bookshelves of educated families next to those of Wieland, Schiller, Goethe and Heine, links up with *Jung-Wien*, the literary movement of the *fin-de-siècle*. At last, in Austria the bourgeois century was producing its bourgeois writers. The middle-classes were growing in prosperity. Wars were no longer fought since the Austrian defeat at Königgrätz. And Metternich's police state, which had driven creative talent to the not yet censorable art of music, had been changed into a much more flexible body, able to give way when popular pressure became insistent. Now the sons of industrialists, hungry for culture and contemptuous of the businessman's outlook which had helped their fathers to educate them so well, found themselves with enough money, leisure and freedom to write. And at once, as artists will do, they turned round and bit the hand that fed them. Not for them the glittering drawing-room comedies, uncritical of social inequalities, which at that time flourished in England and France. Austrian dramatists during those last decades of the old Empire sensed, before anyone else, the fragility of their affluent epoch. They described the hollow moral pattern and empty conventions of a doomed society, or turned away from a reality which seemed to them too crude and insecure.

At this point two roads diverge. Towards the end of the century, Austrian literature was cut in half and drifted apart, not to be united again until after the Second World War. A gulf opened between town and country. On one side stood the Viennese and the German writers in Prague, gathering up the harvest of Austrian worldliness and *savoir vivre*, yet successively growing more introspective and refined until they lost touch with many of their countrymen. And on the other side stood the provincials, rustic, lusty and robust, much more in tune and agreement with the people, given either to realistic descriptions of everyday life or to a primitive mysticism of Christian or pagan origin. Among them were Ludwig Anzengruber (1836–89), a regional writer though he came from Vienna, who in some ways foreshadowed modern social drama, as well as Karl Schönherr

(1867–1943) from Tyrol, the author of adroit peasant tragedies like *Weibsteufel* (*The Devil Woman*) and *Glaube und Heimat* (*Faith and Fatherland*), depicting poverty, greed and lust. These men were far from sophisticated, but while they were still religious, they were morally safe. It was only when—like Richard Billinger (1893–1965)— they fell back on a dubious clod-hopping mysticism, that they were paving the way for the cult of 'Blood and Soil'. It is hardly surprising that the outside world of letters more readily welcomed the urban groups of Austrian writers. They grew from an atmosphere admirably suited to their craft.

The whole intricate web of Viennese society was faithfully, and wistfully, described by Arthur Schnitzler (1862–1931), with Hofmanns- thal the scion of *Jung-Wien*. He was aware of the flaws, the frayed fringes, the outworn patches. In May 1873 the fraudulent specula- tions encouraged by the age of prosperity were unmasked, and on the fateful Black Friday of that month the stock exchange crashed. At the same time, a world exhibition which had long been planned was opened in the Prater. And so, on the tottering edifice, amidst general bankruptcy, the whirl of amusements began. Schnitzler was then a boy of eleven, but he must have sensed what was going on. When, many years later, under the influence of Hermann Bahr and his younger friend Hofmannsthal, he turned away from medicine and devoted himself entirely to writing, there was in his attitude a scep- ticism engendered by early disillusionment.

Schnitzler wrote of his time and for his time. If his plays, like his stories and novels, are firmly fixed in their period, it is because the society they depicted does not exist any more. Their conflicts are out- moded. Unhappy love-affairs, as a rule, do not now end in suicide. Duels no longer form part of the Austrian army code. Anti-semitism has largely, if not entirely, disappeared, mainly for want of Jews. And yet the people involved in all these bygone dilemmas are still with us; the basic make-up of the Austrian character, so lucidly described by Schnitzler, has not changed at all. His legends have survived, if in another shape and form. The legend of Anatol, a lazy, charming, sensitive, self-absorbed and gently ruthless young man. The legend of the *Süsse Mädel* (*Sweet Girl*), a sweet and unselfish, tender-hearted girl who, in the end, is always deserted. Even the legend of the 'femme fatale', a lovely and well-married, but usually scheming and utterly faithless creature, a much more fitting partner for the passionate but heartless Anatol. The merry-go-round of his *Reigen* (*Round Dance*), with its distinct disparities of class, mulled over in the years between the wars, seems true to life again in the snob-ridden second Austrian republic. In fact, the pattern, if not the problems, of Schnitzler's *beau monde* has been revived. His plays, notably *Das weite Land* (*Vast Country*), *Liebelei* (*Love Affair*), *Der einsame Weg* (*The Lonely Road*), *Anatol,* have added a large share to Austrian social history. But more than that: in his part of the world, Schnitzler introduced social criticism into fiction.

As a dramatist he ranks far above his contemporaries. Yet the most delightful modern Austrian comedy was written not by him, but by Hugo von Hofmannsthal (1874–1929) who in England is still known chiefly as the author of Richard Strauss's libretti. Indeed, Hofmannsthal's reputation rests neither on these alone, nor on that exquisite play *Der Schwierige* (*The Difficult One*) nor any other single work of poetry, prose and drama. He must be considered as the only truly universal figure in Austrian letters, an heir to varied and often conflicting traditions, and a mediator of European thought. His early poems, his verse plays—*Der Tor und der Tod* (*Death and the Fool*) and others—took Vienna by storm. His essays on Walter Pater, Swinburne, d'Annunzio and Maurice Barrès, written while he was still under 20, were the first to acquaint his countrymen with these contemporary writers. He was at home in all periods, though he preferred the Austrian and Venetian baroque. His prose was of a classical beauty unsurpassed in his own sphere, except by Stifter. In his poetry, as well as in his mythological plays, he was equally measured and serene. Only in his comedies, in *Der Schwierige*, *Der Unbestechliche* (*The Incorruptible One*) and in *Rosenkavalier* (*Cavalier of the Rose*), the Viennese temperament broke through. In the 'Difficult One', that peculiar kind of Austrian whose prototype was Grillparzer, the shy, gracefully helpless, retired kind is portrayed to perfection. Count Bühl, a man of 40, constantly ties himself into knots by trying to clear up the tangle of his emotions. Though he goes through life wishing to hurt no one, he leaves a trail of broken hearts and misunderstandings behind. He is convinced that one cannot open one's mouth without creating an unearthly confusion. Everything one utters is indecent. At certain moments it may be impudent even to live. All this, as his nephew tells him, may be a *bizarrerie,* but it very nearly leads to his undoing. Still, this is a comedy, so all ends well.

Hofmannsthal wrote the play eight years before his death, and when he had travelled far from the days of his youthful genius. In middle-age, while he reaped world-wide honours with his Strauss-libretti and his—somewhat arty-crafty—adaptation of the old *Everyman*, he had been assailed by doubts and difficulties similar to those of his reluctant hero. For if his most ambitious prose work, his novel *Andreas*, remained a fragment, it was because he too, like Count Bühl, allowed himself to become entangled in a lot of intricacies. The same fate, though it was finished in several drafts, befell his hoped-for dramatic masterpiece, a tragedy called *Der Turm* (*The Tower*) which did not reach the stage in his lifetime, and honourably failed when it was first produced at Salzburg in 1959. Over and over again, Hofmannsthal was defeated by the richness of his own imagination. He saw too many possibilities and not one single certainty. It was only in his later years that he was able to overcome his own failure, sublimating it in the character of Count Bühl.

Both Schnitzler and Hofmannsthal, like most of the members of *Jung-Wien*, were deeply concerned with the interchangeability of life and dream, of semblance and being. As one of them wrote, 'they more often watched the reflection of wax candles in Venetian glass than the stars mirrored by a quiet lake'. Yet Hermann Bahr (1863–1934), for a while their figurehead, made his mark very realistically as a pioneer of modern art and a writer of pleasant comedies—*Das Konzert* (*The Concert*)—while the sensitive Richard Beer-Hofmann (1866–1945) was best known for his well-shaped tragedy *Der Graf von Charolais* (*The Count of Charolais*). All these, and the playwrights who followed in their wake, among them Max Mell (1882–1972), Anton Wildgans (1881–1932), Felix Braun (born 1885), Ferdinand Bruckner (1891–1958), Rudolf Henz (born 1897) and, in his few stage works, Franz Werfel (1890–1945), whether they wrote historic or social drama, pursued, as it were, the path of Tamino, somewhat at a distance from popular taste and relying on educated 'High German' rather than their native Viennese vernacular. Curiously enough, it was that apostle of pure language, Karl Kraus, who elevated Austrian slang to the rank of an artistic medium, thereby setting the pace for generations to come. His titanic attempt to describe the entire social scene of Austria at war, *Die letzten Tage der Menschheit* (*The Last*

Days of Mankind), written in 1922 and never staged in its entirety, makes use in its dialogue of all the various idiomatic distortions of German current in the old Austrian monarchy, alternating with passages of sublime poetry. Here Tamino walks hand in hand with Papageno through the trials of water and fire.

The playwright who extracted the most dramatic tension, the deepest psychological truth from Austrian everyday language, Ödön von Horváth (1901–38), has only very recently been accorded his full eminence. Born at Fiume of Hungarian parents, brought up in Belgrade, Budapest, Bratislava and Vienna, he was a true son of the Habsburg Empire, yet at the same a leading symbol of his age. It was in Germany where he spent many formative years, that he watched the rise of the Nazis and became their bitter foe. From Vienna he went into exile in Hungary, Czechoslovakia, Yugoslavia, Italy and France. And by a sinister stroke of fate, reminiscent of Greek tragedy, he was fatally hit by a falling tree on the Champs-Elysées soon after he had settled in Paris, thereby robbing Austria of its most important dramatist since Schnitzler and the German stage of its only rival to Brecht. His antecedents are not in doubt; he has himself acknowledged his debt to Nestroy. 'One would have to be a Nestroy in order to be able to define all that which, undefined, lies in one's path.' But it is obvious that he had learnt from Karl Kraus the revealing quality of lower middle-class jargon. His plays, among them *Geschichten aus dem Wienerwald* (*Tales from the Vienna Woods*), *Italienische Nacht* (*Italian Night*), *Kasimir und Karoline*, *Der jüngste Tag* (*Judgment Day*), by employing the clichés in daily use, tear the mask from petit-bourgeois hypocrisy. His social analysis is as exact as it is merciless. Yet Horváth was a humanist and, in his Southern, somewhat sloppy way, a Christian, whose vision of a better society, a purified collective mind, led him to fight falseness, injustice, brutality at the core, in the individual mind as well as in its generalized form practised by the Fascists.

Horváth's friend, the lovable vagrant Franz Theodor Csokor (1885–1969), though more prolific, never achieved the success accorded, most posthumously, to his younger contemporary. One play only, *3 November 1918*, a moving and ably constructed account of the break-up of the old Austrian army as reflected in a number of multi-national officers marooned in a rest-home high in the mountains on the Carinthian-Slovene border, has survived its time of origin, which was 1936. Yet Csokor who never shook off the eruptive phrasing and rhythmic diction of his Expressionist youth, was tireless in exploring the great social myths of the past and present, and imbued his works with a humane fervour unequalled by any other Austrian man of letters during his time. His plays, his novels, his poetry, his many accounts of the odysseys this brave and noble fighter of Fascism underwent after the fall of Austria, though none of them put him in the first rank of literature, collectively brought him eminence. Perhaps he was destined to represent his country as a venerable figure rather than an outstanding author, as indeed he did for two decades as President of Austrian P.E.N.

In the years between the wars, while Schnitzler, Hofmannsthal, Bahr and Beer-Hofmann were still alive and active, Austria did not lack great dramatists. Her two most promising younger playwrights however, Ferdinand Bruckner, author of historical plays like *Elisabeth von England* or topical ones like *Krankheit der Jugend* (*Malady of Youth*), and Arnolt Bronnen (1895–1959), a writer of violent, aggressive stage works who later joined the Nazi movement, went to live in Germany. The light-hearted comedies of Alexander Lernet-Holenia (born 1897)—*Österreichische Komödie* (*Austrian Comedy*), *Ollapotrida*—were always subsidiary to his elegant prose and beautiful poetry. And Franz Werfel, who had followed up his early Expressionist drama with historic tragedies like *Juarez und Maximilian* and *Das Reich Gottes in Böhmen* (*God's Realm in Bohemia*) as well as Biblical plays, more and more turned to novel-writing in the thirties; his great drama of Jewish exodus, *The Eternal Road*, was produced by Reinhardt, in 1937, only in America. What dramatic talent remained in the years between 1933 and the Anschluss went underground, under the impact of the Austro-Fascist regimes of Dollfuss and Schuschnigg. In the little theatres and cabarets which flourished in the cellars of Vienna, political satire was acted out in a vain attempt to stem the tide. In their brilliant caricature of the wayward petit-bourgeois already infected by the Nazi bacillus, young playwrights like Hans Weigel (born 1908) and Jura Soyfer (1913–39) showed that they had learned the lesson of Karl Kraus's *Last Days of Mankind*.

When in 1938, after the rape of Austria, the great watershed divided its men of letters into more or less willing exiles and more or less loyal citizens of the Third Reich, hardly a major dramatist was left in the country. Those who stayed were either welcomed by the new masters for fitting the image of the *volksnahe* writer, like Billinger or Mell, or tolerated as the providers of harmless and pleasant comedies in the Austrian tradition, like Friedrich Schreyvogl (born 1899). It must be stressed that no notable playwright appeared on the Austrian scene to promulgate Nazi thought in his plays, as did Hanns Johst, Hans Rehberg and many others in Germany. On the other hand, those who had gone abroad were condemned to silence. While prose writers were able to make known their work through emigré publishing houses or in translation, dramatists found it difficult, if not impossible, to reach the foreign stage. Only one example is known of an Austrian play having been produced on Broadway, Werfel's *Jakobovsky and the Colonel*, and it took many years after it was written until the risk of backing it was taken by the New York Theatre Guild.

1945. Tabula rasa. The allied powers occupying Austria were trying to revitalize cultural life, to open those theatres which had been closed, by order of the 'Patron of German Culture', Goebbels, from August 1944. Had anything been written clandestinely during the dark years that could now be resuscitated? Not so: the drawers were empty. Yet succour was near. With no other luggage but a rucksack Hans Weigel returned from Switzerland illegally, before official permission had been given, and in that rucksack brought with him the first Austrian post-war drama, describing the self-searching dream of a middle-class sinner and bearing the symbolic title of *Barrabas*. It was performed at the Theater in der Josefstadt in its first season, and even reached the Hebbel-Theater in Berlin. Otherwise the Vienna theatre started again as it had ended in the late thirties: with social satire and political cabaret. Those who, next to Weigel, had provided the little cellar-ensembles with sketches and songs—and had gone on to do so in London's war-time Austrian theatre 'Laterndl' ('The Lantern')—among them Hugo F. (Königs) Garten and Rudolf Spitz, did not intend to leave their English exile. But new talent arose. With the young Helmut Qualtinger (born 1928), with Michael Kehlmann, later on Carl Merz and Gerhard Bronner began to a new era of cabaret, a form of dramatic expression which claimed most of the creative urge within the country for a decade or more.

Outside Austria, however, a hitherto unknown playwright from Vienna set out to conquer the world stage with a drama written in Zurich during the war. Fritz Hochwälder (born 1911) who, after some minor dramatic attempts, had been forced to emigrate in 1938, seemed to have acquired an almost uncanny skill in exile. His play *Das heilige Experiment* (*The Strong Are Lonely*), dealing with social justice and God's reign on earth as exemplified by the Jesuit state in Paraguay around 1770, combined all the virtues of a well-constructed historical problem play. Another, *Der öffentliche Ankläger* (*The Public Prosecutor*), built round Fouquier-Tinville, was no less proof of the sound craftsmanship this former master-upholsterer applied to his writing. A number of similarly solid works, among them *Hotel de Commerce* after Maupassant, *Donadieu* and *Meyer Helmbrecht,* supported and justified his plea for an 'unpretentious anti-anti-theatre' for the masses. Twice however he ventured out into experimental drama, in his modern mystery play *Donnerstag* (*Thursday*) and in a sort of post-expressionist Don Juan-fantasy called *1003*, both times without great success. Hochwälder, incidentally, is one of the few authors, beside those employed in cabaret—notably Qualtinger in his satiric monologue *Herr Karl*—to tackle the problem of guilt and punishment of Nazi criminals, as in *Der Befehl* (*The Order*) and *Der Himbeerpflücker* (*The Raspberry Picker*). With him, though they had no immediate connection with this refugee writer who never returned to his native country, may be mentioned a few other playwrights more or less true to the traditional theatrical form, such as Kurt Klinger (*Treibjagd auf Menschen—Battle for Men*), Hans Friedrich Kühnelt (*Ein Tag mit Edward—A Day with Edward*), Harald Zusanek (*Die Strasse nach Cavarcere—The Road to Cavarcere*) and Johannes A. Boeck (*Jeanne 44*). They all emerged during the fifties, but their reputation mostly remains confined to Austria.

Two young women who quickly rose to fame in the whole German-speaking world, supported by the 'Gruppe 47' to which they belonged from the outset, Ilse Aichinger (born 1921) and Ingeborg Bachmann (1926–73), brought a very personal poetic vision and formal daring to the radio play. Though their main achievements lie in other fields, they helped develop the medium of sound broadcasting in a novel way, by making it express surrealist or Kafkaesque thoughts and situations in adequate terms. While they sided with their contemporaries across the border, seeking to merge into the mainstream of new German writing, in Vienna another literary circle was formed. In the early fifties H. C. Artmann (born 1921) and Gerhard Rühm (born 1928) got together, read and discussed the works of Arno Holz, Scheerbart, Schwitters, Raoul Hausmann, Arp and Gertrude Stein, interested themselves in dadaist, surrealist and constructivist writers everywhere, formulated manifestos and invented the art of 'poetic demonstration', a first form of Happening. In 1954 Rühm wrote his programmatic play *rund oder oval* (*round or oval*) in which he applied the principles of concrete poetry to drama. Three other young men, Friedrich Achleitner (born 1930), Konrad Bayer (born 1932) and Oswald Wiener (born 1935) joined them in what has since been called the *Wiener Gruppe*, a loose literary movement which barely lasted a decade but has influenced Austrian writing to this day. Though its prophets were international, it was this group which made use of an essentially provincial or regional tool: local dialect, written in a phonetic way. Tamino, as it were, now talked suburban slang. Artmann's volume of poetry *Med ana schwoazzn Dintn* (*With Black Ink*, 1958) was the breakthrough. When six years later in the 'Chattanooga' bar in the midst of Vienna, their *kinderoper* (children's opera) was performed by them before a riotous crowd, most of the members of the group had in fact already moved to Germany.

Most of what is now considered significant in Austrian writing can be traced back to the discoveries and innovations of the Vienna group. It evolved both 'linguistic' and dialect writing, thereby setting the course for the two main schools of modern Austrian literature. Artmann's, Rühm's and Bayer's plays, mostly short one-act pieces, combine the two elements. Artmann's humour, as displayed in his *Kasperlstücke* (*Harlequin Plays*) *kein pfeffer für czermak* (*no pepper for czermak*) or *die missglückte luftreise* (*the miscarried airtrip*), owes as much to the early *Hanswurstkomödie*—'Kasperl' being the name of the Austrian Harlequin—as to Nestroy. Bayer even called a play *kasperl am elektrischen stuhl* (*harlequin in the electric chair*). To have made local patois fashionable as the raw material of formal experiment, not in the sense of Horváth's use of everyday petit-bourgeois jargon, but so undiluted that it amounts to a secret code, goes to their credit. When in the sixties a new literary centre called 'Forum Stadtpark' was established in the provincial capital of Styria, Graz, the five writers of the Vienna group—one of whom, Bayer, committed suicide late in 1964—were its lodestar. Within or around

Forum Stadtpark arose the so-called 'dialect wave', a movement which produced such dramatists as Wolfgang Bauer (born 1941), Harald Sommer (born 1935), Franz Buchrieser (born 1937) and Peter Turrini (born 1944), all of whom, despite their attachment to some kind of regional slang, have been welcomed, in a linguistically purified form, by the German-speaking stage.

Wolfgang Bauer's *Magic Afternoon*, his first play dealing with a languid, hash-ridden, pop-crazy young generation, derived as much force from the brutal manners of Austrian provincial youth as from the Anglo-American musical idiom. 'Bang bang, you shot me down' was the monotonously repeated number to which a tortured girl stabbed her lover. *Change*, Bauer's second drama also using an English title, was based on the idea of two young men each trying to drive the other to suicide. None of his more recent work has made so much impact, though Bauer's talent may not be exhausted yet. No doubt under his influence, Harald Sommer wrote *A unhamlich stoaka obong* (*a gruesomely strong exit*), another cruelly realistic description of life among young hooligans in Graz. Buchrieser's *Hansel*, the rather more sensitive account of a father-son relationship, has not been followed up so far by a play of equal value.

The most interesting of these dialect-dramatists repeatedly breaks out of their magic circle: Peter Turrini, author of *rozznjogd* (*rat hunt*), a two-character play of a boy and girl who divest themselves verbally and literally of all vestiges of civilization until, stark naked, they are shot down like rats. After writing *Sauschlachten* (*Slaughter of the Pigs*) in a similar vein—the tragedy of a dumb peasant boy which shows a strong affinity to works by the Germans Martin Sperr and Franz Xaver Kroetz—Turrini has turned to adapting Beaumarchais and Goldoni from a contemporary point of view. In an earlier attempt, *Zero Zero*, he tried his hand at a kind of neo-expressionist drama, and in a short study of a child-murderess, *Kindsmord* (*Child Murder*), aimed at propagating the principles of Women's Liberation.

While these writers of the dialect-wave are, to some extent, exploiting the deep-rooted leaning towards violence—usually masked by its proverbial charm—within the Austrian temperament, a number of extremists went the whole hog and turned it into action. Otto Mühl, Herbert Nitsch and Günter Brus have performed what were probably the goriest happenings of their kind, using the blood of animals and the filthiest possible conglomerate of ingredients to cover the naked bodies of young women in a sort of initiation rite. 'Orgies-Mysteries-Theatre' is what Nitsch calls his Saturnalia, by the help of which he wants to transmit the whole breadth of sensual experience, the 'syn-aesthetics as synthesis' in Oswald Wiener's term. Austria's actionists merely drive *à l'outrance* a tendency inherent in most of its dramatic literature, at least since the years under totalitarianism loosened all instincts and brought much latent cruelty to the fore. Yet there is a difference between description and identification, as there are differ-ences of degree. Thus, it is as a distant and rational observer that Elias Canetti (born 1905), the eminent prose writer who made his home in England after leaving Vienna, draws a dehumanized household in his play *Hochzeit* (*The Wedding*), written in 1932 but only recently produced in Austria. In this as in other dramatic works *Komödie der Eitelkeit* (*Comedy of Vanity*), *Die Befristeten* (*The Dated Ones*), he combines great inventiveness of plot with a certain helplessness of treatment, while his early admiration for Karl Kraus makes itself felt in the dialogue. Another writer of vivid imagination whose drama-tic efforts, in advanced age, are but a sideline to his prose, Albert Drach (born 1902), in his comedies (*Der Vortritt* [*Preference*], *Gottes Tod ein Unfall* [*God's Death an Accident*]) echoes Nestroy and the old *Volkskomödie*. The same goes for Lotte Ingrisch (born 1930), who in her *pièces noires* (*Vanillikipferln* [*Vanilla Pastries*], *Die Wirklich-keit und was man dagegen tut* [*Reality and how to Act against it*]) displays a gracefully melancholic if macabre humour sparked off by Austrian lower middle-class demonology.

And so to the two outstanding playwrights of present-day Austria, Peter Handke (born 1942) and Thomas Bernhard (born 1931), both single-minded, unattached to any movement and highly original. Handke, it is true, began his career as a young and inconspicuous member of the *Gruppe 47* in whose midst he first spoke up at a meeting in Princeton, USA, and as a protégé of Alfred Kolleritsch, founder of Forum Stadtpark and its magazine *manuskripte*. He also chose the linguistic approach to literature, as Rühm and Artmann had done, but went right back to the sources, to Wittgenstein and the 'reflexion of language' pursued by Hofmannsthal and the Austrian philosopher Fritz Mauthner; went farther forward as well until he was no longer concerned with palpable reality, only with the reality of words. His plays, notably *Kaspar* and *Der Ritt über den Bodensee* (*The Ride Across Lake Constance*), deal with language as a brutalizing or pattern-forming factor, and in *Das Mündel will Vormund sein* (*My Foot My Tutor*) language stops altogether, authoritative terror becomes mute yet even more frightening. Critics have pointed out the similarity of Kaspar's situation—no Hanswurst, but the legendary foundling Kaspar Hauser who in Handke's play starts off with one sentence, 'I want to be someone like somebody else was once', then becomes swamped by words—with that of Lucky in *Waiting for Godot*. But Handke has taken no cues from living playwrights; his obsession with the self-sufficiency and separate existence of language, which he shares with Wittgenstein, Hofmannsthal, Mauthner and Karl Kraus, can be traced back to the mistrust for, and rejection of the outer life always felt by Austrian writers, to their escape into another self-created and independent reality. In his prose, it is true, Handke has recently returned to the simple, factual story. But it is doubtful whether he will do the same in the theatre, where his purpose lies in showing up the formal suppressive mechanisms of a cliché-ridden society.

Even more detached from contemporary writing, both in his own country and elsewhere, Thomas Bernhard follows his own solitary path, or rather one long straight furrow ploughed in a vast field of nothingness. Obsession as well—not however with the second reality of language, but with the negation of reality altogether, its nonsensicality in the face of death. Here at last is an Austrian writer who feels death, talks death, writes death at every moment, who on receiving the Great State Prize made the Minister of Education storm from the room by replying to his *laudatio* with the seemingly ungrateful sentence : 'Everything is ridiculous when one thinks of death.' First in his prose, then in his plays—and he has written four, of which two were performed to date—he has, to use another topographical metaphor, rotated round it, inexorably fixed in orbit round death as the earth is round the sun. Both *Ein Fest für Boris* (*A Feast for Boris*) and *Der Ignorant und der Wahnsinnige* (*The Ignoramus and the Madman*) are written in free verse and thus—not only by their subject matter—recall Hofmannsthal's early play *Der Tor und der Tod*. But there all resemblance to any other Austrian dramatist ends. In creating his own hermetic world, Bernhard comes closest, of all writers in his national sphere, to Kafka. In *Boris*, a play with sixteen characters of whom only one is not crippled, he has most in common with Bunuel, whose ritual banquet in *Viridiana* is mirrored here. Yet Bernhard's poetry, as his philosophy, is his own, an exhibitionist despair his message, and the artificiality of the situations he creates no obstacle to their exemplary significance. In *Der Ignorant und der Wahnsinnige* the soulless perfection of an opera singer, bared of life and turned into a mere coloratura machine, is contrasted with the ice-cold and precise account of an anatomic dissection. Nothing happens but a verbose progress towards the inevitable catacylsm. A play of this kind can grip an audience only by some magnetic power, the power of penetrating, stabbing words such as are at Bernhard's command.

In tracing the course Austrian drama has taken since the 18th century, it may have become evident that to call it a 'contribution' to the German stage is somewhat misleading. Despite a far-reaching similarity of language, there were, for a long while, few cross-currents between the two literatures, and it is only in recent times that Austrian dramatists have not merely filled the repertoire of German playhouses but are being claimed by German literary historians and critics as their own. Grillparzer, Schnitzler, Hofmannsthal used to be considered, no less than Nestroy, as outlandish in some degree. Apart from those who moved to Berlin, capital of the German-speaking theatre in the twenties, no Austrian playwright captured and dominated the German stage until Horváth posthumously came into his own. Beside him, Handke, Bernhard, Bauer, Sommer and Turrini now form an indispensable part of German dramatic writing, Hochwälder is regularly played, Canetti's early efforts were first resuscitated in the Federal Republic, Nitsch's and Mühl's slaughter of innocent lambs is allowed to shock onlookers in Bavaria and the Rhineland, and even Lotte Ingrisch's poisoned pastries *à la Viennoise* appreciated there as much as they are nearer home. What the *Anschluss* did not achieve, the post-war theatre has brought about : a truly unified German drama, to which Austrian and Swiss writers are no mere contributors but which they have helped to create.

Arrigo Subiotto : THE SWISS CONTRIBUTION

It is an irony that the Swiss—renowned as a small circumspect nation
—took the role of pacemakers in postwar German literature with the
ascendancy in the theatre of two authors, Max Frisch (born in 1911)
and Friedrich Dürrenmatt (ten years younger). Only once before, in
the 19th century, can Swiss writers (who have first to gain recognition in Germany, their major reading market, before they can hope
to achieve international success) be said to have played a part in
German culture out of all proportion to the size of their country.
Gottfried Keller, Jeremias Gotthelf, C. F. Meyer and Carl Spitteler
(the latter more recent and a Nobel prizewinner) all exerted a formative influence on German prose writing a hundred years ago, giving it
that serious dialectic stamp of individual responsibility to moral laws
and to the community that reflected the 19th century ethos of the
middle classes. The regionalism of these authors was their strength,
for the relatively stable social structures of Switzerland were a comfort
in the swiftly changing world of accelerating industrialization and
colonial and military competiton.

Dürrenmatt and Frisch broke through immediately after the war
and were only overtaken by that generation of playwrights who in
1963 initiated the 'documentary drama' trend of the sixties—Peter
Weiss, Rolf Hochhuth, Heinar Kipphardt. It is even more of an irony
that both Frisch and Dürrenmatt are largely concerned with issues
that trouble the German conscience : the immediate political past,
the sense of guilt, the economic miracle. Yet no one denies them the
right to make pronouncements on such subjects, perhaps because
their formulations and the images of society they present have a much
wider application beyond national frontiers; in this they continue the
tradition of their 19th century countrymen. It is, of course, possible
to speculate that Frisch and Dürrenmatt had a head start over German

writers since neutral Switzerland had maintained her cultural continuity throughout the Second World War and had not had to overcome the absolute nadir of 1945. These playwrights were able to
exploit in their drama a unique combination of detachment from the
German catastrophe and sensitive affinity through geographical
proximity and a common language.

Although both have achieved success with novels, their international fame rests almost entirely on two plays each: *Biedermann
und die Brandstifter* (*The Fire Raisers*, 1958) and *Andorra* (1961) by
Frisch, *Der Besuch der alten Dame* (*The Visit*, 1956) and *Die Physiker*
(*The Physicists*, 1962) by Dürrenmatt. All four plays seem to have a
narrowly provincial, even parochial setting that conjures up the
realities of present-day Switzerland. The authors themselves, however,
vehemently deny that they are alluding to their own land more than
to any other. These plays are parables, realistic but not real, and
can thus accommodate the ambivalent attitudes of Frisch and Dürrenmatt to their own nationality, insofar as they need to come to terms
with the society to which they belong; at the same time they aim
beyond the narrow boundaries of a small nation to establish a wider
relevance for their work. Both are very conscious of being Swiss and
very critical of Switzerland. Frisch, by profession an architect, is widely
travelled and concerned with technological man; all his writing reveals
the love-hate magnetism of the modern city, the structures of mechanized society with its effects on the individual consciousness, and he
believes that man can control his environment and himself. Much of
the tension in Frisch's work derives from the awareness and rejection
of nationality, that he is a citizen of Switzerland and of the world.
He expressed this most clearly on accepting the Georg Büchner Prize
in 1958 when he declared that he and others were 'emigrants' like the
revolutionary refugee dramatist Büchner in 'not being able nor wanting to speak on behalf of our fatherlands ... We feel our domicile in
the world as it is today, and whether we change it or not, to be temporary ... We ask only one thing: that wherever we reside we should
retain the unspoken feeling of not belonging. Or as Friedrich Dürrenmatt put it very simply when a Swiss critic asked him his attitude to
the problem of being Swiss: "You are wrong, Sir, I'm sorry to say
I don't find Switzerland a problem but just a comfortable place to
work in".' Frisch then summed up this sense of alienation and critical

detachment in the phrase : 'We have become emigrants without leaving our homelands.'

Whereas Frisch did live in Rome from 1960 to 1965 and elsewhere for long periods, Dürrenmatt is only imaginable in a Swiss setting. The thread of Swiss conditions runs through all his work; he handles the mythology of affluence, the worship of banking and security, but also the strain of primitiveness and brutality behind the cover of a well-ordered nation. He probes beneath the surface image of a rational, wealthy society to the instinctive, irrational forces that, because they are suppressed, plague the modern citizen in unexpected ways. The mental home of *The Physicists* is not only symbolic of the lunatic atomic arms race. Dürrenmatt sits in his villa above Neuchâtel, seemingly in perpetual judgment on his fellow-men, devising conflicts of an elemental nature, larger than life and unnaturally distorted. He was born the son of a Protestant pastor, and possibly for this reason absolutes motivate and permeate his work, creating apocalyptic pictures of final instances in bizarre surroundings. His countrymen are wary of him and he is a figure of controversy—but exportable and therefore valuable.

Like Frisch, Dürrenmatt too acquired his theatrical reputation for writing on 'public' themes. One associates Frisch with warnings against complacent attitudes regarding defence security (*Biedermann*) and the persecution of minority groups (*Andorra*), while Dürrenmatt castigates the moral disintegration born of greedy materialism (*Der Besuch der alten Dame*) and depicts the lunatic situation of the scientist caught between super-powers armed with his destructive inventions (*Die Physiker*). But in the past decade both have turned increasingly to private concerns, though their general validity is usually implicit in the formulation. Dürrenmatt relentlessly pursues his vision of the individual crushed by overwhelming forces in a faceless society, while Frisch has now transferred the 'problem of identity' (what he ironically calls his 'literary trade mark') from the novels to his most recent and very successful play *Biografie, ein Spiel* (*Biography, a Game*, 1967). Both playwrights aver their 'commitment'—and demonstrate it forcefully in what they write—but they refuse to be tied down to a clear-cut *political* stance, asserting instead the independent function of literature as a critical, clarifying but ultimately private process. Dürrenmatt states his own position unequivocally in his most important theoretical pronouncement, *Theaterprobleme* (*Problems of the Theatre*, 1955):

> For me, the stage is not a battlefield for theories, philosophies and manifestos, but rather an instrument whose possibilities I seek to know by playing with it... The problems I face as a playwright are practical, working problems, problems I face not before, but during the writing.

It is important to bear in mind this programmatic statement of Dürrenmatt's experimental approach, for it is all too tempting to search for inner meanings and make profound analyses of his plays. Dürrenmatt insists that he presents on the stage a three-dimensional world, a situation for its own sake; and he retains the sovereign right to create 'models' of society which may or may not contain moral questions. In the brief notes that accompany *Frank V* he says:

> Of course every play contains a statement, or more precisely, statements. Unfortunately, the producer (or critic) often makes the mistake of thinking the dramatist must always start off from a problem... He may start from subjects that *contain* problems. There is a difference here... The value of a play lies in its problem potential, not in a single, clearly-defined meaning.

Dürrenmatt thus tends always to attach primary value to the stage as a *visual show*, not merely the vehicle for the presentation of an argument. On the other hand, literature and the theatre do have for him a social function and relevance in so far as the fundamental question drama must answer is 'how can it adequately reflect the world today?' The reflection is not mindless and purely arbitrary, and it is far from being mimetic, for it must stimulate the intellect and appeal to the senses through its individualistic structuring of the elements of reality. (Brecht took up Dürrenmatt's question polemically with the answer that reality could be reproduced only if it was shown as subject to change.)

In *Der Autor und das Theater* (*The Author and the Theatre*, 1964) Max Frisch in his turn picked up Brecht's statement while asking rhetorically what it was that impelled a playwright to the exhausting task of writing and putting on plays:

> We do not create a better world on the stage, but one that can

be acted and grasped, a world that allows room for variations and in that sense can be changed, at least in the area of art.

On the one hand, Frisch claims that all literature is committed though not in the narrow, directly political sense. It is already a commitment, a criticism of ideology, for the writer to sound the language of everyday to test how real it is. On the other hand, the domain of literature is what cannot be grasped by sociology or biology—the self who experiences the world as an individual, who is incorporated into statistics but cannot voice himself through them; and Frisch strikes a blow for the modishly denigrated 'private' preoccupations of literature:

Are 'private' concerns irrelevant and no subject for literature? If that were true, sociology would be enough. But is it enough? Society, even the most desirable, is made up of people who live their lives, and living takes place in the first person singular.

In their different ways both Frisch and Dürrenmatt maintain that the writer can only be 'subversive' in contemporary society by retaining his personal freedom and independence of fixed positions. This is the attitude emphasized by Frisch in his Büchner speech where he talks of the 'combatant resignation' that prompts the truly committed writer to struggle in every work 'against abstraction, ideology and its deadly fronts':

We cannot write the arsenal of weapons out of the world but, the more clearly we write, the more concretely, the more we can cause chaos in the arsenal of catchwords that are needed in every camp to wage war.

While Frisch refers specifically to life-cramping aspects of the modern world such as the distortions of language, the manipulation of individuals through the mass media, and procrustean ideologies, Dürrenmatt tends to a metaphorical, sometimes almost metaphysical assessment of human life. His dramatic work is inevitably conditioned by his philosophical attitudes which themselves demonstrate a basic pessimism about the state of the world and the 'goodness' of human beings, our social structures and the motives of men's behaviour. There is a certain religious, Old Testament quality about his virulent depictions of human activity, yet he would not want to be seen as a thundering prophet; he offers no belief in a divine order, no faith outside men, no panaceas, and as a result the disasters he presents seem inescapable. It is the chaos of the contemporary world that arouses Dürrenmatt's opposition; he suggested (in a speech accepting the award of the 1960 Schiller prize) that the individual has lost control over his political and social destiny, that he is blotted out by forces too great to be directed by any single person, and that he is consequently filled by an immense feeling of powerlessness. One of the few possible modes of action left is to lie low in order not to go under, but the opportunities of criticism, protest and resistance must be seized when they arise :

> The universal escapes my grasp. I refuse to find the universal in a doctrine. The universal for me is chaos. The world (hence the stage which represents this world) is for me something monstrous, a riddle of misfortune which must be accepted but before which one must not capitulate.

Dürrenmatt claims it is still possible to show man as a courageous being; his pessimism is not a negative sign of cowardice but reflects the integrity of a realism refusing to take refuge behind the easily erected façades of philosophy, religion and politics. In this relentless exposure of life Dürrenmatt's plays have a strong affinity with those of Samuel Beckett : they typically close with the smell of death and a morally or physically devastated world; unnatural, artificial figures remain on stage, symbols of impending doom—the total alienation and stultification of the individual. In *Der Besuch der alten Dame*, an extravagant millionairess, Claire Zachanassian, returns to the now dilapidated village from which she was cast out, and corrupts the solid citizens with the lure of a fabulous sum to murder her former lover, Ill, the mayor. At the end scruples are suppressed by greed and this over-lifesize and thus lifeless heroine is left to transport her victim's corpse to a villa on Capri. In the gangster opera *Frank V* the owners of a bank put into effect a deadly business principle : their clients are killed off after depositing their wealth. *Die Physiker* presents a logically irrational method for nuclear scientists to escape from the moral predicament of their activities by taking refuge in disguise in the anonymity of a mental asylum; but it turns out that the deformed woman doctor-owner knows and controls all their secrets and they have merely delivered the world into the hands of un unpredictable madwoman :

My Trust will conquer and rule every country, every continent, it will ransack the solar system and reach out to the Andromeda nebula. The pay-off is here, and it's not in favour of the world but of an old hunch-backed spinster.

More recently still *Porträt eines Planeten* (*Portrait of a Planet*) is reminiscent of Beckett's end-situations; here we find four gods bored with infinity who barely raise an eyebrow when the earth is destroyed through the explosion of the sun ('It just went pop', says one of them). Indeed, Dürrenmatt's latest play, *Der Mitmacher* (*The Conniver* first performed in 1973), brings his most macabre contraption to date on to the stage—a machine called a necrodialysator which simply dissolves corpses together with their coffins into water. In his stage directions he calls it a 'modern gate of hell', cold and sterile, and it is put to nefarious criminal use in the play. At the close, Bill, the son of the machine's inventor, voices a probable opinion of the playwright's: 'In a lunatic world you need a lunatic method. Our struggle is aimed against every political system, every social structure. None of them is worth a damn.'

Der Mitmacher is not a political play; indeed, Dürrenmatt never engages in specific political themes or so-called documentary drama. What he provides is images of our world, however far-fetched, that fundamentally capture political and social realities. Embedded in *Der Besuch*, that 'comedy of boom times', is a sharp critique of the capitalist economy and the runaway affluence after 1945; while the confrontation of East and West and the absurdity of piling up armaments as a precaution against having to use them is a major motive force of the action in *Die Physiker*. Dürrenmatt clearly sees it as the duty of the writer to make his voice heard in warning though he cannot sway events. He likens mankind today to a reckless car driver who ignores all the rules of the road, has probably stolen the car and may not even have a driving licence; if the writer is a passenger it is useless for him to indulge in descriptions of the beautiful landscape through which the vehicle is hurtling: 'he must shriek out loud in fear, anxiety and above all anger'.

Theaterprobleme, in which this quotation appears, touches on Dürrenmatt's central preoccupations and methods. In it he ranges in his usual compressed manner over a wide field of topics: the Aristotelian unities and the relevance of tradition and the classics, epic theatre, the hero in drama, the relationship of history and literature,

the forms of comedy and tragedy, and the theatrical methods of parody
and the grotesque. At the core of his musings is the search for a
dramatic mode adequate to the contemporary world. He rejects
tragedy in the various forms we have inherited as no longer valid for
the dramatist who cannot slip unobtrusively into this shell and write as
Sophocles, Corneille or Schiller. A shaped and coherent world is
reflected in tragedy, but now shared values, fixed beliefs and a supra-
human order (such as the Greeks possessed) have disintegrated and
disappeared. Scepticism has replaced faith, there are now no co-
ordinates to determine the tragic hero:

> The world today as it appears to us could hardly be encompassed
> in the form of the historical drama as Schiller wrote it, for the
> reason alone that we no longer have any tragic heroes, but only
> vast tragedies staged by world butchers and produced by slaughter-
> ing machines. Hitler and Stalin cannot be made into
> Wallensteins ... True representatives of our world are missing. Any
> small-time crook, petty government official or policeman better
> represents our world than a senator or president.

Having rejected the tragic mode, Dürrenmatt argues that comedy is
the only form attuned to our times since to cope with our present
reality at all we must have distance and objectivity, not identity:
'Comedy ... presupposes an unformed world in the process of taking
shape and breaking down, a world about to pack up like ours.' All
the elements of comedy and satire—powerful, explosive stylistic factors
like the grotesque, paradox and parody—are exploited to mirror the
fracturing of rounded philosophies and enable us to face up to a
world which we are in though it may be none of our making. Dürrenmatt anticipates possible reactions to this approach: since comedy
reflects 'the senseless and hopeless aspects of the world' people might
see it as an expression of despair. He argues instead that despair is not
a consequence of but an answer to the world; another answer would
be not to despair, to determine to withstand and hold one's own in the
face of chaos. Further, even if 'pure tragedy' is not possible, the
dramatist can still achieve 'the tragic' in comedy, as a 'dreadful
moment', 'an abyss suddenly opening up'—as Shakespeare did in his
comedies.

In his analysis Dürrenmatt undoubtedly defines the characteristics
of the most widespread forms of contemporary drama: black comedy

and the theatre of the absurd. (The vestiges of tragedy linger in the neo-realism of tendentious theatre like documentary and 'kitchen-sink' drama.) His own writing accords perfectly with the contemporary mode; every important play by this Swiss dramatist relies heavily for its effect on the uncovering of a frightening web of facts, motives and fantasies beneath the surface of an exaggeratedly mundane situation. Beckett, Pinter, Shaffer and Ionesco all, in their different ways, exploit this discrepancy between the accepted world and the unexpected reality lurking within it. In Dürrenmatt's *Romulus der Grosse* (*Romulus the Great*, 1949) the eponymous Roman emperor has thoughts only for the chickens he rears in his dilapidated palace; when the Teutonic hordes overrun the last remnants of his empire he is sent into ignominious retirement on a pension. The placid eventless village life of Güllen flows on in *Der Besuch* showing not a ripple of the murderous hunt for a victim and scapegoat. The ordered private sanatorium of *Die Physiker* slowly reveals itself as a prison in which a silent struggle for world power is being enacted, while behind the respectable façade of the family bank in *Frank V* a gangster jungle of killings lies concealed. A leading characteristic of Dürrenmatt's plays is the enormous gap between the two levels at which the audience is involved—everyday situations that lull into complacency and the sudden irruption into them of startling and macabre happenings. The effect is deliberately unsettling and the spectator is thrown off balance—alienated yet curiously participant.

The means by which Dürrenmatt reaches his aim is through the manipulation of an 'Einfall'—an unusual, idiosyncratic idea or 'conceit'—so that the distance necessary to comedy is achieved by unexpected, erratic twists and turns of plot or a grandiose idea embracing a whole play. Though Dürrenmatt said provocatively 'I find I can only write haphazardly, at random, into the blue', his randomness is in events, not in the action and dialogue. Once devised, the fanciful situation is developed with a strictly logical cause-and-effect pattern. This dramatic procedure recalls the farce or fairy-tale tradition of Aristophanes, Rabelais, Swift and the Viennese popular comedy of the 19th century; it is not surprising that Dürrenmatt has such a high regard for these authors for he stands firmly in their heritage. Like them, he creates social satire in terms of a fantasy world, but insists at the same time that he is depicting our world, not selling a message.

Typically, he falls back on the simile of the chicken and the egg to describe his position:

> It is my sometimes unfortunate passion to want to put on the stage the richness and variety of the world; so my theatre often becomes ambiguous and seems to bewilder some. Furthermore, misunderstandings creep in when people desperately search in the chicken-coop of my plays for the egg of meaning which I stubbornly refuse to lay.

The spectator is often overwhelmed by the huge variety of incidents, happenings and persons on stage (though recently *Der Meteor* and *Porträt eines Planeten* show Dürrenmatt as more economical) which correspond to his mannerist, baroque imagination with its enormous appetite for eccentric, individual images. Since Dürrenmatt operates in terms of disguised satire such metaphors can nevertheless be related to perfectly real concerns; under the comedy of two leaders and historical destinies in *Romulus der Grosse*, for instance, there lurks the perpetual choice of the individual's duty to the state or to his own nature and also a questioning of what counts in history. The oddness of this approach to a perennial problem—the individual and society—as formulated in, say, *Romulus der Grosse*, is a hallmark of Dürrenmatt's imaginative processes. Here his mind swoops from emperor to chicken-breeder and this juxtaposition—even collision—of extremes recurs consistently. The same can be seen in Dürrenmatt's manipulation of the time dimension; he introduces deliberate anachronisms (gas-light in ancient Babylon) in order to link epochs, or measures the brief span of action in *Die Physiker* against light-years so that the urgent couple of hours filling the stage are suddenly reduced at the end to a speck of insignificance among the solar systems.

It is no coincidence that Dürrenmatt has a lively dilettante interest in astronomy for he works on a grand scale and does not flinch before the huge dimensions demanded by his predilection for extremes. In the creation of characters he is led to types, however odd they may appear, since individuals are heterogeneous, not immediately distinguishable and not amenable to fitting a role neatly. His personages are representative through job, dress, rank and speech, and they thus establish an affinity with mystery and morality plays. Dürrenmatt would be at home with a modern *Everyman*, for in the distribution of roles he allots fixed positions so that king and beggar, judge and

accused, murderer and victim, highest and lowest, stand in an unvarying relationship to one another in a social firmament. The spirit
of the Old Testament is often evident in the scale and power of
Dürrenmatt's handling of his subject-matter; everywhere in his work
is the sense of an avenging God (stylized in the shape of a human
being: hangman, judge, emperor or tycoon) overshadowing puny
individuals transgressing some rigid law that may well be uncom-
prehended. This is the existential face of the social satire, where sin
and expiation are unstated and ineluctable.

The inescapably dominant theme in all Dürrenmatt's work is that
of justice (and therefore freedom), whether it is cast in a social,
political, religious or philosophical configuration. In 1969, a year
after the adaptation of Shakespeare's sombre tragedy of politics,
King John, he delivered a *Monstervortrag über Gerechtigkeit und
Recht* (*Mammoth Lecture on Justness and Justice: a short dramaturgy of politics*), in which he distinguished between the 'Wolf game'
—free-for-all freedom to struggle for survival in a capitalist context
—and the 'Good Shepherd game'—justice for all in a State-planned
Marxist system. They are equally intolerable absolutes, and each
represents a special quality of hell in Dürrenmatt's vision: 'the world
of absolute freedom a jungle where man is hunted like a wild beast,
the world of absolute justice a prison where man is tortured to death'.
It is irrelevant that Dürrenmatt may privately believe one of these
systems to be preferable; he makes it abundantly clear that his task
as a *dramatist* is to create an image of the baffling monstrosity of
the world:

> I think in dramaturgical terms. That is to say, my technique of
> thinking as a dramatist consists in transforming social reality into
> theatre and thinking further with this transformed reality. I think
> out the world by playing it out. The result of this thinking process
> is not a new reality but a construct for the stage in which reality
> appears in analysed form, or more precisely, in which the spectator
> sees himself analysed. This analysis is governed by imagination,
> intellectual experiment and the joy of acting; it is not therefore
> strictly scientific, but in many respects frivolous and for that very
> reason useful ... Dramaturgical thinking investigates the inner
> tensions of reality. The more paradoxically reality can be presented
> the more suitable it is as material for the theatre. Dramaturgical

thinking is dialectic, but not in any politically ideological sense; ...
applied to politics (it) attempts to discover its rules, not its content.

In our world where 'things happen without anyone in particular being
responsible for them', where we are all 'collectively guilty, collectively
bogged down in the sins of our fathers and forefathers', comedy alone
is suitable as a dramatic form and its vehicle, most congruent with the
paradoxical nature of the contemporary world, is the grotesque.

The grotesque involves discrepancies, incongruities, exaggeration,
unnaturalness and artificiality, and its widespread prevalence in all art
forms in recent decades suggests that it is one of the few aggressive
techniques left through which the artist can articulate the inconsistencies of a society which constantly threatens to engulf the individual.
It is a method that disturbs and provokes and leaves the audience
uneasy by knocking the bottom out of a seemingly sensible, well-
ordered and manageable world. For some the grotesque, in its un-
familiarity, appears to be a flight from reality; but for Dürrenmatt it
is necessary, if uncomfortable:

> The grotesque is a great opportunity to be precise. It cannot be
> denied that this art has the cruelty of objectivity, yet it is not the
> art of the nihilist but of the moralist, not of decay, but of salt.

Dürrenmatt's black comedies, pulling out all the stops of the grotesque,
attack injustice, whether individual or collective, through laughter
and wit. Laughter, however bitter, guarantees for him the objective,
critical perspective we need:

> In laughter man's freedom becomes manifest, in tears his necessity.
> Our task today is to demonstrate freedom. The tyrants of this
> planet are not moved by the works of a poet. They yawn at a
> poet's threnodies ... Tyrants fear only one thing: a poet's mockery.

Dürrenmatt may be a Don Quixote tilting at invisible tyrants (who
may be in each of us), and they probably do not even hear him; but
this does not negate the value of his gesture though it may appear
absurd and vain. Like so many writers accused of nihilism, like
Büchner, Camus, Kafka, Dürrenmatt is a true realist and a moralist.

In his different way Max Frisch too is a moralist, though like
Dürrenmatt he vigorously defends the autonomy of what is presented
as a play: 'the only reality on the stage is the fact that something is

being enacted there. Play-acting permits things that cannot happen in life.' Dürrenmatt is more uncompromising in the pursuit of his interpretation of reality in dramatic terms—hence the greater obliquity of his non-realistic approach—while Frisch repeatedly stresses the primary importance for him of facing an actual audience in the theatre: 'I must see my public, I have to be present at the moment of impact between play and public. This is not everything, but neither is it the least fascinating thing for me in the theatre, namely the frank, open, visible confrontation of a work with its contemporary audience.' Frisch is thus highly susceptible to the reactions of the public and to the involvement of the theatre in society. He calls it a political institution in so far as it presupposes a *polis* that has continually to examine and come to terms with itself; in a way the function of the theatre is to act as the conscience of society, to pose questions and provoke answers. The aggressive aspect of this function emerges too in Frisch's relationship to his public: he seeks reactions, even hostility, rather than the patronising, complacent indifference of a liberal-minded apathy; when he is faced by a wall of cotton wool the writer begins to scream and rebel.

In the early years of writing plays Frisch noted in his *Tagebuch* (*Diary*) *1946–49*:

As a playwright I would think I had achieved my aim if I ever succeeded in putting a question in a play so powerfully that from that moment on the audience could not live without finding an answer, their own answer, which they could only provide in their own lives.

In a more direct, less complex and ambiguous manner than Dürrenmatt, Frisch made a worthy, honest attempt in his plays (more private themes dominate his prose writing) to state and analyse some of the uncomfortable problems left in the wake of the Second World War. Above all he tried to elucidate the process of 'how it came about', 'how it could come to this', with guilt, inevitably, as the central motif in every case. Frisch subtitled his second play, *Nun singen sie wieder* (*Now They've Started Singing Again*), written in 1945, 'Attempt at a Requiem': in the German soldiers who shoot helpless hostages and the Allied airmen who bomb defenceless civilians he portrays and deplores the mentality that sees the enemy as totally black and satanic. But the humanistic pacifism of this play lacks a trenchant

cutting edge—at most it is to be found in the flagellation of the
'culture as alibi' syndrome which Frisch also inveighs against in his
Tagebuch. The character of the schoolmaster mouths the hollow
phrases about beauty, truth and greatness while condoning the shabby
deeds of war. Here are the germs of a critique proper to the writer—
unmasking the manipulation of consciousness through language which
induces ready-made opinions and a distorted apprehension of reality
in the service of vested interests. Frisch's skill and awareness in fulfilling
this task become of overriding significance in *Biedermann* and
Andorra.

A year after *Nun singen sie wieder*, in a 'farce' entitled
Die Chinesische Mauer (*The Great Wall of China*), Frisch
pursued a theme related to that of culture as an alibi
for barbarity. Confronted by atomic weapons he now set out
to show the powerlessness of the intellectual, the uselessness of literature as a means of influencing events. This is the first of the plays
that achieved an international reputation for the Swiss dramatist
and in which, prophet-like, he utters warnings to mankind : 'We have
to choose whether there is to be a human race or not. The Flood can
be manufactured.' Frisch was aware very early in his writing career
that stylistically, in both prose and plays, the old forms were superseded. Two of the figures freely acknowledged by him to have influenced his drama profoundly, Brecht and Thornton Wilder (the latter
rekindling his youthful passion for the theatre after a personal meeting in 1948), provided him with that theatrical vehicle, epic drama,
which was best suited to carry an analytical, intellectual content. Like
Brecht, Frisch looked to the parable for the most effective form of
drama 'to serve up a serious content in a palatable way'. In other
words, they both valued the didactic function of parable but were at
the same time loath to relinquish its 'fictional', inventive aspect. The
consideration of instruction and entertainment, *dulce et utile*, prompted
both playwrights to exploit the parable on the stage. Frisch did,
however, recognize the inherent danger of the parable limiting the
imagination; in an interview published in *Die Zeit* in December 1967
he outlined his attitude to the parable form :

> *Biedermann* and *Andorra* are both parables. This is a well-tried
> way of avoiding the theatre of imitation, that pitiful type of theatre
> that hopes to achieve reality by imitating reality. The parable

works in another way: instead of pretending to be reality on the stage we are made conscious of reality through the 'meaning' that the play gives it. The scenes themselves are openly ahistorical, they are invented as examples or models, and artificial. This is all right, only it has one disadvantage: the parable overdoes the meaning, the play tends to a *quod erat demonstrandum*. When this happens it's little use trying to cover myself with the subtitle 'Lehrstück ohne Lehre' (morality play without a moral). A message is always implicit in the parable, even if I'm not trying to put one over.

The subtitle was, of course, that of *Biedermann*, a play Frisch wrote as an interlude between the novel *Homo faber* and *Andorra*, which he had been contemplating for a long time. The immediate success of *Biedermann*, which appeared on over 70 German stages and many more throughout the world, took Frisch completely by surprise; he had not expected 'to live off this hair-oil swindler'. This figure, the chief protagonist of the play, is a wealthy hair-oil manufacturer, Gottlieb Biedermann (a modern commercial philistine parodying Everyman), who through fear, cowardice, hypocrisy, guilt feelings and pretended liberality allows a pair of disreputable, brazen characters to insinuate themselves into his household. With barefaced effrontery, coupled with threats and cajolery, they proceed to stack the attic with cans of petrol and openly proclaim their intention of setting fire to the house and town. Biedermann refuses to believe they are serious and ignores the veiled warning of one of the incendiaries: 'Joking is the third best camouflage. The second best is sentimentality . . . But the best and surest camouflage, I find, is always the plain, naked truth, oddly enough. No-one believes it.' With the undeviating, single-track logic of a morality play the plot unfolds until the final holo-caust, when the spectator recalls the lines of the firemen's chorus in the opening scene:

> Many things catch fire,
> But not every fire
> Is caused by inexorable fate.

This contemporary fable lends itself to many interpretations. Although it has several Pinter-like elements—the mundane setting in a private house, the irruption into this 'safe' world of disturbingly provocative outsiders, the colloquial dialogue concealing an ominous content—it can be related in allegorical manner to specific political and historical themes, while a Pinter play explores the startling subtleties of personal human relationships. *Biedermann* can be seen as a metaphor of Hitler's legitimate 'seizure of power' or of the way in which the nations of the world are playing with nuclear bombs as deterrents (Lindsay Anderson's London production in 1962 ended with the projection of film of an exploding atom bomb). It also offers a 'model' of liberal societies allowing freedom of action, in the name of liberty, to extremist elements in their midst (whether of right or left) whose avowed aim it is to destroy those societies. The model can even fit the contemporary situation of many advanced industrial states which depend heavily on immigrant labour and at the same time close their eyes to the dangerously explosive social stresses they are fostering.

The warning note sounded in *Biedermann* was followed in 1961 by *Andorra*, another parable, this time explicitly generated by the phenomenon of anti-semitism and its catastrophic expression in Nazi Germany. Andorra has nothing to do with the country of that name; indeed, the setting is virtually a village, where every individual might expect to be accepted for his true value as a person. Instead, the opposite is revealed to happen. The Teacher passes off his illegitimate son as a Jew whom he had saved as a child from the 'Blacks' in the neighbouring country. With mounting pressure from the 'Blacks' on Andorra, the inhabitants demonstrate their latent anti-semitism by detecting in the youth Andri all the preconceived semitic traits they covertly hate. Gradually he is forced into conforming to this false image until the point comes when he actively and defiantly identifies with it. An invasion by the 'Blacks' leads to his sacrifice, almost as a scapegoat, and only after his death do the townspeople realize their separate and collective guilt in distorting reality to fit their rigid prejudices. An epic technique reminiscent of Brecht is used effectively to keep the issue alive : between scenes all the people who had actively or tacitly participated in Andri's persecution, the Priest, the Soldier, the Doctor, the Carpenter, etc., appear one by one in a witness-box to exculpate themselves from what happend 'in the past'—a procedure that has been gone through *ad nauseam* by Germans since the Second World War. With masterly sensitivity Frisch exploits the banal clichés that serve to cloak the true attitudes of peeople in their social relationships. The Doctor mouths the unspoken thoughts of latent racism everywhere and at all times, for the fate of the Jews is only one of many models, useful for being historically specific :

I admit, we were all wrong at the time, which of course I can only deplore. How many times must I repeat it? I don't like atrocities and never have done. Anyway, I only saw the young man a couple of times. I didn't witness the beating-up that is supposed to have occurred later. Even so, I deplore it, naturally. I can only say it wasn't my fault; added to which his behaviour—unfortunately, one can't conceal the fact—became more and more—let's be frank— Jewish somehow, although the young man was an Andorran like the rest of us, that may be. I don't deny at all that we were the victims of a certain fashion, so to speak. It was an eventful time, don't let's forget that. Speaking for myself, I never took part in the beatings nor did I encourage anyone else to. I hope I may be allowed to state this publicly. A tragic case, no doubt about it. It's not my fault that it ended like it did. I believe I'm speaking for everyone if, in conclusion, I repeat once again that we can only deplore the course events took at that time.

It would be mistaken to view *Andorra* principally as an indictment of anti-semitism; of greater concern to Frisch is the threat to the individual. More frightening than the persecution of Andri is his own gradual acceptance of the role of the Jew; slowly he withdraws from his own identity to conform to a stereotyped image until he too accepts this as his true self. The parable is a cry of warning to beware of preconceived notions and role-playing that obscure and distort the freshness and vitality of the individual identity. In this respect the theme of *Andorra* lies in close proximity to much of Frisch's prose work. The novels are largely about the threats that surround personal identity and constitute a continuous search by Frisch for certainty.

The significance of his latest play, *Biografie, ein Spiel*, which was first performed in 1967, is that Frisch has apparently abandoned 'public' themes about the individual's guilt and responsibilities in society, and turned instead to his own doubts and self-questionings as an introverted 'specimen'. Kürmann, a behavioural scientist, makes use of that freedom the stage has to offer of repeating, altering, experimenting, to investigate the possibilities of altering the course his life has already run. Under the supervision of a sort of compère, called the Recorder, he enacts variants of past scenes, especially of the key encounter with Antoinette, his future wife. Ultimately, Kürmann comes to realize that all the permutations he tries out in the conviction that 'he knows exactly what he would do differently' are no improvement on the real events, imperfect though these were, and that none of them has the vibrant quality of actually having been lived. Appropriately, the form of the drama is 'experimental', dispensing with the normal plot along a temporal co-ordinate in favour of rehearsals of variant possibilities—the technique of repeated laboratory experimentation. In both theme and form Frisch married in this play the modern technological age of cybernetics and computers with the intensely private world of erratic and unique individual experience.

Frisch, like Dürrenmatt, has been a major force in German drama for the generation since 1945. Both have capitalized on their Swiss nationality to contribute a detached, critical and authoritative view of German topics, at the same time wrestling with the constraints of a restrictive minor state that militate against breadth of vision. Despite their biting criticism of bourgeois forms of culture and their deeply felt social commitment, they clearly reject the communist state in which their individual voices might scarcely be allowed to speak. In devising ingenious models to articulate international concerns these two Swiss dramatists have depicted the weaknesses of individuals and societies with theatrical insight and skill. They have also achieved a combative stature that totally belies the cautious neutrality which we have come to associate with their country.

9

Clive Barker : THEATRE IN EAST GERMANY

The theatre in the GDR is a well-organized, smoothly operating institution. A system of generous state subsidy to supplement box-office receipts, and security of employment for theatre-workers, give stability and a strong sense of continuity. The economic freedom however has not given rise to a corresponding freedom to experiment or to establish any wide variety, and one provincial theatre tends to resemble any other in its repertoire, style of presentation and acting, and design. There is nothing which corresponds to the Fringe Theatre in Britain or the experimental groups in France and West Germany. Although it would be possible for a group of actors to break away and form their own independent company, no one has attempted this.

There are five drama houses in East Berlin along with a children's theatre, two opera houses, a musical theatre, and a variety theatre. Throughout the rest of the country there are around sixty local theatres. The work of these local theatres is not restricted to straight drama and frequently maintains a mixed repertoire of plays, opera, ballet, and children's theatre. The larger cities of Leipzig and Dresden have separate opera houses of a very high standard. Variety is often introduced into the repertoire by having different sized auditoria in the same city. Rostock, for example, with a population of just over 200,000, has two major auditoria, a small Intimes Theatre, a small theatre for chamber opera, and operates a small drama house at War-nemunde a few miles outside the city, each with its own repertoire. It also maintains its own mime troupe. The theatres are lavishly staffed with large acting ensembles and orchestras and forty-three cities have separate facilities for opera and/or music theatre.

There is full employment for actors, on yearly contracts. Before joining a company they all undergo a three-year training course in one of the state schools and a further year's work in a studio attached to a theatre. The training in all the drama schools is standardized, and includes a high level of individual tuition for students.

The theatre season runs from September to late-June, presenting plays in repertoire and allowing for the carry-over of plays into the next season—in Berlin theatres plays often stay in repertoire for several years. This gives freedom for extended rehearsal periods for new productions and allows the actors to work in other media. In Berlin the theatre actors undertake a considerable amount of work in radio, television, and films. The system however makes unequal demands on actors. At the time of writing, Ekkehard Schall is carrying six major roles in the Berliner Ensemble repertoire, each of which comes up about once a fortnight, in addition to work in other media. Lesser actors will be carrying no more than very minor roles in several productions.

The GDR theatre audience is lively and responsive, but respectful, and theatre-going is clearly regarded as a formal social occasion. Seat prices in the Berlin theatres range from 15 marks at the opera down to 1 mark. Even at the present false rate of exchange 1 mark is valued at 17 pence, and its real value in relation to the standard of living is certainly less than this. The cheapest seat at the opera is only 35 pence at the prevailing exchange rate. Prices are considerably reduced outside Berlin and also for abonnement bookings and party bookings through schools, clubs and trade unions. Theatregoing is a very cheap form of entertainment, and performance times are varied to suit the demands of block bookings by various organizations and for special performances for young people. Ticket sales indicate an average of eighty-five theatre visits a year for every 100 people but this should be compared with a level of 600 visits to the cinema.

There are very few dramatists living purely on earnings from the theatre, most combining writing with some other form of work, often in journalism, publishing, or the theatre itself. There is a wide range of publications on the theatre in which writings on or by Brecht proliferate, but the great body of this material is about the GDR theatre itself, and there is not a great deal on the theatres outside Eastern Europe.

Historical factors have materially shaped the nature and direction of the GDR Theatre, and any examination and assessment will be confused and limited if these factors are ignored. In common with other Eastern European countries, the GDR has moved from capitalist to socialist economy and government, but only the GDR moved directly from Fascism to Socialism, and lacked the strength of national resistance to Nazi domination that other countries had. Although, in common with the GDR, the Federal German Republic was created out of the ruins of Fascism, the formation of a new capitalist state meant the continuation of the same social system as the old Germany. Progressive writers and directors, and returning exiles like Erwin Piscator, returned easily to a situation and line of work that was in essence very like that which they had left in 1933. In the GDR a new and unique situation faced both State and theatre. The lack of any clear precedents and tradition on which to build, and the problems arising out of this situation, have given both the State and theatre their own specific character. The strengths, deficiencies, and problems of the GDR theatre appear very different to those involved from the way they appear to the outside observer.

The working conditions of the Berliner Ensemble, with its six-month rehearsal periods, constantly varied repertoire, and, above all, economic security, will probably fill any actor with envy, but the long periods of rehearsal are paid for by keeping productions in repertoire for a long time (*Arturo Ui* was first performed in 1959 and Schall has now been playing that role once a fortnight for fourteen years). The ensemble system functions upon the unselfish work of many actors who continue playing minor roles year in and out. The visits of the Berliner Ensemble to this country have inspired British directors to emulation, and failure, because the British actor, used to a large degree of freedom in personal interpretation in his role and the short high-pressure rehearsal period, has not acquired the sustained discipline necessary to achieve the theatrical effect that is there in the Ensemble's work.

Most Western critics, admiring and negative alike, have tended to respond positively to the theatrical excellence of the GDR theatre whilst rejecting or ignoring the political content and intentions that sustain it. One should be careful of disparaging Brecht's statements about the theatre as a didactic instrument for bringing about social change and his commitment to the building of a socialist state, by dismissing them as political lip-service or re-interpreting them as a generalized liberal hope.

The theatre is taken seriously in the GDR as an instrument of political education helping to bring about social change. With the possible exception of China, no other country in the world gives its theatre such serious attention. Manfred Wekwerth, Brecht's pupil and successor, says, 'The working class and their allies are building a new society. It is one of the purposes of our performances, one defined by Brecht, to enable the people of this German state to master the new, complicated reality with the aid of artistic means'—a principle which is at the core of the practice of the GDR theatre. What the purpose of the theatre should be is in no doubt. If one discounts the emigration to the West of those who disagreed with the principle before the frontiers were closed, there is a surprising unanimity among GDR theatre people upon the aims and objectives of their theatres and an extraordinarily high level of political commitment. What is in doubt is the means by which this intention should be pursued, and in this area there is a great deal of discussion, disagreement and sometimes confusion and contradiction.

In the immediate post-war period, when the state was still under the control of the Russian military authorities, there was less disagreement. The theatres re-opened, playing a combination of imported Soviet plays, and plays which had not been performed during the Nazi period. To these were added new anti-fascist plays such as Günther Weisenborn's *Die Illegalen* about the resistance movement and Fred Denger's *Wir heissen Euch Hoffen* about fascist terrorist groups still in existence after the war. The first play dealing with the role of the individual in the new society—Annemarie Bostroem's *Die Kette Fällt* (*The Chain Falls Off*) was written in 1948. The theatre had a large potential repertoire of plays unperformed for twelve years which made a clear contribution to the policy of replacing the previous ideology with a socialist ideology and in this context the presentation of such plays as Lessing's *Nathan der Weise* and Wolf's *Professor Mamlock* and *Die Matrosen von Cattaro* (*The Sailors of Cattaro*) took on a violently didactic nature as a direct assault on the values of the previous regime. Time and changes in society have blunted the attack but the principles of a return to a Humanist Realist Theatre, laid down then as the basis of the GDR Theatre, still predominate in its work, and the presentation of plays from world drama in this tradition form the major part of the theatres' repertoires. Allowing, as in other theatres, that there are successful and unsuccessful concepts and productions, this is the strongest and most satisfying aspect of the GDR repertoire, particularly since the range of plays selected is wider than I have found in other countries, giving many opportunities for seeing rarely-performed masterpieces. The critical didactic approach, laid down by Brecht, allows neither archaic museum reconstructions of the play in its time nor tricked-out contemporary versions and reinterpretations, but tries to grasp the fact that we are no longer living in the time when the play was written but that that moment and our own age are parts of a continuing historical development. The approach is to explore the dialectical relationship between those factors which shape the play because of the historical situation in which it was written and those elements which show the movement of society from feudalism to capitalism, and from capitalism to socialism.

In 1949 the Russian authorities handed over control of the state to the GDR government, and the earnestness and lack of security felt by the government was reflected in the formation of a State Commission for the Arts which began shaping the theatre as an instrument for political, social and ethical teaching, which correspondingly reflected a shift of emphasis from destroying the old ideology to building the new. The succeeding years have reflected the growing security and social unity of the state by the replacement of the Commission for the Arts by the Ministry of Culture in 1954, and the arrival of the present position when the 8th Party Congress defined the State's responsibility to lay down the political direction of the country, leaving it to the theatre Intendants to interpret this theatrically. Along the way there has been a great deal of discussion and argument, and there have been both positive gains and mistakes. Plays have been stopped and political discipline has been brought to bear on some theatres, but the question of political censorship is not one that seems to concern people working in the theatres so much as the terms of the debate. Nor does there seem to be any thought that the problems of the new drama have been solved. In fact the growing stability of the socialist state and the diminishing threat of outside enemies have in some ways complicated these problems. The problems of the new drama are not simply those of dramaturgical advance but are concerned with adapting the methods of the critical realist theatre to a new situation and of finding the most productive role for the theatre to play in the new society.

In the period of Soviet control and the early years of the GDR government, the problems were clearer, and the GDR was fortunate in having Brecht to clarify and enrich the discussions. Attempts were made to impose a narrow concept of socialist realism on the GDR theatre, and it is accurate to say that the state fell foul of Brecht, rather than that Brecht fell foul of the state. Brecht never opposed the concept of socialist realism, but he strongly opposed the dictum of 'typical figures present in typical surroundings' and the consequent attack on 'formalism' in his work.

The most productive outcome of Brecht's arguments and discussions has been the freedom to use the full range of stylistic resources in staging plays, and the lessons learned from Brecht's theory and practice of stagecraft have given the GDR a rich inheritance.

The standards of production and stage presentation (with the exception of lighting which is often clumsy and sometimes inept) is very high and often revolutionary, as it is with Walter Felsenstein's productions at the Komische Oper where opera is treated as a total theatre art instead of simply a vocal art. The production demands of directors like Besson, Wekwerth, Berghaus and Felsenstein push actors and singers into areas of high physical and vocal skills. When the baritone playing the drunken Puntilla, in the Berghaus production of the Dessau opera version, sings his opening aria swinging back and forward across the stage hanging on a chandelier, one's concept of opera enters a different world. The playing of Hilmar Thate as Galy Gay in *Mann ist Mann* brings the agile clowning of Chaplin back into the legitimate theatre.

A conspicuous strength of the actors lies in their ability to use extrovert and comic skills in plays which have a serious content and intention, to juxtapose styles of acting within the same piece, and to preserve the tension between different levels of engagement both on stage and in the audience. There is very little that is earnest and sombre. It is a cool theatre, which is not to say it is not an emotional theatre. The Berliner Ensemble productions of *Mutter Courage, Die Tage der Commune* (*The Days of the Commune*), and *Der Brotladen* (*The Bread Shop*) I would class among the half-dozen most moving experiences I have had in the theatre, but the audience is never allowed the undiscriminating emotional experience of becoming empathically involved with the suffering or triumph of the protagonists. The production of *Die Tage der Commune* is a clear example of this in action. Brecht, and the directors knew that they could rely heavily on the audience's wish to identify politically and emotionally with the Communards, but throughout the performance the audience is constantly addressed directly as the bourgeois of Paris. There is no gestus applied to the proclamations and addresses that would allow the audience to shrug off the role in which they are cast through irony or satire, and the result is to maintain a distance between the viewer and the object of his sympathy. A dialectical tension is evoked between the wish for the Commune to succeed and the critical assessment of the reasons why it didn't and couldn't succeed. The lesson of Brecht's demand that the theatre should delight and should combine instruction and entertainment has been well learned by a number of his pupils and some younger directors, and the (so far) definitive production of Brecht in this respect is considered by people who worked with him to be the production of *Der Brotladen* (which Brecht left as a dramatic fragment) by two young directors, Manfred Karge and Matthias Langhoff.

Where the system occasionally breaks down is in the indiscriminate application of these techniques to plays which were written with directly opposing tendencies. Thus Berghaus's production of Brecht's *Die Gewehre der Frau Carrar* (*The Rifles of Frau Carrar*) was an unsatisfactory catalogue of alienation devices applied to a play which was not written to distance an audience but to involve them in the Republican struggle during the Spanish Civil War. At the same time new light is thrown upon plays from past historical periods, which enhances the audience's enjoyment without obscuring or perverting the plays' essential content and significance.

The inheritance of Brecht is also revealed in another staple element of the repertoire—new plays written upon historical subjects. It is in this area that Peter Hacks, the finest of the contemporary writers, has most clearly revealed his talents in plays like *Die Schlacht bei Lobositz* (*The Battle at Lobositz*) and *Der Müller von Sanssouci* (*The Miller of Sanssouci*), which are the only post-war GDR plays to have received widespread production outside the country, if one discounts the later plays of Brecht, which were completed or first performed after 1945. In some ways the application of lessons learned from historical situations to the contemporary situation has proved happier ground for contemporary playwrights than the current situation. Hacks and Heiner Müller particularly have taken refuge here, and in adaptations of classic plays, from the difficulties their contemporary plays have run into. In this they appear to have the sympathy of the public. In Hacks's adaptation of *La Belle Helene, Die Schöne Helena,* Homer, entertaining the Greek leaders, complains that everyone asks for adaptations but no one is interested in new plays. The night I saw the production the audience cheered.

The early discussions between Brecht and the authorities at least laid down the lines for the new dramaturgy, and this is clearly expressed in his statement that the theatre 'must uncover the elements of crisis, of that which is problematical, rich in conflicts within this new life, else how can we ever show that which is creative in it?' The post-war history of the GDR theatre is a living proof that it is more easily said than done.

In one respect Brecht himself has been of little help. Towards the end of his life he said that he seemed to have spent so much of his life destroying the myth of the Gods that he hadn't had time to sing the glory of man. The critical realist theatre, such as the parable plays of Brecht, draws its political relevance and validity from making explicit in the theatre what is concealed in politics. In revealing the inhumanity of capitalism and the need for change, it is in advance of the political position of the state. In this respect it might seem that the Brechtian method is of more value in this country than in the GDR, where an attempt is being made to effect the social changes that Brecht called for. A major aspect of the debate on the new drama has centred around this point: whether a socialist society can employ critical means, or whether it should discard these in favour of an inspirational theatre that sings the praises of socialist Man. The early terms of this debate were based on a narrow definition of the critical theatre, and in theory Brecht's broader concept of a critical theatre, reflected in the quotation above, have found total acceptance, but this has only complicated the debate. The dramatist who makes explicit in the theatre what is already explicit in the politics of the state finds little favour with the audience. The dramatist who gets ahead of state politics runs the risk of being accused of utopianism or anarchism. The balance, in Brecht's terms, is 'the simple which is very difficult to achieve'.

The simplistic terms of the early stages of the new drama were satirized in 1952 by Heinar Kipphardt, then dramaturg of the Deutsches Theater, in *Shakespeare dringend gesucht (Shakespeare*

Urgently Sought) in which he attacked both the restrictions of political bureaucracy and the restricted vision of dramatists. A conference in 1956 of theatre workers, called by the government, laid the blame on bureaucracy, and reforms resulted. The Bitterfeld Conference of 1959 threw the responsibility back on the dramatists, who were not producing the goods. The depressing aspect of the current situation is the tendency of dramatists and theatres to play safe, producing plays which are neither theatrically nor thematically interesting nor satisfying. The encouraging aspect lies in the wide public interest in the new drama and the fact that dramatists, like Hacks, Müller and Volker Braun, in spite of the difficulties that some of their plays have encountered, go on tackling the problem with no loss of commitment.

The most interesting new plays have dealt with the relationship of the individual to the community, and in this there have been two significant shifts of emphasis. First the shift from the problems of adjustment to a new society and secondly—clearly expressed by the audience—from plays which suggested solutions to social problems to plays which clearly articulate the exact nature of the problems without necessarily suggesting solutions.

Playwrights who have explored the problems of adjustment to the new social and political situation include Helmut Baierl (whose *Frau Flinz* (1961) is a reverse of Brecht's *Mutter Courage* in showing a woman who does learn from her mistakes and experiences), Rainer Kerndl and Friedhold Bauer. The problems of the individual in the new situation have been tackled by Horst Salomon, in *Katzengold* (1964) and *Der Lorbass* (1967) using conflicts between generations to find a compromise method of integrating the individual's gifts in the social structure. Both plays were highly successful with audiences. More problematical, and more interesting, were a series of plays which criticized society's inability to cope with the Gargantuan social ambitions and appetites of the individual. These include Hacks's *Moritz Tassow* (1961, produced 1965), Müller's *Herakles 5* (1965), and Volker Braun's *Kipper Paul Bauch* (1966).

The GDR theatre appears to have declined from the high standards of ten years ago, and there are signs in the GDR that the theatre is approaching a period, if not of crisis, of a critical re-assessment.

Certainly there is little complacency with the work they are presenting, and a wide and open criticism of their present position.

One area of criticism and discussion centres on the theatre's relationship with its audience. There is a general dissatisfaction that the percentage of industrial workers in the audience is not higher, although by Western standards it is high. There is a feeling that more productive methods must be found to introduce young people to the theatre, although again here, by Western standards, the percentage is high. On the one hand the high standard of political education within the schools, and on the other the intrusion of Western Pop cultural forms have tended to diminish the appeal of the theatre for young people. There have been some—I think misguided—attempts to attract audiences by the presentation of almost boulevard plays in the repertoire. It is something of a shock to find Bill Naughton's petit-bourgeois drama *Spring and Port Wine* in the repertoire of the Deutsches National Theater at Weimar, on the tenuous strength of its passing reference to the nineteen-thirties Hunger Marches.

More positive steps have been taken in some theatres, notably Halle and Magdeburg, to carry discussion into the factories and to enlist the help of workers in the planning and mounting of contemporary plays, and in post-production criticism. There is a general regret that the processes of discussion between the theatre and its audience are not stronger, and some criticism that the gradual withdrawal of the state from the control and direction of the theatre has in part created this problem. Anyone who sees the participation of the state in active criticism as an intolerable and crippling censorship of artistic freedom (and Brecht certainly didn't see it that way) must explain the paradox that as it has weakened standards of writing have generally not improved but declined. The policy of treating the Intendant as responsible for following the political direction of the State, but allowing him to find his own methods for doing so, has led to criticism of Intendants for being too earnest and unadventurous in their policies and not open to problematic forms. There are criticisms of directors for developing their own styles of working and being unwilling to discuss their work outside their theatres. On the other hand, Horst Schönemann, a young director with very clear ideas of what he wants to do and how he wants to do it, was able to bring out Plenzdorf's *Die Neuen Leiden des Jungen W* (*The New Sorrows of Young W*) in Halle, and then to bring it to Berlin when he moved to the Deutsches

Theater. This was the success of the season, and is critical of social development of the GDR, reviving very sharply the old problem of the state's utilization of the individual's creative resources when he is at variance with the accepted collective method. There is hope that wider discussions between theatre and audience can be set up, but it is felt that this will take some years to achieve.

Within the theatres, during the last few years, there has been a considerable movement of actors between companies. There are signs of a growing dissatisfaction among some actors, and this is often expressed as a dislike of, or a lack of confidence in, one or other of the younger directors. The German theatre, in general, has a tradition of autocratic directors and it is interesting to find cracks in the system appearing simultaneously in East and West.

In general terms it would appear that younger directors lack the ability that the older directors possessed, to work with actors, and in a few productions, for example Wekwerth's *Richard III*, at the Deutsches Theater, the icy hand of the director's 'concept' becoming the *raison d'être* of the production to the detriment of the ensemble playing of the actors seems to be creeping into the GDR. It is said that only Wolfgang Heinz (the last of the old school) still works to develop the actors. This may well be a subjective or over-pessimistic view, and certainly the work of Benno Besson seems remarkable for the spontaneous creative freedom given to the actor within a very clear and precise production framework. But the work of Besson would be outstanding in any theatre, and he himself is obviously by now a senior director. What seems likely is that the older school of pre-war directors such as Brecht, Engel and Wolfgang Langhoff, commanded more respect from the younger actors than directors of their own and younger generations, and there is a considerable movement between theatres of actors in search of directors they believe they can work with. Regrettably some actors, including Wolf Kaiser, one of the best European actors of his generation and a pillar of the old Berliner Ensemble, seem to have left the theatre to work entirely in the other media.

Of the dramatists, Hacks appears to have retreated into areas of mythology and linguistic complexities (philosophy dramatized). It will be interesting to see what Plenzdorf produces next, but the key figure is probably Heiner Müller. His unproduced version of *Macbeth* has attracted strong support and opposition in print, and a new play *Cement* is announced for première by the Berliner Ensemble. The controversy over *Macbeth*, printed in 'Sinn und Form' showed that there is still no general agreement about the direction and form that the new socialist drama should take but an increasing proliferation of views. The debate, as they say, continues.

10

Ronald Hayman : BRECHT IN THE ENGLISH THEATRE

The more pervasive an influence becomes, the harder it is to hypos-
tasize, but if Shakespeare can be called the most important playwright in German drama, Brecht must be acknowledged as the most
important in the post-war English theatre. He has exerted more
influence than anyone else not only on playwriting, design and style in
production, but on our whole approach to the theatre. The question
'What is the object of the work we are doing in the theatre?' is all
too seldom seriously posed, but our fundamental thinking, such as it
is, is very much more Brechtian today than it was in the decade after
the war.

But then the word 'Brechtian' needs immediately to be redefined in
a way that exculpates Brecht from complete responsibility for the
ideas that have been canvassed in his name. The greater part of his
theorizing—like the greater part of his best playwriting—was done
during the thirties and forties, when he was living outside Germany
but still reacting against the bombastically rhetorical histrionics that
had dominated the German theatre in the late twenties and early
thirties. As Martin Esslin has pointed out,[1] his theoretical writings
were not available in English until John Willett's selection of them[2]
was published here in 1964, so the majority of playwrights and directors, unable to read German, had to rely on approximate and in-
accurate secondhand accounts of what Brecht had actually said.
Nevertheless, his name was used as a password and his ideas as a
passe-partout to all that was new and desirable in theatre.

What had been available at first hand was the experience of seeing
the three Berliner Ensemble productions that the impresario Peter
Daubeny brought to the Palace Theatre in August–September 1956
—Brecht's own production of *Der kaukasische Kreidekreis* (*The
Caucasian Chalk Circle*), *Mutter Courage* co-directed by Brecht and
Erich Engel, and *Pauken und Trompeten* (*Drums and Trumpets*)

Brecht's version of Farquhar's *The Recruiting Officer*. As Peter Palitsch, Brecht's Assistant Director at the Berliner Ensemble, has pointed out, Brechtian theory was never fully applied there. Brecht used to say that it would take four years to acclimatize an actor fully to his methods, and even the Ensemble's leisurely rehearsal periods did not allow enough time for that. In England, the main impact was made by the sheer power of the productions, but distorted ideas of Brechtian theory played a large part in the period of influence that ensued, as playwrights, directors, designers and actors went on asking themselves how the Berliner Ensemble had achieved its results.

Undoubtedly the season at the Palace Theatre was a turning-point in British theatre history, whether we regard it as the chief cause of the changes that followed or merely as a catalyst for tendencies that already were powerfully at work underneath the surface and away from the centre. In so far as our theatre was a temple of middle-class romanticism, there was already a resistance movement, led by Joan Littlewood, who was trying, rather unsuccessfully, to attract a working-class audience to the Theatre Royal, Stratford, E14, and she was using songs and music-hall techniques rather in the way that Brecht was using alienation effects—to confront the audience directly, breaking down the pretence that the action on stage was life being lived out in a room with a transparent wall. Meanwhile Kenneth Tynan had been using his influential drama column in the *Observer* to launch a series of broadsides on Establishment theatre, using Brecht's name as a battle-cry.

The most immediate impact of the three Berliner Ensemble productions was visual, and the most direct influence was on designers. The pictorial detail and the cult of atmospheric enchantment that prevailed in the English theatre during the late forties and early fifties has now come to look almost Pre-Raphaelite. The setting that Teo Otto and Heinrich Kilger designed for *Mutter Courage* had a simple white cyclorama instead of a backcloth, and in effect there was no set at all except for Mother Courage's wagon, which reappeared in different positions and at different angles. No coloured gelatines were used in the lighting and the colours of costumes and properties were almost Puritanically subdued—greys, browns and discreet pastels. Property master and wardrobe mistress had patently been trained into the habit of making objects look handled and clothes look worn. Realistic sweat-stains and unglamorously embedded grime made simple but shatteringly effective statements of their own. Today we are habituated to this visual verismo; in 1956 we were suddenly made aware of the falsification in appearances we had accepted as realistic.

The most influential designer in Britain during the sixties was John Bury, who worked for Joan Littlewood at her Theatre Workshop, first as an actor and then as her designer from 1954 to 1963, when he was appointed by Peter Hall as Head of Design for the Royal Shakespeare Company. Unlike most English designers he did not train as a painter; his approach was more like that of a sculptor or an engineer. He thought in terms of shapes, materials and textures, regarding a set as a machine. In his designs for the RSC's production of *The Wars of the Roses* (1962) the council tables, trucks and ammunition boxes were used very much like the wagon in *Mutter Courage*, creating a locale and a realistic atmosphere by planting a shape three-dimensionally in the foreground. The central metaphor in the production was the steel of war, and, as John Bury put it himself, 'On the flagged floor of sheet steel, tables are daggers, staircases are axe-heads and doors the traps on scaffolds.' Like Jocelyn Herbert, who designed most of the best sets at the Royal Court, Bury has thoroughly digested what he has learnt from Brecht's designers— and especially from Caspar Neher. Neither Bury nor Herbert is a mere imitator. They have learnt that economy in background, in detail and in colour makes it possible for objects and textures of materials to contribute powerfully to the statement of a play; in applying this lesson they have found ways of making visual images work like imagery in poetry.

By the end of the fifties heroic drama would have been in decline anyway in England, irrespective of the example of the Berliner Ensemble. John Osborne's *Look Back in Anger* had been produced at the Royal Court earlier in 1956, and Jimmy Porter was the first of the new anti-middle-class anti-heroes to capture the imagination of the new generation of theatregoers. But the Berliner Ensemble must have done much more than Kenneth Haigh's performance as Jimmy did to change preconceptions about what an actor ought to look like and sound like. In 1950, if there had been any physical equivalents among English actors to Angelika Hurwicz and Heinz Schubert, who

played the daughter and the younger son in *Mutter Courage*, they
would never have been cast in leading parts. Brecht's actors all looked
more like people one would have met on a bus or in a Labour
Exchange than people one would have paid money to see in a theatre.
But by the end of the fifties conventional good looks were suddenly
out of fashion on the stage, and gritty provincial accents were outnum-
bering educated RADA voices. When Arthur Miller was in London
in October 1956 for the production of *A View from the Bridge*, he
complained that it was hard to find English actors who could be
convincing in Common Man parts. Five years later he would have
been more likely to find difficulty in casting kings or aristocrats, were
it not for the fact that by then casting policy had moved in the
direction of Berliner Ensemble practice. By casting David Warner
as Hamlet and Ian Holm as Henry V, as he did in 1965, Peter
Hall was developing an existing tendency to put the emphasis on
what Shakespeare's royal heroes had in common with the common
man, not on what differentiated them from him. Tony Richardson
went further still in his production of *Hamlet* in 1969, encouraging
Nicol Williamson to play the part with a working-class Birmingham
twang.

Directors generally were becoming more anti-heroic in their
attitudes, concerning themselves more with the 'social sub-text' of a
play and shifting the focus away from the central figure towards the
group that surrounded him—partly because of Brecht's doctrine that
each play should be approached as a piece of history. Instead of
using supporting characters as figures to be grouped around the leading actor so as to form an effective stage picture, directors now tended
to go some way in the direction Tom Stoppard took when he made
Rosencrantz and Guildenstern the central characters in his play,
relegating Hamlet to a small part.

Meanwhile leading actors adapted themselves to the new style.
After encouraging Laurence Olivier to play Othello and then giving
him Dr Leavis's essay 'Diabolic Intellect and the Noble Hero',[3]
Kenneth Tynan said 'I think Larry would have played Othello quite
differently twenty years ago. This is an unromantic Othello, a wild
animal, unheroic. This wouldn't have been possible in the pre-Brecht
period.' Similarly, Olivier's Brazen in William Gaskill's very Brechtian production of Farquhar's *The Recruiting Officer* (which might
never have been staged at the National Theatre but for *Pauken und*

Trompeten) was much more calculating and unglamorous than Olivier would have made him before 1956. The production was conceived more in terms of social and economic pressures, less in terms of comic theatrical effects. Again, in Congreve's *Love for Love*, Olivier's characterisation of Tattle, with pasty complexion and grubby lace, broke away from the romantic tradition of playing Restoration comedy.

In another context[4] I summed up the change in English acting as a shift from Stanislavskian spirituality to Brechtian materialism. Generally the Brechtian approach tended to push the focus away from inner life and personal relationships towards exterior pressures and generalisation in which each character emerged as a representative of a social situation. When she was playing Kattrin in *Mutter Courage* Angelika Hurwicz found she had to discard the textually justified idea of presenting the dumbness as the result of an injury done to her tongue during childhood. It would have been wrong to give the audience an impression of retarded development. 'What was important was to show that intelligent people, born to happiness, can be crippled by war. Precision in portraying an individual case had to be sacrificed for this general truth.' English actors might seem to be temperamentally immune from any temptation to sacrifice precision in portraying an individual case to general truths, but a great deal has changed since 'The Method' was in fashion. It would be simplistic to say that the Stanislavski-Freud-Lee Strasberg tradition has been discarded in favour of the Marx-Brecht tradition, but our actors do seem generally to be moving towards approaching their characters less in terms of what differentiates them from other people than of how to indicate common ground. Paul Scofield has said 'I find myself being much more interested in finding in a character something which is common to a lot of people.'[5] Alec Guinness, similarly, is no longer content to exploit his skill in disguising himself with crepe hair and nose-putty. He defines his aim now as being 'to cut out all unnecessary frills ... to try and refine something down and eliminate the unnecessary'.

The results of the Brechtian influence on English playwrights are easier to demonstrate. In John Osborne's work, for instance, there is a very clear tidemark between the two early plays *Epitaph for George Dillon* (written in collaboration with Anthony Creighton) and *Look*

Back in Anger and the next two, *The Entertainer* and *Luther*. The first two are 'well made plays' with the action situated in living-rooms that can be represented by box sets and spread neatly between three acts, the third culminating in a pregnancy followed by an ironic-ally happy ending. The construction of both *The Entertainer* and *Luther* is Brechtian : each act is divided into short, nearly self-con-tained scenes, and even if a box set were used for the boarding-house scenes in *The Entertainer*, Archie Rice would have to step outside it to play directly to the audience in the music-hall scenes. In Tony Richardson's original production, a big figure lit up alienatingly on either side of the stage to tell us which 'number' or scene we were watching. In *Luther* the alienation effects are still more obvious, and on the surface it is a very Brechtian play. It is divided into twelve watertight scenes, each being introduced by a Knight who comes on stage with a banner to announce the time and place. Like Galileo, Luther was an intellectual revolutionary who succeeded in changing the course of history, but more by his ideas than by his life, which was not lived out on the same level of consistency. Osborne's Luther is more belligerent and more successful in his skirmishes with authority than Brecht's Galileo—he refuses to recant but lets the peasants down in their rising against the princes. And both plays end with a scene showing the hero passive in the comfort of a home, being waited on by a woman who is salving his bad conscience with good food.

Not only the construction of *Luther* but also the treatment of the plot is modelled closely on Brecht's *Galileo*. But Brecht's treatment of history is Marxist, and the scene in which the once friendly Cardinal Barberini becomes depersonalised in both appearance and attitude as he dons the papal vestments is a classical theatrical illustration of the way individuality can be blotted out by history and social position. In John Osborne's perspective, personality stands right in the fore-ground. The determining factors are psychological and physiological, not social or economic, and *Luther*, like *Look Back in Anger*, is a play conceived mainly in terms of monologue. Except in the scene with his father, Luther is never seen in collision with anything except him-self, God and history. He becomes involved, often enough, in argu-ments, but compared with the arguments in *Galileo*, they are very deficient in dramatic give-and-take. The effect is that the hero is put on a different level from everyone else in the play. Tony Richard-son's production of *Luther* used history only as a backcloth, ignoring the ordinary life of the ordinary people. Many of Joan Littlewood's productions had paid far more attention to it, and been enriched accordingly. The same could be said of the best RSC productions, like Terry Hands's *The Merry Wives of Windsor*, with its loving realism about domestic life.

Robert Bolt shares with Osborne what might be called a personality attitude to historical subject matter. Of all our playwrights who have resorted to it, he is the one who suffers most by comparison with Brecht, yet he is the only one who has explicitly challenged it. 'The style I eventually used,' he wrote in the Preface to *A Man for All Seasons*, 'was a bastardised version of the one most recently associated with Bertolt Brecht.' The only Brechtian feature of the construction is that the action is spread out over a long span of time and a wide range of places, none of which is established in detail by scenery. There were also devices that produced alienation effects—baskets of props and costumes were lowered from the flies, and the Common Man, a chorus figure, joined in the action, playing a number of different roles, and changed his costume in front of the audience. He addressed us directly, introducing the scenes, not announcing them like Osborne's Knight but providing a humorous linking commentary. But whereas Brecht's projections of place-names and plot summaries deliberately interrupt the action by highlighting the division between one scene and the next, the Common Man provides continuity. Bolt's construction is less 'Epic' (in Brecht's sense) than cinematic, with the alienation effects embroidered in ornamentally. Far from wanting to alienate the audience from Thomas More, Bolt really wants to invite the closest possible identification.

John Arden is a much more deeply Brechtian playwright. Like Brecht he is basically a poet and basically more interested in the group than the individual, while his historical imagination projects itself naturally on a grand scale. The main theme in both *Armstrong's Last Goodnight* and *Island of the Mighty* was the supersession of a primitive civilization by a more advanced one and the waste of animal energy that occurs when historical progress forces a group into a more sophisticated form of political organization. When Arden was asked in 1961 by the editors of Encore whether there was any modern play he would particularly like to have written, his first answer was '*Mother Courage*' and he went on to say how impressed he had been by the Berliner Ensemble production. In the same interview,[6] he also compared the alternation between verse and prose in Brecht's dialogue with the alternation in his own. 'I see prose as being a more useful vehicle for conveying plot and character relationships; and poetry as a sort of comment on them. I find it difficult to carry this out in practice. Brecht, for instance, is usually very, very distinct between the two. I haven't always found it possible to be so.'

Whether it was Brecht's example that encouraged him to divide his plays as he has done between prose dialogue and snatches of rhyme and song is an unanswerable question. In any event the influence is so well digested that he seems not to be copying from Brecht but writing in the only way that could have come naturally to him. He is also Brechtian in his deep basic desire to influence his audience's habits of thinking. He was impelled to write *Serjeant Musgrave's Dance* partly by an incident in Cyprus when a British soldier's wife was shot by terrorists. Afterwards, according to newspaper reports, some of the soldiers ran wild and people were killed in the rounding-up. Like *Mutter Courage*, the play Arden went on to write is didactically aimed against war and the way it nourishes aggressive and acquisitive instincts.

Arden is also Brechtian in his dependence on folk-songs, folklore and the ballad tradition. It is not only in his interpolations of rhyme that he draws on these, but his choice of subject matter and his technique of story-telling derive from them. In *Serjeant Musgrave's Dance* the scene in which Annie is rejected by each of the three soldiers in turn is conceived not as a realistic projection of how these people would behave in these circumstances but as a three-dimensional extension of a ballad-like progression. And the attraction of the Arthurian legend, which had fascinated Arden for years before *The Island of the Mighty* was produced in 1973, must have resided partly in the folkloristic quality of the deeds of primitive heroism that provided the main substance of the physical action. Like Brecht in *Kaukasische Kreidekreis*, he approached a mythical society as if he were a social historian.

In some respects Arden's technique is more Shakespearean than Brechtian. He often weaves stage directions into his dialogue, and, especially in *Armstrong's Last Goodnight*, he uses the combination of language and action to evoke a vivid sense of locale with no help from the scenery. But, ironically, one of the main functions of Brecht's

Shakespeare on the German stage: *Much Ado About Nothing*,
Frankfurter Schauspielhaus, 1974

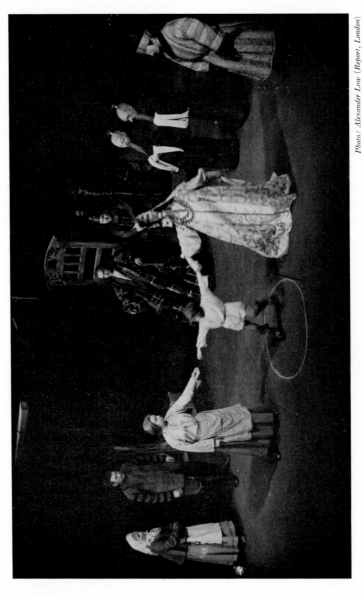

Photo: Alexander Low (Report, London)

Brecht on the English stage: *The Caucasian Chalk Circle,*
Aldwych Theatre, 1962

influence on the English theatre has been to promote a revival of the anti-illusionist techniques of our own Elizabethan theatre from which he learnt so much.

Edward Bond is another playwright who could not have written as he has if Brecht's plays had not existed first, but the superficial evidence of influence is less important than the deep infiltration. Like Arden's early plays *The Waters of Babylon* (1957) and *Live Like Pigs* (1958) Edward Bond's *The Pope's Wedding* (1962) and *Saved* (1965) were mainly naturalistic—grounded on a verismo reproduction of working-class dialogue—though Bond was already deeply interested in Brecht's work. The influence is first discernible in *Early Morning* (1968) although 'Brechtian' is not a word one would apply to it until one comes to look at it in the perspective of his later work. The cannibalistic heaven and the Lesbian relationship between Queen Victoria and Florence Nightingale then come to seem like a pair of outrageous alienation effects as we see how Bond is using British history. It was his first play to be pitched away from the present, but it was in no sense a historical play, though he boldly announced 'the events of this play are true'. He was, in fact, trying to historicize in a Brechtian way, building a monstrous distorting mirror to show the present its own image, disguised as a Victorian grandparent. It is a play about capitalism, imperialism, authoritarianism and social injustice—themes that Bond was to take up again, more directly, in *Narrow Road to the Deep North* (1968) a play that is more obviously Brechtian in its stylized use of masks and its unrealistic use of oriental history, the distance of the civilization from our own itself acting as a means of alienation. As in *Kaukasische Kreidekreis* children are used lovelessly as pawns in a power game, while colonials and coolies, priests and pupils are represented very much as they are in the *Lehrstücke* (didactic plays).

Bond's *Lear* (1971) is Brechtian in different ways. It reworks and updates a Shakespearean plot, shifting the focus away from personal issues towards social and political issues, as Brecht did in his version of *Coriolanus*. The King is de-individualized into a representative of Commanding Officer authoritarianism, while both the 'Epic' succession of more or less disconnected episodes and the vignette characterization of peasants who appear only briefly are reminiscent of *Mutter Courage*. In William Gaskill's original production at the Royal

Court, the groupings, the lighting, the colours of the decor and
costumes and the overall visual economy all seemed to derive from the
style Brecht evolved at the Berliner Ensemble.

In the work of the younger generation of British playwrights it is
harder to pinpoint instances of the influence, mainly because it has
become so strong that the prevalent view of the theatre's function is
much more Brechtian than it was in 1955, when none but the most
radical of our playwrights would have felt anything but derision for
Brecht's idea that the value of a play lay in the effect it had on the
audience. Today it is more exceptional for a young playwright to
challenge the view that the main purpose of writing is to encourage
change in society. Tom Stoppard is quite conscious of his heterodoxy
in maintaining that all art is useless, and one of his main objects in
his 1974 play *Travesties* was to construct a kaleidoscope to shake up
memories of James Joyce, Tristan Tzara and Lenin and their conflicting opinions about the relationship between progressive art and
social change. But many of the important new plays by important
young writers make it almost impossible to distinguish between art
and agitprop.

Howard Brenton, for instance, may still be open to attack from Communist critics for not having a more positive vision of how society
could be improved, but even his best plays, which are among the
best being written, verge on propaganda. Like Brecht, he is writing
not for posterity but for a specific social and political situation, which
is changeable. Some of his characterization is very subtle and some
of his situations are ingeniously constructed, but his main concern is
with the viewpoints that the characters represent. The two poles of his
1973 play *Magnificence* are a Conservative Cabinet Minister and a
boy who develops from a squatter into a terrorist. *The Churchill
Play* (1974) argues that the greatness which won the war was that
of the English people, not of their leader. The action is set in a British
concentration camp in 1984, but (like *Early Morning*) the play is
mainly about the present, its chief concern being with the avoidable
erosion of liberty in this country. 'The Churchill Play' is written and
performed by prisoners in the camp—a device that may derive from
Peter Weiss's *Marat/Sade*, which was itself strongly influenced by
Brecht. We shall soon be at a stage where the red thread of Brechtian
influence, however strong, can no longer be untangled.

NOTES

1. *Brief Chronicles*, Temple Smith, 1970.
2. *Brecht on Theatre*, Methuen, 1964.
3. F. R. Leavis, *The Common Pursuit*, Chatto, 1952.
4. Ronald Hayman, *Techniques of Acting*, Methuen, 1969.
5. Ronald Hayman, *Playback*, Davis-Poynter, 1973.
6. *Encore.*

III

STRUCTURE AND THEATRICAL PRACTICE

Peter Fischer: DOING PRINCELY SUMS—STRUCTURE
AND SUBSIDY

'Make the best theatre in Germany and tell me the cost', Prince
Hardenberg, chancellor of Prussia, is reported to have said, just after
the Napoleonic wars, to the director of the Royal Theatre in Berlin,
Count Brühl. Even if the great democratic reformer was thinking
more of spectacle than of artistic excellence, his phrase seems like a
motto setting out two of the basic factors which have nourished German theatrical life to this day—public munificence and regional rivalry.
While Germans take them for granted, they never cease to amaze
foreign observers. 'The Germans take theatre and opera more seriously
than we do. What other conclusion can one draw from the 165
theatres that local authorities there subsidize to the tune of £35
million a year?' asked a columnist in the *Guardian*, impressed by a
London exhibition of post-war German theatre architecture in 1968
(since when the sum has been substantially increased). An American,
Alex Gross, reported to the *International Times* in 1967 : 'There are
more new American plays being done in Germany than in America,
often as many plays from continental countries as in the countries
themselves, and in terms of spectators probably a larger audience for
new English plays than in London ... The possibly unpleasant fact
remains that the things which the Germans do well they do very well
indeed, and one of those things is the theatre.'

This statement also implies that the riches of the German theatrical
institutions are not matched and sustained by a similarly rich flow of
German dramatic writing, and are relying largely on foreign plays,
particularly on the fruits (and fads) of the English theatre, which is so
very much poorer in material wealth. During the 1970–1 theatrical
season in West Germany, Austria and Switzerland, only 858 out of a
total of 2,054 new productions were of German-language plays, including all the German classics. 432 productions were of English and Irish

plays, 320 of French, and 165 of American plays. Again, these figures include the classics, above all Shakespeare, who continues to be the first or at least the second box-office hit each year, with around a hundred different productions in German. Some contemporary English playwrights, notably Edward Bond and James Saunders, have made their real mark in Germany, as well as their German marks which far exceed their royalties in British pounds. Charles Marowitz, some of whose London productions have been made possible by German festival managements, has said, 'It is not all that whimsical to suggest that without the generosity of German cultural interests there might be no experimental theatre in England.'

The close relationship between English and German theatre is, of course, a traditional one, and by no means one-way. German theatrical development since the Renaissance owes its very origin to the troupes of English players that began touring Germany towards the end of the Elizabethan period, soon on a more or less permanent basis, acting on rough-and-ready stages of a shape adapted from the Globe and the Swan in Shakespearean London, and in English (a rare enough event the other way round even in these days of transistorized simultaneous translation systems), and the brand-image of these *Engelischen Comoedianten* continued as a generic name even after they were joined by some native members and, from about the middle of the 17th century, gradually superseded by wholly German itinerant companies using their own language for English as well as other plays. A common origin: yet, theatre in Germany and England has evolved completely diverging institutional, financial and even architectural modes and moulds.

One underlying reason, no doubt, is the absence in Germany of that Puritan strain which in Britain tends to regard theatre basically as an 'entertainment' for which those indulging in such frivolous frills have to be prepared to pay punitive prices, just as they do for their liquors and cigarettes, but which they also feel free to enjoy in comfortable leisure-wear, just like a pint at the pub—and indeed the bar is a vital part of every British theatre. Germans, having exalted theatre to the sphere of *Kultur*, go to pay their religious respects at the Temple of the Muses which authority provides and promotes because it feels it is good for them, and they also go, of course, to parade their festive attire, preferably black, in the imposing pronaos known as the foyer which they use not so much for drinking as for being seen, like church-goers. However, the British do have a similar, though more severe, god whom they call Education, and whom they worship with self-improving devotion in the world's most elaborate system of libraries (provided free out of the public purse) as well as in the great museums with their traditional freedom of charge. But Britain, too, now has a Minister Responsible for the Arts and, ever since Covent Garden was established as a national opera-house in 1946, central and local government have come to recognize the necessity of that public patronage of the arts, including drama, which was already a matter of course to Hardenberg in Prussia and to all the German princes spending princely sums on their court theatres.

This, then, is the other, and more tangible, reason for the difference in pattern between the German and the English theatre. Unlike Britain, where dukes have dukedoms but no duchies, Germany has at no time been a unitary state but, rather, an association of dozens of principalities which developed strong local and regional traditions and rivalries, with each Margrave trying to keep up with the Grand-duke across the border—a patchwork comparable only to that of the Italian principalities and communes which has generated the riches of the Renaissance, and, again as in Italy, civic interest in artistic projects has often been vying in importance with the dynastic one.

In the beginning, of course, dramatic performances, like other festive spectacles, were mounted in the halls or courtyards of palaces for court audiences, and in other buildings or the open spaces between them, where they could cater for a wider range of spectators. But as early as 1603 the first proper theatre in Germany, the Ottonium, was built on the orders of one of the minor princes, Landgrave Maurice the Learned of Hesse-Kassel, in his capital. It was an oblong rectangle with a capacity of 475 and a stage suitable for English itinerants. This was followed in 1641 at Ulm, a Free City of the Empire, by what has been described as Germany's earliest civic theatre building, constructed by Joseph Furttenbach (1591–1667) and soon rearranged for no less than 1,000 townspeople (though it was eventually converted into military barracks). Its stage techniques were directly derived from those pioneered in Florence by Bernardo Buontalenti, that ingenious and industrious architect at the Medici court and organizer of 'choreographic intermezzi' in the Teatro Mediceo he built within the Uffizi Palace in 1585, and carried on by Giulio Parigi. Here is another common source of German and English theatre, for Parigi, in the

second decade of the 17th century, became the mentor of both Inigo
Jones, who took Florentine concepts of perspective home to his masque
designs in Stuart London, and of Furttenbach, the German architect,
who at Ulm applied the Italian system of the *telari* stage. This consisted of two lines of triangular revolving columns called *telari* (i.e.
canvas frames), with sections of different sets of scenery painted
illusionistically on each surface which, for scene changes, could be
turned to simulate two rows of buildings, with gaps for the actors'
entrances and exits, going inward from the corners of the proscenium
arch and narrowing perspectivally towards the painted backdrop—
a forerunner of the movable 'wings' which, in fact, had already been
introduced at Parma by Giovanni Battista Aleotti.

The common element in all these schemes, of course, was the proscenium arch or 'picture frame' with a moat-like orchestra-pit separating the stage from the spectators seated in straight or slightly curved
rows, all their eyes pulled neatly towards a perspectivally represented
but, in effect, two-dimensional image, a comfortably remote picture
of reality. This arrangement, so different from the rounder view
afforded by the semicircular layout of Elizabethan as well as Greek
and Roman theatre architecture, obviously fitted an autocratic system
of society, and the addition of elevated boxes and balconies round
the sides, and the royal box as the focal point, helped to promote
hierarchical distinctions. It has continued as the dominant form of
Western theatre for 300 years. Princes, so numerous in Germany, could
hardly find a theatrical setting more suited to impress the populace
with the glory of their crowned heads, and they took it to their
generous hearts.

As there was no more spectacular type of theatrical performance to
demonstrate the splendours of the Baroque era than opera, the major
theatre buildings of this period were, in fact, opera-houses, such as
those in Vienna (1652), Regensburg (1653), Munich (1654), Dresden
(1667), Hamburg (1678), Hanover (1690), Berlin (1742), Mannheim
(1742), and the Markgräfliche Opernhaus at Bayreuth (1748) which
survives intact, while the exquisite little Rococo theatre in Munich
(1751–3) built by François Cuvilliés, the French architect whose name
it bears, was destroyed in 1944 but faithfully reconstructed in 1958 on
a neighbouring site, using the original fittings which had been
preserved. Its sloping stalls floor could be raised to the level of the stage
to form a hall for court festivities. Complicated stage mechanisms with

pulleys, winches, grooves, traps and flies were common, and their
sophistication was matched by the flamboyant decoration of the
auditorium and the elaborate scenery. The extravagance of the
Baroque age, later reinforced by neoclassicist monumentality, may be
said to have characterized German theatre architecture to this day.

In contrast to commercial theatres in London, New York and elsewhere which are integrated into a row of ordinary houses, German
theatres were, and still are, usually free-standing structures, not only
because of their large size, which favours a self-contained site, but
also because they were meant to be majestic temples both to the
Muses and to their gracious benefactor, the ruling prince and his
house. The desire to make them focal points in their urban settings,
facing public gardens or a square, coupled with the availability of
space and the ruler's munificence, determined the magnificence of their
exterior and interior architecture, the grandeur of their façades, complete with statuary of the appropriate classical gods and illustrious
contemporaries, the spaciousness and luxurious decoration of the
foyers. A theatre had to be not only handsome and festive but *re-
präsentativ*, and the palatial character of court theatres was emulated
by the aldermanic councils in the case of Free City states like Hamburg, and even by the citizens of provincial towns wanting to boast
their own theatre, though not all of them established resident companies to play in them.

Nor were *all* playhouses constructed with royal or public funds.
Germany's earliest private theatre building, seating around 800, was
erected in remote Königsberg in 1755 for Konrad Ernst Ackermann
(1712–72), the principal of an itinerant troupe, entirely at his own
expense, although the site was donated by the King of Prussia. He
moved on a year later, after the outbreak of the Seven Years' War,
and in 1765, again at his own expense, opened another theatre in
Hamburg. It was this building which was soon taken over by a
consortium of Hamburg businessmen for the ambitious scheme of a
permanent (though in the event short-lived) repertory theatre—the
'Nationaltheater', which Lessing, its literary consultant, sought to
promote as a civic antidote to ducal dominance and French influence :
and this was what the name implied. Paradoxically, in view of the
connotation of government subsidy which the term carries today, it
was a venture of private patronage. Although it was a failure, it was

followed by a number of other private theatres, owned either by individuals, or by shareholders, or by town councils but run by lessees. In 1824, the rather grand Königsstädtische Theater in Berlin was opened as a private competitor to the Royal Theatre, which had been set up in 1796; but the rival was not permitted to put on classics and had to confine itself to entertainment of a more popular type. By the end of the 19th century, there were fourteen private theatres in the Prussian capital—about as many as there are in the Western part of the city today—and a similar situation evolved in most of the other major centres. However, despite their great importance for the rich variety of theatrical life, the predominant and pace-setting line in Germany has undoubtedly been that of the state and municipal theatres.

As Germany lacked an obvious centre, such as Paris or London, itinerant troupes settled down wherever an opportunity presented itself. An appointment as 'court comedians', together with a subvention, granted in 1751 by Duke Christian Louis II of Mecklenburg to the Schönemann company of players, carried with it an obligation to play at Schwerin for eight months each year, and this background security enabled Konrad Ekhof (1720–78), the eminent actor and champion of his profession, to form an 'Academy' with careful precepts for the art of acting and strict rules for the duties and rights (including voting rights) of members, and he later even envisaged a pension scheme for actors. The first real court theatre with its own resident company came into being in 1775 when Duke Ernest of Gotha retained Ekhof's troupe in his little Ruritanian capital, where, however, it could not survive the death of its dynamic director.

Meanwhile, in 1776, Emperor Joseph II had formally established the Vienna Burgtheater as a 'Court and National Theatre' with a directive to perform 'good and regular original plays as well as fine translations from other languages', selecting them 'with a view not to quantity but to quality'. The theatre, financially attached to the imperial household, had a nobleman as figurehead and his deputy as administrative manager, while the artistic running was in the hands of a committee of five, each of whom took charge for a month in rotation—a remarkably democratic constitution. Although it was abandoned after a while, it seems in retrospect like a foreshadowing of the tendency towards collective or collegiate responsibility that was to become popular in Germany around 1970. However, the uncrowned head of the Vienna theatre was the crowned head himself, the Habsburg Emperor, whose lively interest extended even to details such as the choice of plays and the hiring of actors. In 1791, a former Minister of a Ruritanian duchy in central Germany, Goethe, assumed the direction of the Weimar court theatre and actively exercised it for twenty-six years.

An equally influential example of direct dynastic involvement is that of Duke George II of Meiningen (1826–1914) who, after his accession in 1866, gradually took over personal control of his court theatre, went so far beyond the princely pale as to marry an actress and, assisted by her, welded and ran an ensemble in which even the highest-paid members were obliged occasionally to play walk-on parts. Although the dozen or so new productions, including several new plays, which he put on each season offered ample variety, a capital of a mere 13,000 souls obviously could not sustain a theatre throughout the year, so the company took to touring to show its highly elaborate work with its careful attention to authenticity to enthusiastic audiences in other cities, although the Meiningen style subsequently degenerated to the over-ornate bathos still known derogatorily as *Meiningerei*.

Strong ensemble work and literary quality had also created the reputation of the Nationaltheater at Mannheim in the time of the young Schiller, when it was run as a ducal theatre by Freiherr Friedrich von Dalberg, the President of the Court of Appeal, who also introduced 'committee' meetings (or seminars) on the Vienna model. But in 1817 the Mannheim municipality took over part of the expense, and in 1839 assumed complete control of the Nationaltheater—which has retained its historic name to this day, although it has never been any more 'national' in the modern English sense than the English Stage Company's home in London is a royal court theatre. It thus became the first of the *Stadttheater* or municipal playhouses which were to proliferate throughout the country.

This completed the dominant pattern of subsidized permanent court or municipal theatres with resident companies serving a fairly small population with a choice of plays (and often operas as well) performed in repertory. Public patronage provided a large measure of security to both theatres and actors. In 1871, German actors, to protect and promote their interests, organized the *Genossenschaft deutscher Bühnenangehöriger*, the German version of Equity, the actors' trade union. Twenty-five years earlier, in 1846, an association of managements, the *Deutsche Bühnenverein*, was formed (and its comprehensive compilations are the source of most of the statistical data given below).

This set-up has become so much part of the social fabric of the nation that even the revolution after the First World War, when the Emperor had to abdicate along with all the other kings, granddukes and dukes who had been maintaining their playhouses and operas, left the system virtually intact. Monarchic munificence was simply replaced by republican munificence for the former court theatres, now renamed *Staatstheater*; and the new Social Democratic ministries forking out the old princely sums could take comfort from the knowledge that the theatres they had inherited were already under public control either by city councils or individual states. Not, however, by the central State. It is an incidental but very noteworthy result of the traditional structure that no German theatre has ever been transferred to the control of the central government of the Reich in Berlin, let alone to that of the present Federal Government in Bonn, whose constitutional authority specifically excludes *Kulturhoheit* (jurisdiction over cultural affairs) which is reserved to the *Länder*. In the past, German theatre, like that of other countries, has from time to time been subject to censorship and prosecutions for blasphemy or *lèse-majésté* : but within local limits. On the whole, its autocratic origin has, paradoxically, ensured its freedom from any—or at least from any systematic—influence or interference from the centre of political power in normal times.

The exception, of course, was the Nazi duodecennium when Goebbels, without altering the administrative and budgetary framework, tied theatres firmly to the massive yoke of his Ministry of Propaganda. At the same time, he was clever enough, albeit for purposes of political prestige and efficacy, to maintain and cultivate a high standard of performance, even in war-time, and it may be that this helped to stress and to strengthen the importance of German theatre and its will to survive when Nazi policies ended up by getting nearly all German theatres destroyed.

Wir sind noch einmal davongekommen—literally : We have survived—was the German title of Thornton Wilder's *The Skin of Our Teeth* which soon after the war packed houses throughout Germany with shabbily-clad people torn excruciatingly yet deliciously between a yearning that the performance would go on forever and the gnawing hunger for a warm bowl of watery vegetable soup and a piece of branny brown bread. Houses? Makeshift ones, of course, with acting platforms and hard-backed chairs installed in any old hall, or at best in a still usable wing of a bombed-out theatre building. More than 100 German playhouses had been damaged or destroyed, and only fifteen are reckoned to have remained intact, most of them in smaller places such as Baden-Baden (1862), Bayreuth (Festspielhaus, 1876), Wiesbaden (1894), Fürth (1902) or Göttingen (1890) where the Deutsche Theater, under Heinz Hilpert's directorship, became one of the beacons of the German theatre in the early post-war years. Berlin, cut off and cut up, had lost the position it had enjoyed as the focal point in the German theatrical landscape during its period of being imperial and Nazi capital.

Apart from this, the pre-war situation was restored with minimal delay. Outside observers were struck by the phenomenon of a totally ruined nation flocking to see shows within months after the collapse in 1945. Actors, musicians and other theatrical staff, returning from prison camps and wanting to work in their own professions again, formed companies and needled the authorities for support. There was no doubt of the eager support of audiences who had few escapes from the grime and gloom of reality—no television, few books because of the paper shortage, and not even beer worthy of the name. There was some hesitation, but not much, among civil authorities about according the patching up of theatres or temporary theatres very nearly the same priority as housing, hospitals, schools and industrial plant, and since the reform of the German currency in 1948 set the 'economic miracle' in motion, well over 200 theatres in West Germany and West Berlin alone have been repaired, renovated, improved, expanded, rebuilt or totally built from scratch. Apart from reconstructions in the former style, like that of the neoclassicist Nationaltheater (opera-house) in Munich (1811–25, rebuilt 1963 for 60 million marks), Germany now has the highest density of the most modern theatre buildings anywhere in the world.

What is less certain is whether they are truly up to date in terms of recent developments in the art they are meant to serve. The materials are new—concrete and glass—and they confidently speak the architectural idiom of the mid-20th century, often with flair, aplomb, ingenuity, distinction, even originality and considerable aesthetic success. But planners had to face complex questions of expedience and logistics and find their solutions on the basis of circumstances: the location and size of the site, the size of the population, the funds available, perhaps retention of the well-loved façade of a burnt-out pre-war building, local traditions and ambitions such as the existence of a resident drama company as well as of an opera ensemble, an orchestra and a ballet troupe, all of which may exist in a small German town. There might be

(1) one building containing two auditoria, or even three (the smallest one for experimental productions), but all sharing the same set of offices, workshops and stores, either on the premises or on a different site;

(2) separate buildings for drama and opera (and again perhaps a third one for experimental work), with supporting facilities either in each building, or only in one but also serving the other;

(3) a multi-purpose theatre used alternately for drama and opera —which presents special problems because of their differing requirements but is often found attractive in a smaller community, even one with a drama company only, because it can then accommodate a visiting opera production;

(4) a building solely for the use of visiting companies, with no need for workshops and stores.

Whatever shape and form was chosen by the authorities and architects, great care was almost invariably given not only to the impressive character of the building but also to its social function as a meeting place which is enhanced by the efficiency and elegance of the accessories and preliminaries of an evening at the theatre. The visitor, having passed the box-office, comes upon a long series of alcoves in the vestibule, fully staffed with uniformed ladies and equipped with hooks, hangers and numbered discs, frequently twinned with seat numbers, so that ticket-holders can know precisely where they will find reserved space for their coats and do not have to queue. The foyer, which lies behind and usually above, is totally different from its English namesake, that entrance-hall cramped by the high commercial value of space around Piccadilly Circus and Times Square. A German foyer, directly adjoining or encircling the auditorium, is a vast, resplendent ambulatory where everyone can meet and chat, eat and drink before stepping through one of numerous doors into the inner sanctum of the dramatic cult. Inside, the hierarchical implications of seating have usually been minimized, either by avoiding boxes and balconies altogether and finding the extra room in the upper part at the back of an 'integrated' stalls area, or by building wide-flung, all-embracing semicircles. One of the planners' watchwords has been 'democratization'.

In the service of the other watchword, 'communication', sight-lines have been improved and shortened by such means as a steeper rake of the stalls floor and more strongly curved rows of seats in an auditorium which bulges outward from the corners of the stage to form a roughly oval shape and thus permits a reduction of its longitudinal axis while accommodating a considerable number of spectators and also improving the acoustics. The old rigid separation between stage and stalls is played down, for example, at Bochum (1953) where the architect, Gerhard Graubner, installed a curved safety-curtain in front of, rather than behind, the forestage (which can be uncovered to provide an orchestra-pit) and thus enabled sets and scenes to reach out through the proscenium arch towards the audience.

However, the communication has remained a limited one. The basic fact is that, generally, the old proscenium arch has been re-erected and the orchestra-moat re-excavated. No doubt fire regulations imposed restrictions by requiring a curtaining-off of stage and props from the auditorium. Whatever the reasons, ideas such as theatre-in-the-round have been neglected, not to speak of more way-out flights of fancy like the plan for a 'total theatre' proposed in 1927 by Walter Gropius, the Bauhaus director. There are, it is true, some ingenious solutions such as the theatre at Ulm—the place of Furttenbach's innovation of three centuries ago and now a city of just under 100,000—with its two auditoria designed by Fritz Schäfer (1966), the smaller of which is a hexagonal bowl with variable floor levels allowing infinite seating and stage permutations—scenes can be arranged on any of the sides, in the centre, across the room, or even all around the audience. But it is an audience of a mere 200, and such novel halls for dramatic experiments are exceptional among the vast number of new German playhouses.

Critics have argued that after the near-total annihilation of 1945 the unique opportunity was missed to revolutionize theatre building—and, with it, theatre—instead of just modernizing its style and technology, and that the new forms the authorities and their architects opted for are essentially nothing more than restorative adaptations of the old, although the electronic stage-machinery, the lighting and all the other gadgetry is no doubt the best that money can buy, and certainly the envy of many managers, directors, actors and particularly designers elsewhere.

The gadgetry and all the trappings and trimmings—this may well be the rub. Planners and their clients, the theatre directors, seem on occasion to have been obsessed with the wonders of their expensive new toys, and there is a danger that producers, wishing to make full use of the tax-payers' generous gifts, may end up devaluing the importance of the actor and the import of the spoken word in favour of superficial show effects, or trying to out-illusion the illusionistic theatre of the past. This would be anachronistic in an age when television and the wide screen can use the art of escapist make-believe with even greater refinement, and when theatre in its more advanced forms has reacted by going back to stylization and alienation, simplicity and poverty, and sometimes to direct involvement of its audience as in a market-place. This is not to suggest that contemporary German theatre has indeed succumbed to superficial super-spectacularism. But the hand of the director—always the strongest force in the German theatre—has been further strengthened by the acquisition of this new tool-box of tricks with which to carve a production after his own image and imagination: away from the actors and away from the author's intentions. It is a fact, too, that the German theatre in this period of its amazing technological perfection has, so far, thrown up few of the playwrights who have made decisive contributions to the progress of drama and theatre internationally.

It may turn out to have been the planners' tragedy that they had to do the bulk of their building work in the fifties and sixties and could not foresee the subsequent development of theatrical art which their hardware has probably hindered rather than helped. It may one day appear that their majestic palaces, built at astronomical expense, had, almost as soon as they were finished, turned into a huge herd of white elephants. Yet in 1974, at a time when German theatres, including some of the most aggressively progressive ones, are rediscovering plays of the late 19th century for contemporary consumption, just as London is reviving plays of the twenties, it seems too early to say. It may well be that the new buildings in their massive presence help to cement the traditional pattern of organization, which has lately shown signs of strain and entered a phase of uncertainty and attempts at structural modification. So far, however, its basic features remain unchanged.

In 1971–2, there were, in seventy-seven towns and cities in West Germany and West Berlin, eighty-six publicly-controlled theatre institutions with 192 halls between them—including those for opera and ballet, which it is difficult to separate neatly from drama since they often share the same building and budget, part of the staff and various statistics. There were also seventy-eight private theatres, most of which, too, receive some, though much smaller, contributions from public funds. In a nation of 61 million people, this makes a total of 270 theatres—counting buildings rather than companies, and excluding commercial touring troupes, folkloristic drama companies, satirical cabaret ensembles and 'free groups' on the Fringe (which do exist in Germany but are probably less important than those in Britain, perhaps because the universal availability of other theatres at subsidized prices renders them less attractive for both actors and audiences.

Although most established theatres have many characteristics in common, it is impossible to speak of any one format as *the* typical German theatre: so great is the variety. Out of the 192 institutional theatres, thirty are run by one of the eleven *Länder* or states which make up the Federal Republic of Germany plus West Berlin. Because most of them are erstwhile court theatres there may be more than one of them in a *Land* which incorporates several of the old ducal territories, such as Hesse which has (and has to pay for) the former court theatres at Wiesbaden (the present state capital), Darmstadt and Kassel. These *Staatstheater* enjoy a certain stately prestige, but neighbouring theatres run by local authorities are not necessarily second-best in size, standard and standing. There are 106 of these municipal theatres, generically known as *Stadttheater* and controlled and financed by city councils, often with minor contributions from their state government. In a third group are fifty-six theatres which, although basically subsidized from the public purse and generally regarded just as much as community institutions as the rest, are legally constituted as limited companies or some other form of autonomous organization (*GmbH, AG, e.V.*, etc.) for reasons of accountancy and budgetary convenience such as the fact that they are entitled to receive direct payment for television recordings instead of these fees being paid to their sponsoring authorities. Among them are such major institutions as the Deutsche Schauspielhaus in Hamburg and the Düsseldorfer Schauspielhaus as well as several theatres which are shared by two or more neighbouring towns, in some cases as a result of a recent merger for reasons of economy.

Similarly, this is the legal structure most often chosen for a rather less glamorous sub-group known as *Landesbühnen*—touring companies maintained jointly by a *Land* government and one or more local councils for the purpose of serving communities without resident ensembles of their own. But some of these places without a theatre company do have a theatre building with a fairly regular programme arranged by the *Kultur* officer in the town hall and made up entirely by visiting companies—either the *Landesbühne*, or ensembles from other places in the region (whose managements like to increase their incomes and reputations by operating a system of *Abstecher*, i.e. short-range excursions), or one of the private touring companies.

This vast set-up is supported by equally vast sums of money which in 1971 amounted to:

Income in German marks

	Number of seats	Ticket, programme, advertising sales, etc.	Subsidies from public funds	Subsidies per head of population
192 institutional theatres	c. 120,000	171,203,000	654,642,000	32.99
78 resident private theatres	c. 25,000	no information	11,354,000	0.95
Total subsidies			DM 665,996,000	

This is the equivalent (inevitably very approximate in that year of major currency fluctuations) of $200 million or £80 million—about twice as much as the figure quoted in the beginning. In the same period, the Arts Council of Great Britain as the agency dispensing government subsidies to the arts in a country of roughly similar size and population, was spending £5,731,248 on drama, ballet and opera (the latter accounting for half of it). The National Theatre in London was receiving £415,724: just over a third of the 9,302,000 marks (c. £1,125,000) for the Berlin Schiller-Theater which is just one of several companies of similar size. For a true comparison of the total, of course, one would have to take into account the subsidies which local and regional sources in Britain have recently been adding to those from the central government. In Germany, too, the Federal Government does contribute some grants to theatre, usually for special purposes such as a tour abroad, but these amounted in 1971 to just over 2.6 million marks, or 0.4 per cent of the total.

In no case, however, does public 'control' extend to more than the annual allocation of subsidies, some budgetary supervision, and the appointment of the director known as *Intendant*—or *General-intendant* in the case of a large multilateral theatre with two or three auditoria and ensembles for opera, ballet and drama. Except where a theatre's constitution provides for the director to be elected by the ensemble, he is chosen, from a number of applicants, by a committee of the sponsoring authority, usually after considerable public airing and eager debating in the press, both locally and nationally. His contract is likely to be for three to five years but may be extended. The Director is normally a director, less often a distinguished actor with a taste for directing productions, but has full executive control, assisted by an administrative or business manager. There are some rare cases where this relationship is reversed, with the artistic director being subordinate to a managerial overlord. There is also a *Dramaturg* (i.e. literary manager), or several of them, to assist the *Intendant* in all artistic matters, from the choice and textual preparation of plays to the editing and printing of programmes and posters. There are departmental heads (drama, opera, design, etc.) and often one or more additional resident directors. But it is very much the *Intendant* who is king, and with whose charismatic character and policies a German theatre is as closely identified in the public mind as an American administration is with its President. It is he who appoints the artistic staff, part of which he may bring with him from his previous appointment in another city.

A drama ensemble is likely to number around thirty, considerably more in a few leading theatres with a large auditorium and a smaller one for more intimate or experimental plays. A few actors and actresses, and directors as well, are brought in as 'guests' for a particular production to give it the lustre of a star, or if no suitable talent is available on the resident staff. The majority are given salaried employment, usually for a season (or *Spielzeit*, which means a year minus the long summer break) but they often stay much longer, and after ten years they have won the right to be kept on, although they may be switched to other functions, even to desk jobs, until they are ripe for a retirement pension. The total number of artistic, clerical and manual staff in German institutional theatres is around 24,000.

The security of subsidies and salaries encourages experiment and guarantees the 'right to fail'—within the limits of the sponsoring authority's patience. Another important result is that members of a permanent company, working together in a constantly changing repertoire, are able to develop a group mind or 'ensemble spirit' resulting in closely dovetailed acting which is not easily monopolized by an overbearing star. At the same time, the individuals' experience in a wide variety of parts, between which they have to alternate almost daily, makes for fresher performances and greater versatility than actors are likely to develop playing long runs on a commercial basis. On the other hand, under the German system actors are not normally picked for one specific part, or allowed as much time to enter under a character's skin in rehearsal and during the limited run, and to achieve that natural perfection in which English acting, at its best, is unparalleled. Another danger, for the individual actor as much as for the theatre as a whole, is a certain laxity and lassitude, a sort of *Staatstheater* blues, that comes with job security in a theatrical establishment not dependent on box-office success.

Attempts are now afoot to reform and revitalize the traditional set-up by mobilizing the intellectual and social resources within the company and challenging the autocratic position of the *Intendant*. Such tendencies are inspired by the 'collective' working style promoted by Brecht in his Berliner Ensemble, and by the general drift in German industrial and intellectual organizations, from universities to publishing firms, towards democratic *Mitbestimmung*, i.e. co-determination or participation in decision-making. It was with a production of a Brecht play in October 1970 that the Schaubühne, a small private (but two-thirds subsidized) theatre in West Berlin, opened as a collective allowing all members of its staff, including cloakroom ladies, a say on such questions as new appointments, salaries and the choice of plays. Their views gained a direct influence on the underlying philosophy as well as on the details of the Schaubühne's committed, provocative productions; but the glowing reputation which it soon won for itself is largely due to the personality of its brilliant director, Peter Stein, with whom the Schaubühne became just as much identified as any other German theatre is with its *Intendant*.

An even bolder initiative was taken in a large municipal theatre, in Frankfurt, where the post of *Generalintendant* was abolished when it fell vacant in 1972. The opera became a separate entity under its musical director but continued to share administrative and material facilities with drama which came under the responsibility of a board of three—the chief director and the chief designer, both appointed for four years by the city council, plus an actor co-opted annually by the ensemble as a third director of equal status. Here, too, the ensemble itself—but not the technical staff—assumed an important role in formulating general and artistic policy. The theatre began to emerge from its earlier doldrums. However, it was soon noted that only a handful of the more active members were dominating the discussions and that a certain weariness had set in, and in 1974, the managing triumvirate, while remaining responsible legally, was enlarged for internal purposes to form an eight-man board, mostly by co-opting several actors so as to strengthen the links with the ensemble.

A smaller company in Frankfurt, the Theater am Turm, financed jointly by the *Land* and the city, had been operating for two years as a collective with a three-man executive, and had achieved considerable artistic success, when the two artistic members of the executive dropped out. In 1974, Rainer Werner Fassbinder took over as sole artistic director, and the arrival of this brilliant young playwright and director, arguably the brightest hope in German drama since Brecht but also known to be a somewhat capricious genius, was widely interpreted as spelling the end of the company's participatory character. A roughly similar experiment in Mannheim petered out quickly.

Teething troubles, of course, were bound to occur, and whatever one may think of the practical merits of such wide distribution of responsibilities in so complex an organization, all this internal ferment cannot but be a healthy antidote to any complacency into which German theatres might have been falling after the restoration of their stately pleasure-domes.

Of course, filling close on 150,000 seats seven nights a week is a constant challenge to managements, even in a country where nearly 80 per cent of the total theatre budgets is provided from public funds, and just over 20 per cent through the box-office. It was worrying when in the late sixties audiences dropped by about 10 per cent—just after all the great and glittering theatres had been completed. Had their number and size perhaps been a miscalculation in this new age of television? There were some economy measures, some mergers and even closures. But attendance figures soon picked up again, and by 1970–1 had reached an average of 71.4 per cent of the seating capacity for drama in institutional theatres—which represents 8,745,000 people, or a total of 17,294,000 if opera and other events are included, with a further 4,496,000 in private theatres. Audiences went on increasing the following year in most places. The steepest jump, by over 10 per cent to 78.5 per cent, occurred at Bochum, where Peter Zadek, the recently appointed *Intendant,* had gone all out to capture new social sections in this hard-working industrial city by such means as a nude show thrown into Tankred Dorst's gaudily jazzed-up stage version of Fallada's novel *Kleiner Mann, was nun?* (*Little Man—What Now?*) Yet, he managed to raise the proportion of industrial workers in the auditorium to just about 1 per cent. This estimate—Zadek's own—seems worth quoting in view of the scarcity of definite data on the class components of theatre audiences.

However, if German theatre cannot attract every layer of society, it would be very far from the truth to think that it was still a preserve of the more well-to-do and educated bourgeoisie, as it was during the 19th century and beyond. Theatre has been put within the reach of everyone by a system of subsidized ticket sales whose extraordinary scope and complexity far surpasses that of 'party bookings' in London as well as that of New York 'theater parties'. True, ordinary seat prices for drama may range from about 4 marks to as much as 25 marks (in a few extreme cases). But 'ordinary' tickets number a mere quarter of the total: the casual visitor paying the full price is anything but the ordinary German theatregoer.

For one thing, virtually every theatre runs its own *Abonnement,* or subscription scheme, offering, at reductions of up to 30 per cent, various combinations of selections from the year's productions: a cross-section of everything, opera only, drama only, even classics only or modern plays only, often tied to a specified day of the week, sometimes allowing a choice between alternative productions from the chosen short-list. There are cheap students' tickets. There are several theatre-goers' societies delivering about 5 million attendances a year at subsidized reduced prices—an indirect subsidy to the theatre. The oldest and largest of these organizations, the Volksbühne, goes back to 1889, when a theatre in Berlin began to put on members-only performances—rather like British theatre clubs. This grew into a vast movement linked with the political left, selling tickets for special club performances at reduced but *uniform* prices, with the actual seat allocated by lot. Its local associations throughout the country often provide special coaches to take members to the theatre in another town, and the choice is widened by the offer of plays from the repertoires of several theatres. Managements do not regard them as unwelcome rivals to their own subscription schemes. After all, they do bring in crowds of customers on whose constancy the theatre can rely almost regardless of the type, quality and success of plays and productions. It is this virtual independence of box-office success that enables German theatre to treat entertainment value as a secondary consideration and to cultivate its aspirations to be a 'moral institution', as Schiller postulated in his famous Mannheim lecture in 1784.

The fact that the majority of seats is sold at reduced rates and that nearly four fifths of the theatres' budgets are provided by subsidies has recently led to the suggestion that admission charges might be abolished altogether. The loss in income, it was argued, might be offset by the saving in box-office work. However, there is some fear that free tickets might turn out to keep people away rather than attract them as regular subscriptions do, and in any case, there would be grave damage to the private theatres which could not afford to admit people for nothing.

German private playhouses differ from English and American commercial theatres in that most of them enjoy a certain amount of public money and have a more clearly delineated identity shaped by the personality of the director, who may himself be an actor or a producer rather than an impresario. What they have in common with their London and New York counterparts is that casts are usually hired for individual productions, which are then played *en suite* rather than in repertory, and that the theatres tend to be compact in size and to concentrate on lighter entertainment, leaving expensive heavyweight drama to their institutional neighbours.

Another theatrical vehicle which started rolling in the early nineteen-fifties and has since grown into a real bandwagon is the touring theatres—not so much companies as managements which hire a producer and a cast, or occasionally a complete production from a permanent theatre after it has finished its local run, and send their package round the country. The actors are freelance or are making use of their contractual right to take extended leave from their normal employers. Fees of up to 1,500 marks for a single appearance can persuade even top artists of Martin Held's stature to face the rigours of the road for, say, three months, during which some may earn more than they do in a whole season (autumn to summer) at their regular theatre. The attraction is even greater for slightly fading stars of stage and screen, including retired *Intendanten*, who are still household names able to draw audiences of up to 95 per cent capacity. Smaller towns are the chief clients. Local authorities, especially those without a company of their own, purchase such mail-order productions to the tune of between 3,500 and 7,200 marks per performance, enabling even these purely commercial enterprises to benefit handsomely from public patronage. An estimated 125 touring productions, including operas, are now available each year. Plays are likely to be well-tried successes, including classics and other ambitious works, and the proportion of major contemporary plays has lately been growing, so that touring groups provide a valuable addition to the country's dramatic fare.

If it is public subsidy which makes the stupendous number of plays and productions possible, it is the system of subscription and society schemes which makes that variety compulsory. The number of performances of each production—about twenty or twenty-five on average —is naturally limited by the size of the local community, and subscribers or society members have a right to expect eight or more offerings in their chosen field per season. This requires another first night every three to six weeks at each theatre, adding up to a national total of some 1,000 new productions a year in drama alone. Many of them, of course, are of identical plays—classics or currently fashionable works; but there is also the ambition of every *Intendant* to stick out from among his colleagues and attract the attention of the press by launching a world premiere or, with a foreign play, a German premiere, although occasionally some of the thunder has already been stolen by a 'German-language premiere' in Austria or Switzerland. It is an ambition which may often be wasteful and sometimes give undue support to an unworthy play. But this competitive tradition, inherited from the princely patronage of the past, also encourages experiment, variety and, as a result, an unrivalled interest in the international dramatic scene. Subsidies and subscriptions may not, to adapt Hardenberg's phrase, have made Germany's theatre the best in the world. But it is, for better or worse, the best that money can buy.

Klaus Völker : THE NEW THEATRE BUILDINGS

I

One of Brecht's most important maxims was 'Don't latch on to the good old, but to the bad new'. The wretchedness of the theatre in West Germany has its cause chiefly in the decisive resumption of the 'good old', when, after 1945, there were opportunities everywhere for a new beginning. Many performers today enjoy their memories of the immediate post-war years, when theatre was still an indispensable necessity, a sort of embassy for its spectators. Plays were put on in cellars and emergency shelters. Make-shift halls were heated by briquettes brought by the audience. The actors' inspiration had survived the Nazi years, but they had neither artistic nor political consciousness. The first play to be performed in Berlin after the collapse was a farce, *Der Raub der Sabinerinnen (The Rape of the Sabines)*. The official beginning was more pretentious : Lessing's classic *Nathan der Weise*. It was a significant dual inauguration, illustrating the German post-war theatre's characteristic combination of culture and commercial appeal.

Those years saw the foundation of the much prized 'pluralistic' programming which is still so obstinately adhered to. The need to catch up on plays by German and foreign writers who had been banned by the Third Reich displaced the development of purposive playwriting. Quantity took the place of quality. There was no real starting anew, because the means of performance were the same as they were under the Nazis. It was important that there should be some critical thinking about the new situation and an attempt to develop different structural principles. But the social function of the theatre was ignored. It was precisely then that the theatre ought to have sought a different relationship with its audience. With increasing prosperity the theatre was needed less and less as a dispenser of solace, a substitution for happiness; it again became a solemn event and an abode of education.

Symptomatic for the immediate post-war theatre was the attitude of Achim von Biel, head of both Kurfürstendamm theatres in Berlin's West End. He explained his programme, which embraced Anouilh, Georg Kaiser, Bridie, Schiller, Rattigan, Goldoni, Chekhov and O'Neill, as follows: 'I will not be so presumptuous as to talk of education—or possibly re-education—in respect of such productions. I am satisfied if, by means of the theatre, attention is drawn to *people*. If the theatre has a task to fulfil, it might be this.' Boleslaw Barlog, Gustav Gründgens, Karl Heinz Stroux thought no differently, and almost all the Intendants of West German theatres endorse these sentiments year after year in the brochures put out to woo their season-ticket subscribers.

In 1948, the critic Friedrich Luft was still protesting against the 'anachronistic scandal' which he had to endure on the Berlin stages, the result of the sort of triflingly non-committal conception of theatre purveyed by Achim von Biel: 'No wonder that in their enforced aimlessness the theatres tied themselves down more and more to security, to the familiar, to the time-honoured Theatre of Inertia. Not a truly contemporary theatre.' Returning from exile in America, the director Berthold Viertel passed a similar verdict on the mindless, stereotyped theatre which he encountered in Berlin. 'The style of presentation I have seen at work simply evades anything dramatic.... A cold kind of fervour is audible, but it sounds frozen—a false objectivity left over from Nazi rhetoric. That is bad enough. But even more problematic is the acting style, the choreographic element, which has the outward effect of completeness, postulating a neatly ordered world and setting in motion a smooth machinery of illusion: a world without perspective, without half-light, picturesquely conceived and picturesquely painted.... What this play-acting lacks is any sense of reality, any penetrating motivation or characterisation, any firm and forceful statement.'

At the end of 1947, Brecht returned to Europe from America, determined to resume his interrupted theatre work in the light of the altered social conditions since his exile in 1933. He settled first in Zurich, though from the start his goal was Berlin. First he wanted to explore the opportunities for work there, as well as the political circumstances he had to reckon with. So 'a residence outside Germany' seemed suitable for the time being. In the summer of 1948 he went to a production by Heinz Hilpert in Constance, just over the German-Swiss border. In his memoir of Brecht, Max Frisch has described the fury which seized the playwright after this, his first trip to a German theatre since his return. The vocabulary of the actors of the 'German theatre of Constance', their self-importance and their arrogance reduced him to speechlessness until a remark by the actor Wilfried Seyferth, who had come with him from Zurich, brought him to bursting point: 'Seyferth couldn't understand what was wrong with Brecht. The vocabulary of these survivors, however unencumbered they might be, their behaviour on stage, their cheerful lack of presentiment, the brazenness with which they simply carried on as though it were merely their houses which had been destroyed, their artistic contentment, their premature harmony with their own country—all this was worse than feared.'

Of all the returned exiles Brecht was the only one to succeed in making a really new beginning. At the end of October 1948 he went to Berlin. He had been invited to produce his own play *Mutter Courage* at the Deutsches Theater. He saw that, even in the eastern sector of the city of Berlin, the consequences of the Nazi period had not yet been overcome. On top of that there was the need to combat the old biases on the Communist side, the bad disciples and idolaters of Stanislavsky with their dogmatically interpreted Socialist Realism. No one at that time wanted to give him a theatre of his own, but it was finally agreed, principally at the instigation of the Intendant, Wolfgang Langhoff, and of the Soviet culture officer, Alexander Dymchitz, that an independent troupe should be set up with, for the time being, the right to play in the Deutsches Theater. Helene Weigel busied herself with the organizational problems, while Brecht waited in Zurich for a definite decision.

Brecht was not welcomed with open arms: he had to overcome many obstacles to gain his theatre. He knew why he was going to East Berlin and what was his due once there. His decision was the only possible and sensible one open to him, for, as a playwright outside the GDR he could not have achieved the artistic results that were yielded by the founding of the Berliner Ensemble.

II

The German theatre's lack of any real new beginning after 1945 is borne out by the buildings in which the performances take place. They were rebuilt, not new-built. Yet only pure architectural reconstructions, like the Nationaltheater in Munich (built 1811; reconstructed 1963), or the Deutsche Staatsoper in East Berlin (built 1743; reconstructed 1955) emerge as anything beautiful and fit for their purpose. The brand new buildings are expressions of the compromises between the artistic ambitions of the architects and the wishes of the municipal authorities. Rebuilding meant a continuation of the old style of theatre under a modern coat of paint. The architect's task was to create multi-purpose halls not only for the production of plays and operas but over and above that for the most varied aspects of a repertoire accommodating all styles and genres. The architects created memorials to themselves and the city fathers—temples of the arts, which solidified the theatre as an institution and induced the setting up of an enormous administrative machinery which has meanwhile become a straitjacket for every kind of creative work in the theatre.

There is not one single theatre building that has been planned and built according to the ideas of the people who are working in it. The architects charged with the rebuilding of the theatres were hardly ever conversant with the working methods of the various people concerned in a theatrical production. Their designs simply corresponded to their views on the theatre and were limited to those aspects which had to do with the theatrical 'event' but not with the structuring of a play or with problems of production. Imagination was replaced by ostentatious displays of applied art. The builders of those splendid halls, which carry the bourgeois concept of possession over into the realms of culture, merely showed themselves as poor disciples of the civic theatre architects of the 19th century. The recently built theatres, which are mostly self-enclosed structures, represent vast monuments to art without regard to the city's cultural life. Their location has been dictated by the laws of tradition or by the politics of town-planning. At first sight, the German system of civic theatres seems imposing to a foreign observer, comprising as it does a magnificent number of advantages, which enable continuous employment in the theatre and the use of the means of production on a large scale. The disadvantages consist in the sluggishness of this system and its lack of flexibility. It

considerably restricts creative initiative, demanding from each participant as time goes by only one task, which guarantees the functioning
of the system and only serves to sanction the end already achieved.
Experiments are allowed only so long as they don't call into question
the structure of the theatre.

Meanwhile the individual theatre companies are subsidized public
service industries like the post and the railway, whose constantly
rising budgets stand in inverse proportion to the quality of their
service. The inimical bureaucratization of the theatre has its origins in
the anachronistic structure which has allowed the portion of money
set aside for the productions themselves to shrink to a minimum.
Nearly 80 per cent of the theatre companies' total budget is swallowed
up by standing costs; that is, almost all the monetary resources are
already used up before a single performance takes place.

The more lavishly endowed a theatre building is, and the more it
outwardly manifests its function, the higher are the costs arising from
its use and upkeep. Each wall of glass which has to be cleaned by
window-cleaners makes inroads on the money which would otherwise
go towards scenery and costumes. Each installation of special technical equipment, demanding time-consuming structural alterations
and umpteen personnel to service it, is an additional burden on the
company and needlessly reduces rehearsal time, which as a rule is
already too short. The architects must unquestionably share the
responsibility for the bad working conditions in the theatres that they
have designed and built.

Inseparable from the problem of failing to begin anew after 1945
is the fact that the recent theatre buildings have not improved the
quality of the productions, having merely eliminated opportunities
for improvization and inventiveness, to which theatre people have
formerly been constrained because of unsatisfactory conditions of performance. As a result, empty perfection, unadorned stereotyping, and
lack of quality are all the more apparent in the new theatres. The
architecture seems to contradict the action on stage. If attempts are
made with bold production methods and scenic devices to draw the
whole stage and auditorium together into the action, the modern
theatre buildings prove more obstructive than the old: for instance,
a large part of the audience will have bad sight-lines or hardly be able
to hear. It is not the old theatres that hinder innovations and unconventional solutions. A fine rococo theatre does not prevent the

evolution of new acting styles. Giorgio Strehler's marvellous productions with the Milan Piccolo Theatre's ensemble originated in what can only be called an architectural abomination, and not in the modern, excellently proportioned Teatro Sant'Erasmo. Novel theatre buildings do not yield new forms of theatre, let alone a new and better theatre practice. Brecht worked in the plush-covered Theater am Schiffbauerdamm, any rebuilding or modernization of which he would rightly have considered tasteless. His 'Epic' theatre derived a good deal of its effectiveness from its very contrast with the theatre's architecture. Every old theatre is usable for new theatre. A theatre has only to be arranged according to the respective requirements of the troupe working in it. It is also essential to the quality of a production that it creates its own space in relation to the facilities available.

If interesting productions have recently taken place in Germany and certain ensembles have marked themselves out, this has happened as a rule either in old civic theatres or in premises which became recognizable as 'theatres' only with that production. The famous productions of Peter Zadek, Wilfried Minks, and Kurt Hübner, purveyors of the 'Bremen Style' which caused a stir in the late sixties and early seventies, originated in the Theater am Goetheplatz in Bremen, which had been built in 1950 on the site of the old playhouse and largely according to the old plans. The theatre proved itself to be sufficiently neutral and unobstrusive for the extreme modernity of the stage designs with their collage and pop-art influences either to clash productively with the architecture or to create a fusion between the two. For experimental productions they adapted a disused cinema, the Concordia, in 1970, so as to be free from the pressures of the civic theatre. Because he did not comply with these pressures as fully as the city fathers required, Kurt Hübner did not have his contract renewed as Intendant at Bremen. Since the autumn of 1973 he has been head of the Freie Volksbühne in West Berlin. Although this theatre, built in 1963 by Fritz Bornemann, is generally recognized as the most successful of the new buildings, Hübner still hankers after his Bremen Concordia. Erwin Piscator, the Freie Volksbühne's first Intendant (1963–6), did not achieve a single contemporary production in which the stage space played an important role or made a valuable contribution.

Even Peter Stein has never yet directed in a modern theatre building. As Fritz Kortner's Dramaturg and assistant, he worked in the

Theatre buildings old . . .

Photo: Bundesbildstelle, Bonn

Württembergisches Staatstheater, Stuttgart

'Photo: Fremdenverkehrsamt Munich — E. Zickmantel

Nationaltheater, Munich, during reconstruction

... and new

Nationaltheater, Mannheim

Stadttheater, Dortmund

Photo: Bundesbildstelle, Bonn

Munich Kammerspiele, a beautiful *art nouveau* building of 1901, which remained undamaged in the war. His first productions were done in the workshop theatre attached to the Kammerspiele. The West Berlin Schaubühne, which Stein and his collaborators set up in 1970 and which has outstripped the Berliner Ensemble as the leading German-speaking company, performs in the hall of an externally unattractive, 1960-built multi-purpose workers' welfare building, with the whole acting and audience areas re-arranged according to the conditions of each production. In civic theatres, on the other hand, the set designer has to fight with the administrative director over every seat that has to be removed on account of a projecting forestage.

III

The Mannheim Nationaltheater, built by Gerhard Weber in 1957 and often cited as an example of modern theatre architecture, is the prototype of the showy and unwieldy culture-bunker. The outer shell, which houses two theatres, has been constructed like a fortress on a giant air-raid shelter shielded against the city. For this reason the stage-floors are at first-floor level. The enormous, unencumbered space on the ground floor serves as foyer for both theatres, a comfortless waiting-room whose artistic accoutrement is paltry and commonplace. Because of their enormous breadth and depth, the stages in both theatres are especially suited for 'big' plays. Although they are alterable, it is impossible to achieve the kind of intimate staging demanded by many of the plays one would choose to produce. Also, as in almost all civic theatres, the full depth of the stage cannot be used, because a part of the stage floor serves as a temporary storage area for the scenery from other productions in the repertoire. The smaller theatre, having no circle or galleries, can be adapted for traverse or in-the-round staging, but in practice the requisite alteration is precluded by the way the theatre is run.

So the architect has provided this provincial establishment—provincial from the point of view of its structure and artistic potential—with technical facilities which simply cannot be exploited. It is because one cannot sense the utopian aspect intimated by stage relationships that the building seems so dead. Moreover, workshops, administration, and most of the rehearsal rooms are situated in another building near the theatre complex; so the actors enter the theatre in the evening as if it were a museum—not somewhere they work but where they only put themselves on show. Before and after the performance they wait around in a canteen which is reached by long air-raid passages and which has such a cheerless, tasteless atmosphere that anyone who spends any length of time there will find his aesthetic sensibilities (if he has any) more or less blunted and dulled.

Most of the new civic theatres were planned in the mid-fifties, when the need to catch up on plays from all over the world was being met, and the middle-classes, benefiting from their increasing prosperity, were hankering after more grandiose accommodation for their cultural pursuits. The famed era of theatres in cellars and studios was drawing to an end. There is no occasion to mourn this era, but it is crucial that the new theatres could not then have been evolved from definite programmes and ideas rather than handed over to the artistes as monuments, where they found all the advanced technical gadgets and paraphernalia for which they had hitherto had to think up their own substitutes.

The City theatres in Frankfurt had their best time when the drama side was still in emergency accommodation in the Stock Exchange. On the small and narrow stage there, without a revolve of any kind, Harry Buckwitz mounted productions of Brecht's *Gute Mensch von Setzuan* and *Kaukasische Kreidekreis,* which had sharpness and directness and did not seem at all restricted in stage terms. The confined space was turned to masterly advantage by the designer Teo Otto, and the stage was arranged in such a way that even quite large-scale settings were possible. Fritz Kortner produced Max Frisch's *Graf Oederland* here, which is scenically fairly demanding and, in his production of *Der staubige Regenbogen* (*The Dusty Rainbow*) by Hans Henny Jahnn, Erwin Piscator was able to employ all his customary techniques such as projections and silhouette effects.

With the move in 1963 to the newly built theatre, an architectural complex annexed to the former Frankfurt Schauspielhaus (which was doing service as the opera house after the war), the quality of the productions deteriorated noticeably. The permanent company soon disbanded, the producers came to grief on the vastness of the stage and the technical equipment. Teo Otto said of the undeniably magnificent new working conditions that, in contrast to the old 'pastry-board stage' in the Stock Exchange, he found himself devoid of inspiration. The first Buckwitz production in the new theatre, Brecht's *Die heilige*

Johanna der Schlachthöfe (*St Joan of the Stockyards*) was artistically a fiasco and provided the proof of the absurdity of the new building in revealing all the director's bright ideas to have been provided for by push-buttons already incorporated in the architect's plans. The production was under obligation to utilize all the fantastic technical facilities. The attraction of employing the beloved 'conveyor belt stage', for example, which Piscator first used for his *Schweyk* production in 1928, persists only so long as it is clearly incorporated as a technical device into the overall design and structure of the play. In the scene 'A deserted section of the stockyards' in the Buckwitz production, the actress playing Joan used a conveyor belt to simulate a strenuous march through the snow, which was meant to be indicated by a forest of dangling lengths of string. After a while a second conveyor belt was switched on, on which Frau Luckerniddle appeared, in order to pursue Joan and finally catch her up. What one saw were two actresses good-naturedly toiling away, concentrating closely on their feet, and holding a conversation which, because of the noise of the conveyor belts, was completely incomprehensible to the audience. A dry run for the benefit of the technical apparatus, leaving the actors out in the cold. Not to mention the play itself. Even without the noise of the conveyor belts, the voices seldom penetrated beyond the middle rows. For Buckwitz and his successor, Ulrich Erfurth, the consequences were that from then on the full depth of the stage and the complicated technical equipment remained as good as unused, and the blockings and designs from earlier productions were now moved as far forward as possible on to the forestage for the stage of intelligibility.

Only during the last season or two (since the autumn of 1972) in the productions of Peter Palitzsch, Hans Neuenfels, and Klaus Michael Grüber has the stage been opened up again and something like scenery and production design have been discernible, but the audience feels provoked because hardly any of the text is comprehensible. The new building resists all attempts to create contemporary theatre attuned to a dialogue with the audience. But the present structure, which is strongly adhered to, prohibits alterations to the spatial arrangement. Theoretically it is possible, for instance, to convert the proscenium arch arrangement at Frankfurt into an open stage, since the side walls of the auditorium, complete with their built-in lighting emplacements, are manoeuvrable in and out. But in practice they are content to be able to vary the width of the stage a bit for individual productions.

More demanding alterations are considered impossible in a repertoire theatre, being too time-consuming since the stage is needed for rehearsals during the day.

IV

The more completely a new building is founded in a city as a cultural centre, the greater are the obstacles to productive theatre work. The grandiosity of a building's outward appearance stands in complete contrast to the cramping conditions which the stage itself has to make do with. Far more money is invested in the decorative art adorning the approaches to the theatre than in lighting equipment and other technical apparatus. The Wuppertal Schauspielhaus, built by Gerhard Graubner and opened in 1966, is a striking example of a theatre as a 'total complex'. The front of the building intended to be seen is stepped and segmented in a decidedly lavish manner; the foyer is superfluously extended outwards by means of two Japanese gardens; while the rear of the building facing the River Wupper and the overhead railway has not been contoured at all and has simply been plastered over like an ugly office-block. The theatre was designed for a sliding stage, with the main stage divided into elevatable sections, but its completion—the second side stage is still missing—was held back in favour of a later section of the building. The considerable width of the stalls certainly brings the whole audience close to the stage, but it considerably restricts the view of those spectators sitting at the far sides if the action spreads over the whole of the stage. The modern building demands not only enormous compromises on the part of theatre people but even forces them to adhere to the principles of the picture-frame stage, which hardly need the services of modern theatre architecture.

The extremes to which such senselessness can be carried is demonstrated finally by the new building for the Landestheater at Darmstadt, which came into operation in 1972. Here the architect, Rolf Prange, has enclosed a space of about 217,000 cubic metres. As in almost all cities, the site sets itself apart from the environment as if it were an island. Getting to the theatre is one long obstacle race. If you come on foot, the prospect of finding the entrance is relatively good, but if you come by car, it lands you in the underground car park beneath the theatre, and you must find your way through a concrete labyrinth in order to reach a staircase with an entrance like a firing-slit and placed at the farthest point away from where you come in. The whole set-up can only be compared to the new Frankfurt Airport, but at least there you find your way around more quickly thanks to better sign-posting. Here you are directed to the opera or the playhouse by loudspeakers. A trip to the lavatory is inseparable from the nightmare of getting lost in one of the endless corridors. Should you succeed in reaching the playhouse auditorium, whose overall effect is relatively decent and modest, you are confronted on stage with the old fustian of the fifties. Dust-covered decor, a declamatory style, or chic applied art demonstrate that the civic theatre is stubbornly holding its own in the modern environment. Prussian-trained janitors, with a thousand regulations at their fingertips, mount guard over this concrete fortress and drive out the last remnants of aesthetic pleasure and sensitivity left in the people who ply their art within its walls. The money which was spent on this temple of the muses and which will be needed for administration and maintenance could have been used to mount bold experiments and try out new forms of theatre for the next hundred years in the old Darmstadt Orangerie, which the new building re-placed. Old theatres can be turned into contemporary theatres, but a modern theatre building with a civic theatre-style organization is an anachronism.

It seems that the last possible new building in the sphere of German-speaking theatre is the City Theatre in Basle. The economic situation is for the time being constraining the municipalities to make the greatest economies. In Basle, meanwhile, there is hardly anyone left whose heart beats faster at the thought of the opening of their new theatre. The good citizens were more than a little alarmed to learn that the budget of the new theatre which they so proudly decided some years ago to build will overstep the old budget by more than 50 per cent. In the meantime the new building remains empty until a public referendum has taken place over the theatre administration's unexpected subsidy demands. This referendum took place at the end of 1973. The increased subsidy was rejected by 24,000 to 18,500 votes. The building ought, without further delay, to be let to a supermarket concern, and the present 19th century City Theatre should be maintained as the place where plays are performed. When the current Intendant, Werner Düggelin, was asked what he wanted for the opening of the new theatre, he answered: 'A bulldozer to push the building away.' Düggelin and his team know that the new building will only bring problems and difficulties which have little to do with the aims and aspirations of their theatre work hitherto and which will only monstrously encumber their future working relationships.

As long as there is no contemporary theatre, there can also be no sensible modern theatre architecture. It is important therefore that at least the spaces in which theatre takes place should prove themselves adaptable to the methods and styles of the theatre-makers. The development of West German post-war society is fairly accurately demonstrated in the civic theatre buildings of the time. They offer a particularly conspicuous reflection of the social consciousness of the citizens for whom they were built. They are cultural abodes of the good, the true, and the beautiful, intended to disguise the fact that the confidence of the middle classes in their own inevitability is no longer completely intact. From the aesthetic point of view, the modern theatre buildings are the expression of the artistic ambitions of architects, who have opportunity only for the free development of their ideas in the realm of theatre and church building. With their other contracts, which are tied down by the interests of property speculators, by the regulations attached to housing development schemes, and by the requirements of the individual house-buyer, the architects' dreams can no longer be realized. Modern theatres, like churches, are an anachronistic luxury; they are not needed, yet they are financed because the givers of money and the upholders of law want to have themselves commemorated as friends of the culture to which they otherwise behave like barbarians. The theatre of the future, if it is to be alive and creative, will have to disregard modern theatre architecture, as it is this which has cemented the old conditions and is underpinning the present theatre-makers' terrible harmlessness, immutability and lack of imagination.

(Translated by Nicholas Hern)

Volker Canaris: STYLE AND THE DIRECTOR

The West German theatre of today is a directors' theatre. Yet there is no characteristic West German style of directing. The theatrical standard in the Federal Republic is set by a scant dozen directors, each attempting to find his own style and to realize it in his productions. This is a logical development in a country which, politically and culturally, is organized on federal lines and in which society persists in the fiction of having a pluralistic structure. The theatre reflects the society in which it functions, a society which has no genuine—political and cultural—capital city.

The two other chief participants in a theatrical occasion—author and actor—generally become subordinated to the director's stylistic whim. The resulting danger is obvious : play and performer tend to degenerate into mere vehicles of that theatrical dictator's fancies. The advantage, on the other hand, is equally obvious : only an integrated performance, which has been thought through in all its detail, can provide the spectator with that feast for the mind and the senses, those insights and experiences, of which theatre at its best is capable. A mere glance at the European theatrical scene will show that theatre that matters is Director's theatre, as witness the productions of Giorgio Strehler and Roger Planchon, of Ingmar Bergman and Otomar Krejca, of Benno Besson, Manfred Wekwerth, Patrice Chéreau, Peter Hall and Peter Brook. West Germany has brought forth at least one director of equal rank : Peter Stein. Above all, the system has created the working conditions, under which directorial personalities of such calibre could emerge (as well as outstanding productions) and in which the West German theatre is distinguished as hardly any other in Europe.

It cannot be said that there are no good actors in the West German theatre because the directors' supremacy will not allow them to develop their own potential. The truth is that it is precisely the productions of the last ten years, with their consistency of dramaturgy and staging, that have led to acting performances of outstanding calibre.

A realistic performance will not merely portray the character and its individual qualities, but demonstrate the whys and wherefores of its existence. To do this it must relate to the concrete world—to space and time, to fellow actors and courses of events. It is above all the production, the director's conception of the whole, which provides the actor with this relationship. The time of the star, of brilliant solo performances is past.

One can speak even less of a unified style of acting than of a unified style of directing. The multiplicity of aims and ideas on the part of directors requires a correspondingly wide range of histrionic expression. Besides, the style and techniques of German actors has been extended by having to work time and again under foreign directors (Swinarski, Axer, Krejca, Ciulei, Barrault, Beckett, Blin, Anouilh, Pietri, Strehler, Gaskill and many others), whose ideas and requirements are based on different traditions.

In the post-war Federal Republic the theatre gave its audiences the assurance of being in possession of a secure cultural heritage. Brilliant premières in newly opened houses made the theatre the symbol of the economic miracle.

The directors, who influenced the theatre of the period had become famous in the Weimar Republic; they had lived through the Third Reich (behaving with greater or lesser opportunism); some of them had even held important theatrical posts under the Nazis. Gustaf Gründgens, who was Intendant of the Berlin State Theatre from 1934 until 1944 and who, from 1945 until his death in 1963, remained unchallenged as personification of the Federal German theatre (1947–55 in Düsseldorf and 1955–63 in Hamburg)—this man, who had been a distinguished producer, a great director and an actor of genius, justified his attitude vis-à-vis the Nazi State in the name of Art: he had been concerned to ensure the continuity of German theatrical culture in a time of barbarism. These were the principles according to which the most important people concerned with the Federal German theatre in the fifties conceived their task.

They had all been influenced by that culture. In their joint capacities of Intendant and director they wanted theatre as pure art, the dramatist's work for its own sake, they wanted the grand tradition : Heinz Hilpert in Göttingen, Karlheinz Stroux in Düsseldorf, Boleslaw Barlog in Berlin, Rudolf Sellner in Darmstadt, Hans Schweikart in Munich, Harry Buckwitz in Frankfurt, Hans Schalla in Bochum. However much they differed in their literary aims and the means at their disposal, they were united in one thing : they did not want political theatre. Brecht's demands for a 'correct' theatre were answered by Gründgens with the West German standard formula that he aimed at 'good' theatre. The few brave attempts to perform Brecht's plays (notably by Harry Buckwitz in Frankfurt) were always being justified by referring to their poetic quality which supposedly translated the ideology into a poetic dimension.

It is significant that those men of the theatre, who might further have developed the tradition of politically realistic theatre in the Weimar Republic, either went to the GDR in order to work there (in particular Brecht and Wolfgang Langhoff) or else played the role of outsiders who tended, if anything, to be regarded with amused condescension. Thus it was only in the last years of his life that Erwin Piscator was able to give a new impetus to the Federal German stage, above all with the first performances of Hochhuth's *Stellvertreter* (*The Representative*, 1963), of Kipphardt's *In der Sache J. Robert Oppenheimer* (1964), and of Peter Weiss's *Ermittlung* (*The Investigation*, 1965). And when Fritz Kortner returned from exile, he had to fight for almost fifteen years to get to the top where he belonged : his sense of realism, requiring meticulous attention to detail and insisting on a presentation which would let the idea underlying the text be clearly understood, met with the resistance of the representative Federal German 'culture industry'.

The people of the theatre who had been obliged to emigrate in 1933 must derive considerable, if belated, satisfaction from the thought that the work of the most influential German directors of today is the direct, if inevitable, development of the tradition of Brecht, Piscator and Kortner, while that carefully preserved German cultural drama, which survived the Third Reich, died with Gustaf Gründgens, its most illustrious representative, at the beginning of the sixties.

The trend towards political theatre in West Germany—corresponding to the increasing political awareness of Federal German society in the sixties, culminating at the beginning of the seventies and running parallel to similar tendencies at the universities—did not lead to an improvement or, worse, uniformity in production-styles. On the contrary, the range and variety in the West German theatre today is greater than it was ten years ago. (This view will be supported in the second part of this essay by a description of the work done by the most important West German directors).

It is significant that in the 1971–2 season Brecht was the most performed playwright on the German stage (for the first time taking precedence over Shakespeare) since it means that middle-sized and small theatres now dare to do what they had so long avoided, namely to perform the Marxist 'classical' writer. But the catchword 'Brecht' only shows that the provinces are at last catching up with what twelve or fifteen years ago had become the foundation of today's work in the theatre.

What is meant are Brecht's attempts to put the theatre of the scientific age onto a different basis, to realize it by different methods. These methods, which were closely related to the play's substance, have had far-reaching consequences. The beginning of the new movement in the Federal German theatre was marked by a new dramaturgy.

Brecht had developed and practised it at his theatre in East Berlin, the Berliner Ensemble. The Dramaturg became the director's most important theoretical collaborator. Dramaturgy in Brecht's sense comprises the entire conceptual preparation of a production from its inception to its realization. Accordingly it is the task of dramaturgy to clarify the political and historical, as well as the aesthetic and formal aspects of a play and to convey the scientifically researched material to the other participants : it must give the director, the designers and the actors the necessary 'data' to put the work on stage; it controls the scenic illusion by relating it to an empirically conceived reality— and by making this reality accessible it stimulates the imagination. This procedure enabled the Berliner Ensemble in its heyday to put on productions of quite outstanding merit. And it is no mere chance that such a method, in which theatrical work had been rationalized and formulated into a system, could be detached from the person of Brecht and applied by others. As a director, too, Brecht has had his disciples; four of them are amongst the most important directors of the German-speaking theatre and of television : Peter Palitzsch and

Egon Monk in the Federal Republic, Benno Besson and Manfred Wekwerth in the GDR.

Peter Palitzsch has put his experiences as Brecht's dramaturgical collaborator and as director of the Berliner Ensemble at the service of the Federal German theatre. As a result the Stuttgart theatre, of which he was Senior Producer, was for a period of at least seven years (1966–72) the most interesting stage in West Germany. It was distinguished by its consistently serious treatment of socially relevant material. The plays were carefully prepared on dramaturgical lines which were strictly followed in production; a first-rate cast gave a highly distinctive performance—all this was the result of the method Palitzsch had learned from Brecht, who had taught him to approach his task with scientific objectivity. The rationale of how a play should be presented to a contemporary audience determined not only its conception; the social conscience of those concerned with its production shaped both the outline and the details of the happenings on stage. In this theatre Brecht's thesis of a changeable and changing world was constantly thought out afresh and put before the audience. After prolonged difficulties, the theatre has succeeded not only with the critics, but also with the public. And the principles that are basic to its work have made the company into one of the most intellectually purposeful in West Germany. The current attempt at Frankfurt by Palitzsch and his colleagues at a collectively managed theatre is the logical consequence of the work at Stuttgart.

Besides Palitzsch, directors as different as Peter Zadek and Hans Hollmann, Niels-Peter Rudolph, Hans Neuenfels and Klaus Michael Grüber have worked in Stuttgart. The idea, reiterated by many conservatives, that Brecht's dialectical materialism would lead to the theatre's impoverishment and to the spread of a dogmatic ideology was refuted by the first consistent attempt in the Federal Republic to put these principles into practice.

There is now hardly any important performance in the West German theatre, which has not had the benefit of a dramaturgical adviser, or which has not been conceived on strictly dramaturgical lines. In particular, the critical reappraisal of classical plays, the analytical examination of their historical and structural elements would be unthinkable without such a method. Productions of the classics (from Shakespeare to Chekhov) have always been central to the repertoire of the German theatre, and today they are still the touchstone by which a director's qualities are judged. It is true that the critical examination of an old play in many cases results in emphasizing the theoretical aspects of the drama at the expense of its effectiveness on stage; or else the performance merely serves to illustrate certain theories. But these are the unavoidable disadvantages of a practice which, on the whole, has led to the advancement of the West German theatre everywhere. The most important and the most fruitful presentations in the last ten years—Peter Stein's production of Brecht's *Die Mutter* (*The Mother*); *Peer Gynt*; Kleist's *Der Prinz von Homburg* (*The Prince of Homburg*) in particular, bear the unmistakable imprint of the dramaturgical (and political) work of the theatre at which they came into being: the collectively managed Schaubühne am Halleschen Ufer in Berlin. These productions have succeeded in uniting the intellectual and sensual aspects of the plays, providing the spectator not only with the enjoyment of an experience, but with food for thought. If only one of Brecht's demands has been met in the West German theatre, it is this: the spectator is to be regarded not as 'goggling', but as seeing, sensing and thinking—as an active participant in the play. Even directors who do not define their work as belonging to the school of dialectical materialism subscribe to Brecht's view of the spectator.

The decentralization of the West German theatre has produced a phenomenon which is both revealing and typical of the system: the so-called travelling director. The career of a West German director ran and still runs as follows: he makes a name for himself at one of the smaller theatres by spectacular productions; his aim is to draw the attention of critics from outside the region and thereby that of the talent-hungry Chief Dramaturgen and Intendanten, so that he might get an engagement at one of the larger theatres. As soon as he has made a success at one of the more important theatres, he will sell himself to other important theatres. If further sensational productions have increased his market value, he will be in a position to dictate not only his price, but the play to be produced, the cast and to a large extent the working conditions. Since the system more or less follows the laws of a capitalist economy, its supreme law is the saleability of the offered ware: the director must be able to prove that he is worth his price, that he is different from other directors, that he will bring success to the theatre which has bought him. As the theatre business is widely subsidized, it follows that the success of a production brought about by these means is not measured by consumer interest (the audience), or even by its quality, but by the notice it attracts, by its publicity value. The theatre critics—in Germany by tradition the culture pundits among journalists—assume willy-nilly the role of brokers or PR-agents on behalf of the travelling directors. Even being violently attacked or 'pulled to pieces' by the critics often serves to enhance the director's image : he regards it as a testimony to his exceptional and original qualities.

The system has a considerable effect on the stylistic quality of the productions. Travelling routine-men apart, who merely attempt to copy their previous pattern of success by serving up repeat-performances, the travelling director has to be original in order to be considered good value, and as a result his work tends to be highly subjective. And in view of his brief sojourn at any one theatre, generally lasting not more than six or eight weeks, the travelling director is mostly beyond the reach of the dramaturgical control described earlier, since he can easily excuse himself on the grounds of pressure of work. The production is no longer the result of a carefully thought-out plan, but of the director's 'inspiration'—a single aspect of the play becomes its focal point, which dominates the entire performance; superimposed, purely external effects reduce the piece to a hollow shell, with stereotyped structure and contents. The director's powers of invention and evocation are confined to a few scenes and characters, to isolated moments and situations. This results in performances which are remarkable neither for subtleties of detail, nor for penetrating insights into the thematic links of the drama, because they are intended to fulfil one single purpose : to demonstrate the director's originality.

Particularly popular for such *tours de force* are first nights of new plays or first performances in German; the sensation of a new play is heightened by a sensational production. Often enough it becomes impossible to judge the play on its merits, because of the undue prominence given to that single aspect of it, which has the greatest power to scandalize : the brutal, the obscene, the blasphemous, the 'revolutionary'. 'Updated' classics are admirable for the purpose : when Schiller's *Robbers* suddenly appear in leather-jackets and crash-helmets, the apparently progressive thesis of the unsettling of the educated middle-class would seem to be borne out in that it promptly

reacts to the provocation and—with the help of its political power—
threatens sanctions against the offending theatre.

It is obvious that the alternative to such a style of production is
not the so-called 'faithfulness to the work' beloved of the directors of
the fifties. Divested of their positions as Intendanten, they work in
middle-sized or small theatres belonging to the German theatrical
landscape and polemicize against the mania for innovation amongst
the young, without themselves being able to offer more than repro-
ductions of their erstwhile recipes for success.

Despite all these drawbacks, the system of the travelling directors
has its positive side : they have brought a breath of fresh air into
petrified institutions; they have liberated actors from the conventions
of decades and introduced them to entirely new possibilities; they
have drawn attention to new trends in the theatre and to authors
who would have been overlooked, had a chance not been taken on
their making a stir. The part played by Hans Hollmann in resurrect-
ing the plays of Horvath, by Claus Peymann in gaining acceptance for
the plays of Peter Handke and Thomas Bernhard, by Peter Palitzsch
in disseminating the methods and plays of Brecht, by Hans Neuenfels
in discovering irrational theatrical elements derived from Artaud, by
Peter Zadek in employing the forms of the Anglo-Saxon theatrical
tradition—all these were positive gains for the West German theatre of
the sixties, even if the directors were wandering from theatre to theatre
and working under constantly changing conditions. Yet the fact that
just these men sooner or later chose to make a contract with one
particular theatre surely proves that ultimately they found continuity
to be superior to the system of the travelling director.

An account of the creation of a theatrical centre in a provincial
German town is of some interest. In the sixties Kurt Hübner's theatre
in Bremen, with its so-called 'Bremen style' radiated its impulses over
the entire theatrical system. The people who were working under
Hübner's directorship in Bremen (and to some extent earlier in Ulm)
between 1962 and 1970, today set the standard of the West German
theatre everywhere. They were the directors Zadek, Palitzsch, Hollmann, Stein, Grüber and Fassbinder, the stage designers Minks, Rose
and Hermann, actors like Bruno Ganz and Edith Clever, Jutta Lampe
and Hannelore Hoger, Michael König and Margit Carstensen.

The resulting performances were entirely distinctive in character. Kurt Hübner's own productions of the classics (*Hamlet, Antigone, Macbeth*) set forth the action pure and simple, without in any way seeking to 'interpret' events. Peter Zadek's 'updated' versions were radical both in form and presentation : Shakespeare's *Henry V* under the title *Held Henry* (*Hero Henry*) became agitatorial-pacifist collage; Wedekind's *Frühlings Erwachen* (*Spring Awakening*) a bitter-sweet elegy on the subject of the 'Halb-Starken' (teddy-boys); Schiller's *Räuber* a bloodthirsty, grotesque comic-strip; Shakespeare's *Measure for Measure* an exercise in physical and intellectual excesses verging on exhibitionism. Ultimately on Bremen's stage that famous performance took place, in which, as if focused by a burning-glass, the formal virtuosity, the intellectual niveau and the social impotence of the West German theatre of the sixties was at once vividly realized and exposed : Peter Stein's *Tasso* (1969).

The unifying factor in these stylistically heterogeneous productions was the rigorous artistic sense and rich imagination of their designer, Wilfried Minks, whose evocative sets, aesthetically pleasing as well as intellectually meaningful, offered new insights (passed on meanwhile to other designers and directors) into the potentialities of space on the stage.

The important points are highlighted by the example of Bremen. First, that a decentralized theatrical landscape leads to the formation of several centres, which complement one another creatively and out of which new centres come into being. (In the persons of Zadek, Palitzsch and Stein the most important West German theatres of today have links with the defunct theatre of Kurt Hübner : the Schauspielhaus Bochum, the Schauspiel Frankfurt, the Schaubühne am Halleschen Ufer in West Berlin.) But the example of Bremen also shows that it is impossible to speak of a West German theatrical style. There never was a 'Bremen Style' in the sense of there being a single way of making theatre. There were and are only the different stylistic potentialities of different directors.

These must be seen in the context of the theatrical system. What follows is a description of the stylistic singularities and developments of the nine directors, who—in my opinion—today constitute the quality of the West German theatre : Hansgünther Heyme, Hans Hollmann, Hans Lietzau, Rudolf Noelte, Hans Neuenfels, Peter Palitzsch, Claus Peymann, Peter Stein and Peter Zadek. It is obvious that in addition to the Nine there is an abundance of experts and good craftsmen, routine-men and imitators. The following figures will demonstrate that my choice is not purely subjective. Since 1963 the 'Berliner Wettbewerb' (Berlin Theatrical Competition) has been in existence, in which a jury of ten critics decides on what it considers to be the most important productions of the season (in the Federal Republic, Austria and Switzerland). Of the ninety-four productions selected between 1963 and 1973 forty are by these nine directors. If one deducts the productions of the late Fritz Koztnez and Hans Bauer, as well as those of foreign guest-directors, only thirty-one productions remain, which are not by one or other of the chosen Nine, who can therefore exemplify the styles of the West German theatre at its best.

1. HANSGÜNTHER HEYME (born 1935) was assistant to Erwin Piscator and afterwards Chief Producer at the Hesse State Theatre in Wiesbaden. Since 1968 he has been working in a similar capacity at Cologne.

For years Heyme has been concerned with political theatre. His production of Greek classical dramas (*Oedipus Tyrannus, Oedipus at Colonus, Antigone, The Seven against Thebes, The Bacchae, The Frogs*) are paradigms of social situations, above all of the structure and conditions of authority. Close concentration on the political theme at the centre saves the plays from being mere museum-pieces, while the archaic nature of stage, costumes and masks and the strictly formalized dialogues and choruses leaves them as expressions of an alien world: the world of the plays is not identical with ours, but the latter has evolved from the former.

Heyme pays the same attention to historical detail in his productions of the German classics. His version of Schiller's *Wallenstein* (1969) was one of the most important productions of a classic in the West German theatre. Heyme subjected the text to a materialistic historical analysis using the means of Epic Theatre. At the same time the dramatic approach was as simple as it was effective: into the story of the betrayal and fall of the mighty Duke Wallenstein he inserted scenes from the first part of the trilogy, from *Wallensteins Lager (Wallenstein's Camp)*; in addition he commented on the action with projections from historical writings on the Thirty Years War.

Thus the war no longer appears as mere background to heroic destinies, but as a political contrivance: it destroys the Many in the interest and on the command of the Few. And by making the political interests and ideologies of Schiller's tragic heroes tangible he made them more transparent, more comprehensible—and thereby open to criticism, this *Wallenstein* serves as a model inasmuch as Heyme has succeeded in realizing one of the greatest and most beautiful of German tragedies in terms of Epic and dialectical drama, as political theatre of today. Without doing violence to Schiller or flatly 'modernizing' him, the Tragedy of Fate has become a lesson in politics.

The same emphasis on ideological criticism (in the spirit of Adorno) is apparent in Heyme's productions of the plays of Hebbel and Ibsen: (*Maria Magdalena, Die Nibelungen, Pillars of Society, The Wild Duck*). The common purpose of all these productions is to show how individual behaviour was affected by the social conditions prevailing at that time when our modern middle class became established. Heyme realizes his insights by careful stylization of historical attitudes and modes of expression; the characters appear comic and terrible at the same time; their limitations become comprehensible, because we are shown the social structures in which they originate and which we have by no means abolished, and yet they appear grotesque in their hopeless and helpless subjugation to these conditions. Hebbel's and Ibsen's tragedies on Heyme's stage turn into stories that end worse than is strictly necessary.

Heyme has also directed new and politically explosive plays (Weiss's *Marat/Sade*, Tankred Dorst's *Toller*, Dieter Forte's *Luther und Münzer*). The radical political utterances and the excesses on stage made for powerful and disturbing theatre, which infuriated and repelled one portion of the public, while it attracted and stimulated another.

While Heyme's theatre does not go unchallenged in a town like Cologne, with its middle-class liberalism, his position is secure owing to the social democratic majority in the Council. (His position as Senior Producer has just been confirmed for several years.) Not a few critics object to Heyme's handling of the actors: in order to put across his ideologically critical concepts he often uses the actors as purely functional bearers of certain aspects in his interpretation—at the cost of physical reality, of linguistic and psychological differentiation, of meaningful gesture and expression. There is no doubt, however, that

Heyme is one of the dramatically and stylistically most assured and uncompromising directors in the West German theatre.

2. HANS HOLLMANN (born 1933) is an Austrian. He has acquired his reputation in many parts of the West German theatrical landscape : in Bremen, Stuttgart, Munich, Hamburg, West Berlin. He is regarded as a self-assured and eccentric director, gifted though erratic. Some of his most important recent productions were in Basle. Having been for many years the characteristic travelling director, with all the advantages and disadvantages that this implies, he now works there more or less permanently, as well as at the Schiller- und Schlosspark-theater in Berlin, directing at least two plays every season in each of these theatres.

His productions show an extraordinary virtuosity of style. In Goldoni's *Trilogy of Zelinda and Lindoro* (Bremen 1966) he combined realism and poetry, while he staged *Macbird* (Stuttgart 1968) as satirical and polemical 'Polit-Collage'. In Schiller's *Kabale und Liebe* he has traced the story of human relationships created and destroyed by German militarism (Schiller-Theater, Berlin 1969). He gave Brecht's *Tage der Commune* (*Days of the Commune*) a production of straightforward revolutionary pathos (Stuttgart 1970). In the same season he directed the Brecht adaptation of Marlowe's *Leben Eduards des Zweiten von England* (*Edward II*) as a bloody spectacle of human passions and desires, set in a slaughterhouse-world, dominated by coldly clinical exterminating mechanisms (Münchner Kammerspiele). But Hollmann can also command magic and fairytale—Raimund's *Der Alpenkönig und der Menschenfeind* (Berlin 1973) and occasionally he dazzles us with stylish boulevard entertainment (Feydeau, Anouilh).

He is erratic just because of his stylistic brilliance and virtuosity, which seemingly enable him to master all genres equally well. Not infrequently he loses himself in his first sensational inspiration—as a travelling director Hollmann has studiously avoided being tied down by dramaturgical discipline and thereby tended more and more to be carried away by *idées fixes*. He is an egocentric who cultivates his stardom and his market value. The Berlin performance of Peter Weiss's *Hölderlin* in his hands degenerated into a gigantically inflated Grand Opera. And he made the Basle première of Heiner Müller's historically faithful adaptation of *Macbeth* (1972) into a scandal-spectacle with sex, crime and science-fiction horror. From the very beginning of their stage-career, these two important plays by important German-speaking playwrights were distorted to the point of travesty.

His actors fare no better. To exalt his own ego he mercilessly puts them through their paces in the manner of an animal trainer, forcing them to act in ways which are foreign to their natural talents, and from scene to scene or role to role he makes them alter their style, going from one extreme to the other. He certainly has an exceptional eye for theatrical possibilities, but his virtuosity constantly leads him into excess of vanity.

His good qualities, on the other hand, were made manifest in his productions of plays by Ödön von Horvath *Italienische Nacht* (*Italian Night*, Stuttgart 1967); *Kasimir and Karoline* (Basle 1968); *Geschichten aus dem Wienerwald* (*Stories from the Vienna Woods*, Düsseldorf 1971). Through a theatrically effective and realistic portrayal of the behaviour of ordinary German and Austrian citizens he illuminated the rise of Austro-German Fascism with inexorable clarity; by using pointed gesture and language, by veering from searching analyses to scenes wallowing in *Gemütlichkeit*, by permeating private postures with conventional attitudes he achieved carefully balanced performances, which provided not only aesthetically satisfying theatre, but also penetrating political insights.

In recent years Hollmann has made repeated attempts at Shakespeare—translating, adapting and directing him. *Titus Andronicus* became a colourful spectacle about power as a political means. (Under the title *Titus Titus* it was played in 1969 in Basle against a background of Western European student revolt.) In *Coriolanus* (Residenztheater, Munich 1970) he exposed the tendencies of European Imperialism at the turn of the century by means of cabaret, satire and political caricature. *Troilus and Cressida* was served up as a pacifist drawing-room piece, and *Richard III* as a multi-coloured showbooth-spectacle (Thalia Theater, Hamburg 1970 and 1973). And ultimately Hollmann demonstrated the splendour and misery of his gifts with *Julius Caesar* (Berlin 1972). The production was packed with theatrical and political ideas : Caesar (played by the comic Horst Bollmann) appeared as a jovial dictator à la Mussolini; the conspirators and their adversaries were portrayed as élitist cliques, squabbling for power. The manner of its realization literally killed the conception : each idea was repeated several times, every stage effect drummed in ad nauseam, every emphasis was made more emphatic, every point

driven home more forcefully and each revealing gesture revealed yet
more clearly. The performance thundered, shouted, sweated and raged
above the heads of the audience. One could no longer see or hear
anything, because eyes and ears were saturated; one no longer understood anything, because every thought had been spelled out. Bertolt
Brecht had a phrase for it: *Menschenfresser-Theater* (cannibal
theatre).

3. HANS LIETZAU (born 1913) began his career as actor, but for
thirty years he has been working almost exclusively as a director. He
has done longer service in a senior theatrical post than any of the
other eight directors. From 1954 until 1963 he was Chief Producer at
the Schiller- und Schlossparktheater in Berlin. From 1964 until 1969
he held a similar position at the Residenztheater in Munich. After an
interlude of six months as Intendant of the Deutsche Schauspielhaus in Hamburg, Lietzau returned to Berlin as Intendant of West
Berlin's State theatre, the Schiller- und Schlossparktheater.

Lietzau's professional life illustrates both the advantages and disadvantages of a German stage career. His period as Chief Producer
in Berlin was characterized by a pronounced predilection for so-called
'difficult' authors (Barlach, Adamov, Genet); in later years he tended
more and more to stagnate in painstaking but uncommitted routine.
The change of scene to Munich, with the additional stimulus of collaboration with the former theatre critic Ernst Wendt as Dramaturg,
led to a revival of Lietzau's theatrical imagination. In Munich Lietzau
achieved productions which combined the classical virtues of the
German theatrical culture in the Gründgens tradition (supreme formal
assurance, richly-varied ensemble-work, and intellectual precision) with
dramaturgical consistency and with an imagination and vitality, which
were astounding for an apparently 'finished' routine director.

Lietzau's production of Claudel's *Le Soulier de Satin* (1966) combined sensuous force with a lightness reminiscent of a Mozart opera.
The Prussian Lietzau traced the rich catholic inventiveness of the
work to its powerful baroque roots. Ionesco's *Les Chaises* (1967) was
made into an artistic study for two performers. He directed two actors
who seemed much too young for their parts, Martin Benrath and
Elisabeth Orth, into giving a gymnastic demonstration on the large
empty stage, of a comically macabre, precise and unsentimental requiem for two old clowns. This ability to translate the bodily move-

ments of his actors into a highly lucid and at the same time stylized and expressive theatrical language was shown to great effect in what is probably Lietzau's most perfect production to date—the première of Heiner Müller's adaptation of the *Philoctetes* of Sophocles (1968). Müller's extremely difficult German was made visually explicit in the action of the three performers (Helmut Griem, Martin Benrath, Wolf Redl). In Lietzau's production the complicated dialectic of a parable of domination and freedom became visually and intellectually comprehensible.

In 1968 Lietzau directed Genet's *Les Paravents* in Munich (after directing the first performance in Berlin in 1961). In Munich, together with his designer Jürgen Rose, he utilized the products of our industrial society—refuse, tin, scrap metal, steel structures and placards—as well as the gestures, expressions and psychological manifestations typical of an exploited, estranged and destitute society. Lietzau wanted to show the relevance of Genet's parable of revolution to the Federal Republic of 1968.

With all its theatrical and histrionic brilliance his last great Munich production, Schiller's *Räuber*, showed an unmistakable tendency towards star and prestige theatre. Griem, Benrath and Gisela Stein were the protagonists. Instead of a clear dramaturgical interpretation, he provided a coldly dispassionate reading of the text. Artistic directorships in Hamburg and Berlin beckoned—and Lietzau's constant aim had been a return to Berlin. Until now Lietzau has succeeded neither in Berlin, nor during his brief stay in Hamburg, in producing anything as remarkable as his Munich productions. His *Prinz von Homburg*, which had to stand up to direct comparison with Peter Stein's inspired version of the same piece only a few weeks later, was academic and lacked assurance. And while his most rounded achievement in Berlin, Edward Bond's *Lear*, showed a return to the elemental methods of presentation, which had distinguished *Les Chaises*, *Les Paravents* and *Philoctetes*, they served here merely as props to save a weaker piece.

There can be no doubt, however, that Hans Lietzau, who is now in his sixties, is still a theatrical personality to be reckoned with. He took over the Berlin State theatres from Boleslaw Barlog, whose regime had lasted for twenty-five years, and already in his first two seasons as Intendant, Lietzau has given new impulses of vitality to all areas of the theatre.

4. HANS NEUENFELS (born 1941) first made a stir in the provinces, at the municipal theatre in Krefeld. After two years in Heidelberg (1968–70) he entered into partnership with Peter Palitzsch, first in Stuttgart and since the autumn of 1972 in Frankfurt. Of the young West German directors, Neuenfels is liable to go to the most violent extremes. His Krefeld productions—Bond's *Saved*, Handke's *Publikumsbeschimpfung* (*Offending the Audience*), Claudel's *Le Soulier de Satin*—showed his undoubted gifts : on almost empty stages, with few props or costumes, using only the bodily movements and the language of his actors, he can evoke locales and worlds which come to life in the imagination. As long as Neuenfels's own theatrical imagination remains in harmony with the author's poetic vision, the audience will be riveted by the tension that develops between what is happening on the stage and its underlying meaning. In productions like these, Neuenfels proves himself to be the only director in the West German theatre to make meaningful and productive use of Surrealism. However, his sign-language is often so remote from the play that the audience remains alienated from the action. *Troilus and Cressida*, for instance, was staged by Neuenfels as an insoluble riddle, composed of quite heterogeneous phantasy elements. His idea of the war as damaging if not destroying all the characters' powers of communication, induced him to atomize the story and its concrete situations, so that they became a confused mosaic of sometimes beautiful, but mostly hermetic, signs and symbols.

With realistic plays, too, Neuenfels's phantasy performs complicated gymnastics. At the German première of Sean O'Casey's *The Plough and the Stars* (Wuppertal 1971) this wonderful play was distorted and mutilated almost beyond recognition. What remained was an abstract piece, with extreme histrionic poses, with folkloristic elements treated ironically and with characters reduced to hollow, incomprehensible stereotypes.

Neuenfels shows his considerable talent to best advantage in plays which go to extremes in form and content. An ideal example of his potential was the production in Stuttgart of Vitrac's *Victor* (1970, with Ulrich Wildgruber in the title role). In a larger-than-life bourgeois interior (table and bed dominate the stage) the characters are exhibited like extraordinary specimens of a familiar species. The rather vague postures and dialogue, reminiscent of boulevard theatre, are suddenly focused so sharply and distinctly that they stand out with photographic clarity. In this way the conflicts hidden beneath a super-ficially harmonious surface are delineated in microscopic detail. Sud-denly the normality of that institution called 'family' appears as monstrous, its rationality absurd, its order chaotic.

Neuenfels dealt with his two most successful recent productions in a similar, if still more elaborate, manner. He presented Ibsen's *Doll's House* (with Elisabeth Trissenaar and Peter Roggisch) as a critical parable on the subject of middle-class marriage; the estrangement between Helmer and Nora was stripped down into sudden stylistic outbursts, bizarre gestures and situations verging on the allegorical. The characters, whose basic behaviour consisted of well-rehearsed set-pieces, appeared both as perfectly functioning tools of bourgeois ideology and as its denatured products. (Stuttgart 1972 and Frankfurt 1973). With Ibsen's *Hedda Gabler* (Frankfurt 1973, again with Tris-senaar and Roggisch) Neuenfels apparently contented himself with presenting a tasteful drawing-room piece with all the rhetorical splen-dour and all the histrionic refinement proper to the genre, but the tension produced by superimposing this smooth exterior on to the catastrophic sequence of events achieves the effects and revelations which are the hallmark of Neuenfels's surrealism. The production is entertaining and keeps an ironic distance, and at the same time it is destructive and full of aesthetically and intellectually calculated malice.

5. RUDOLF NOELTE (born 1921) is the only conservative among the important West German directors. He is a pupil of Jürgen Fehling; after spending many years in Berlin and Munich and a brief period as Intendant at the Freie Volksbühne in West Berlin (1959) Noelte has for years been working exclusively as a freelance director—especially in Stuttgart, Munich and Berlin.

Despite his conservatism, Noelte differs from the routine directors who dominated the West German theatre in the fifties and early sixties. Noelte does not make it easy for anyone, he is uncomfortable, he exacts adequate working conditions, he fights against inefficiency and red tape. He has planned more productions that have not materialized than he has actually brought to fruition. But even his political adversaries, and especially the critics whom Noelte brands as 'red', testify to the complete integrity and high artistic standard of his work. However inexorably this Don Quixote fights against the system, he is a highly sensitive director, who carefully observes and probes every human emotion. In his tightly constructed productions, every move is thought out and planned, every utterance taken seriously, every nuance listened for. Decisive events occur in silences, in glances, in barely perceptible, yet clearly discernible movements. In the figurative as well as the actual sense, Noelte's figures are bathed in a melancholy light. They are isolated, lonely, desperate and resigned. For them and for Noelte the world ends at the footlights.

Noelte's stage is not concerned with historical realities. Individual aspirations and the impossibility of their achievement are the measure of his picture of the world and of Man. When this picture collides with texts, which apparently satirize certain types of social behaviour, Noelte's method of humanization proves to be productive. In Carl Sternheim's works (particularly in *Snob* and *Cassette*) Noelte succeeded in portraying codes of conduct in the Kaiser's Germany realistically as well as revealingly.

Noelte's favourite author, however, is Chekhov. His *Three Sisters* (Stuttgart 1965) and *The Cherry Orchard* (Residenztheater, Munich 1970) are among the most admired productions on the West German stage during the last ten years. Slowly and agonizingly, Noelte uncovers the individual truths of human beings and their relationships. He represents the situation of the dying Russian bourgeoisie at the turn of the century as an elegy on the death of beauty and humanity. Released from their historic context the figures appear as the representatives of the existential needs of modern man : they are sensitive, but unable to communicate; avid for life, but hopeless; vulnerable, but too weak to effect change. There is tension between this symbolic interpretation and the wealth of realistic detail, with which Noelte brings the characters to life. Suddenly, through the back door of his working ethos, as it were, Noelte captures gripping and precise formulations of human attitudes. A perfect example is his Berlin production of Strindberg's *Dance of Death* (1972). In Noelte's hands (and the acting of Bernhard Minetti as Edgar) the psychology and symbolism expressed in Strindberg's vision of 'Life's Hell' become the realistic portrayal of the situation of an old married couple.

The extent to which Noelte's conservative view of the world endangers his style became evident in the summer of 1973 in his Salzburg production of Molière's *Le Misanthrope*. The review of the play by the critic Benjamin Henrichs can be taken as a critical summing-up of Noelte's work as a whole : 'Noelte's theatre celebrates moods (the most beautiful and solemn in our theatre today), but he refuses to reflect—to reflect on a reality other than his own. In other words, a rather misanthropic mythology : theatre which no longer reacts to its surroundings, which constantly presents its own unvarying vision; theatre which no longer risks exploring new avenues, but merely describes dead ends. This may perhaps be the reason it is so sensitively insensitive, despite all tenderness, lacking in humanity.'

6. PETER PALITZSCH (born 1918), is Brecht's most distinguished pupil apart from Benno Besson and Manfred Wekwerth. For ten years, from the beginning of the fifties, Palitzsch worked with the Berliner Ensemble, first as Dramaturg and editor of the publication known as BB, then as director. Brecht's Hitler-parable *Der aufhaltsame Aufstieg des Arturo Ui* (*The Resistible Rise of Arturo Ui*) in 1958, on which Palitzsch worked in collaboration with Manfred Wekwerth, is one of the great productions of European theatre; five hundred performances and fifteen years later (with Ekkehard Schall still in the title role) it remains in the repertoire of the Berliner Ensemble.

In the Federal Republic, where he has been working exclusively since 1960, Palitzsch directed Brecht's plays at many theatres and thereby contributed materially towards defeating the Brecht-boycott, a legacy from the cold war. Having studied and practised with Brecht a theatrical method which postulates a precise dramaturgical and scientific analysis, Palitzsch has introduced it not only into the Federal German theatrical system, but developed it further in his own work.

His later Brecht productions—*Herr Puntila und sein Knecht Matti* (*Puntila and his Servant Matti*, Cologne 1965); *Schweyk im zweiten Weltkrieg* (*Schweik in World War II*, Ruhrfestspiele, Recklinghausen 1967); *Mutter Courage* (Stuttgart 1970) already showed the development of the Brecht models to advantage. Jointly with the designer Wifried Minks, Palitzsch found new ways of staging Brecht's classics in such a way that they come across as fresh and full of attack, and above all as theatre of physical action.

It is interesting to see how Palitzch applied his Brechtian experiences to other playwrights, notably Shakespeare. In Stuttgart Palitzsch produced a number of the historical dramas : *The Wars of the Roses* (on two evenings—comprising the three parts of *Henry VI*, 1967); *Richard III* (1968); *Henry IV* (1970). The production of *The Wars of the Roses* was the beginning and culmination of Palitzsch's efforts

to stage Shakespeare for today's audiences. Minks's sets were divided
into variable segments, which allowed for the simultaneous presentation of scenes and for film-like cuts in the action, as well as for wide
perspectives and intimate individual scenes. On this stage Palitzsch
directed Shakespeare in accordance with his dramaturgical and philosophical views, with the result that the Histories became plays about
the dialectic of history, showing actions and events affected by political
mechanisms and people as both the masters and the servants of such
mechanisms. The materialistic aspect of history was presented by
Palitzsch in a series of richly human and intellectually meaningful
tableaux (Peter Roggisch played the vulnerable, human-inhuman
King Henry VI).

In his last Stuttgart production, *Hamlet*, with Roggisch as the
Prince, Palitzsch summed up, as it were, his period as Senior Producer
in Stuttgart (1966–72). It had been characterized by battles against
bureaucracy, against reactionary criticism and the bourgeois public,
and for a self-critical, socially responsible and committed theatre. His
Hamlet became an acute and painful analysis of the difficulty encountered by anyone who, with intellectual means, with words and
thoughts and the imagination, consciously and conscientiously, sets out
to change the world.

Between the two extremes, Brecht and Shakespeare, Palitzsch has
directed a rich variety of plays, in which he examines the human
condition in specific social circumstances. Although in the course of
the years Palitzsch's style has become less severe, more relaxed—he
has never ceased to insist on the precise analytical portrayal of social
conditions without forgoing psychological realism. (Babel's *Marya*,
1967; Horváth's *Glaube, Liebe, Hoffnung* (*Faith, Hope and Charity*,
1969); Gorki's *Barbarians,* 1973; Wedekind's *Frühlings Erwachen*,
1973). For these performances Palitzsch was able to assemble a cast
unparalleled in the West German theatre of the sixties (Hannelore
Hoger, Peter Roggisch, Elisabeth Schwarz, Traugott Buhre, Ingeborg
Engelmann, Hans Mahnke, Enst Jacobi, Hans Christian Blech).

In the end, both as Chief Producer and director, Palitzsch has come
down unequivocally on the side of politically progressive plays by
important German-speaking authors. He was the first to direct plays
by Walser, Weiss, Hochhuth and Dorst, and because his productions
give a clear account of the action and do full justice to the quality

of the plays, they have secured for many outstanding works (Dorst's *Toller*, Weiss's *Hölderlin*) a firm place in the West German theatre.

7. CLAUS PEYMANN (born 1938) is one of the few directors in the West German theatre, who has successfully made the jump from student-theatre to the big stage. The start of Peymann's career was sensational, although it took place at one of the smaller theatres, in the Theater am Turm in Frankfurt, where he directed the first performances of Peter Handke's plays—*Publikumsbeschimpfung (Offending the Audience*, 1966), *Kaspar* (1968), and *Das Mündel will Vormund sein* (*My Foot My Tutor*, 1969). *Publikumsbeschimpfung* marked the beginning of that period in which—inside the theatre and from the stage—the effectiveness of theatre as such was called into question. Peymann's flexible production, which provocatively manipulated theatrical material, and freely played with words, phrases gestures and movements, in the overheated and charged atmosphere of the 'Experimenta' week, acted like a catalyst. Handke's doubts, whether reality could be presented in the theatre, were formulated in Peymann's production with cheerful impudence—and the result was, that in the years that followed, the Federal German theatre examined its relationship with the public so radically that, in the meantime, a new type of audience seems indeed to have grown up.

Peymann's original production of Handke's *Kaspar* was reviewed by the critic Botho Strauss in the following terms: 'At the Theater am Turm, Claus Peymann and his principal actor Wolf R. Redl have made the sound decision to liberate the stock figure of Kaspar from his traditional role and let him come to life on the stage. An Arlecchino in reverse—thus does he stumble through the drop-curtain and start back horrified at the sight of the spectators.' At its best Peymann's theatre is still distinguished by such electrifying moments of tension between stage figure and stage situation.

After leaving the Theater am Turm, Peymann worked as guest-director at nearly all the larger theatres. He had become one of those travelling directors, who are obliged to put their originality to the proof again and again. Thus the first night of a by no means unimportant play—Harald Mueller's *Grosser Wolf* (*Big Wolf*)—provided the occasion for Peymann to stage a series of tableaux, in which he made use of the Theatre of Cruelty, but largely mutilated the text in the process. He showed great imagination in his tableaux on the theme

'Children and War', but the realism of language and scenery was negated by violence and an excess of 'ideas'—thus hampering the progress of a good play by a gifted author.

Peymann's handling of other plays (Weiss's *Hölderlin*, 1971 in Hamburg, and Bond's *The Sea*, 1973 in Frankfurt) was hardly more restrained. And his attempt at becoming co-director at the collectively managed Schaubühne am Halleschen Ufer in Berlin came to grief after a very few months, soon after his first production. Handke's *Der Ritt über den Bodensee* (*The Ride Across Lake Constance*) was Peymann's highly artificial farewell gift to the Schaubühne: the complicated structures of this word and sense play had been translated into moments of high classical affection.

In the meantime Peymann has entered into a firm contract with one theatre: at the beginning of 1974 he became Senior Producer at the Württembergische Staatstheater in Stuttgart. And in Thomas Bernhard he has found an author who, like Handke, stimulates him to ideas which are both congenial and advantageous to the play. Already the first performance in Hamburg of *Ein Fest für Boris* (1970) has helped the prose writer Bernhard to become established on the stage, thanks to Peymann's production. The first night of *Der Ignorant und der Wahnsinnige* (*The Ignoramus and the Madman*, 1972) helped to renew Peymann's reputation as a director of importance. The première did not, however, pass without a scandal, because the Salzburg theatre refused to play the scene in total darkness, with even the emergency lights switched off. But the performance had great style, and the actors, notably Bruno Ganz and Ulrich Wildgruber, did their utmost to do justice to the emotional and linguistic extremes of Bernhard's world. On this occasion the scandal, which could be described as the result of the defiance by genius of authority and middle-class values, had a purpose: it drew attention to the author's highly complex text; the production was transferred to the Deutsches Schauspielhaus in Hamburg and invited to take part in the theatrical competition in Berlin; the play was successfully performed at several large theatres. Peymann's still youthful and rather immature inclination to show off has been set aflame by the searching earnestness of Bernhard's pessimism—and disciplined by it.

8. PETER STEIN (born 1937) is the most important director in the West German theatre today. He studied in Munich, where he partici-

pated in student theatre and subsequently he became assistant director
(to Kortner, among others) at the Kammerspiele. Within a space of
barely seven years Stein has achieved an undisputed pre-eminence.

His productions are faultlessly, almost frighteningly perfect, each
as beautiful and clever as the last. In addition they are highly successful both with audiences and critics. His first independent production,
Bond's *Saved* (1967, in a Bavarian dialect version at the Kammerspiele in Munich) was chosen as performance of the year by the
periodical Theatre Heute. No less than eight of his first twelve productions have been selected for the Berlin Theatre Festival. And it is
due not least to his genius and success as director that the most daring
and most progressive theatrical experiment, the collective management
of the Schaubühne am Halleschen Ufer, has so far been a success.

Stein is not a solitary worker but likes regular teams. Until now he
has worked at only four theatres and with the same stage designers—
in Munich, Bremen and Zurich they were Jürgen Rose and Wilfried
Minks, and in Berlin Klaus Weiffenbach and K. E. Herrmann. Since
his first two productions, the same actors have continuously played
leading roles for him: Michael König and Bruno Ganz, Edith Clever
and Jutta Lampe. He has also worked successfully with established
actors of the older generation (Joana Maria Gorvin, Peter Lühr,
Therese Ghiese). And when he gives very young actors important
parts to play—in *Optimistische Tragödie* (*Optimistic Tragedy*),
Fegefeuer in Ingolstadt (*Purgatory in Ingolstadt*) they arrive immediately at a more advanced stage in their development (Angela Winkler,
Elke Petri, Rüdiger Hacker). Since the Zurich period, the Drama-
turgs Dieter Sturm and Botho Strauss have collaborated in almost all
his important productions.

Peter Stein's artistic development has therefore to be considered in
relation to that of a team. His career has not been without setbacks.
Three times—in Munich, in Bremen and in Zurich—his radical and
forthright political views have brought him into conflict with the ruling
class. He left Munich because a collection on behalf of the National
Liberation Front, which would have followed logically on his production of Peter Weiss's *Vietnam Diskurs*, was prohibited. In Bremen,
immediately after the première of *Tasso*, he opposed the Intendant,
Kurt Hübner, in a dispute about collective working-terms. In Zurich
his production of Bond's *Early Morning* showed up all the monstrosities of the piece without restraint, tracing their roots back to middle-

class society. It aroused such strong feelings in the conservative Supervisory Council of the theatre, that the Intendant, Löffler, who had engaged Stein, was dismissed after a few months—and, naturally, Stein with him. In Berlin, Stein and his colleagues have at last achieved the working conditions which enable them to work continuously and in relative freedom at their plan for a progressive and emancipated theatre. This admittedly is only because the great success and outstanding quality of their work are an attraction which West Berlin would not willingly lose. Otherwise even the work at the Schaubühne would probably have been stifled after the first production—Brecht's *Mutter* (*The Mother*)—by a reactionary coalition in the Senate.

Stein's theatre is dialectical in the sense that his critical and partisan interpretation brings out the play's historical or topical quality, underlining the resemblance between its situation and the current actuality as the contrast between them. Brecht's *Mutter*, for instance, which Stein co-directed with Frank Steckel and Wolfgang Schwiedrzik in 1970 for the opening of the new Schaubühne, became an object-lesson in revolutionary work, in individual and collective processes of consciousness, in the relationship between theoretical and practical reason. It did not make out that Russia of 1905 and Berlin of 1970 could be equated—it insisted on the historical differences—but at the same time it offered the examples of public and private behaviour for examination as to their relevance to the present day. The production was aimed at communicating a clear propagandist message. And in the role of Pelagea Wlassowa, Therese Ghiese was able to show her great artistry at character portrayal in depicting and proclaiming the learning process Wlassowa undergoes, transforming her from helpless worker to revolutionary, in all its historic beauty and greatness.

While the production of another revolutionary piece, the *Optimistische Tragödie* by Wsewolod Wischnewski, clearly emphasized the need for Bolshevik party discipline, it also expressed sadness at the defeat of revolutionary anarchism. Stein fastened on the exact moment when this defeat had been necessary for the sake of saving the revolution. He also took the liberty of celebrating the contradictions and the historical productivity of this process with both great romantic pathos and the tense excitement of an adventure story.

When in 1971 Stein presented *Peer Gynt* in two parts, his production displayed a narrative skill and delight in storytelling appropriate to a 'tale from the 19th century'. The central problem, the question of self-realization in an industrial age, was handled unobtrusively, but to great theatrical effect by a simple trick : the part of Peer was played in eight consecutive stages by six different actors.

When Stein directs a play about religious and adolescent delusions (Marieluise Fleisser's *Fegefeuer in Ingolstadt*) he simultaneously depicts the characters as they are and shows why they have become what they are, because—wrote Benjamin Henrichs—in this production 'the actors think with their bodies'. And when he directs a farce by Labiche (*La Cagnotte*) he makes sure that underneath all those side-splitting comic effects we do not lose sight of the realistic situation of petit-bourgeois aspirations and their frustration.

All the virtues of Stein's work were concentrated in his *Prinz von Homburg* (1972), the perfect example of the production of a classic. It specifically places the opening situation in the occupied Prussia of 1811; the timeless conflict of the individual versus society is then rooted into this historical context. Stein and his Dramaturg, Botho Strauss, used Kleist's dream-symbolism to set the entire play inside the mind. There it acquires Utopian dimensions and visions are enacted of a future resolution of the conflict, but they must end in inevitable disillusionment, brought back into the perspective of present reality.

Despite Stein's inventiveness and his ability to discover the appropriate style for each play, there are certain constants in his repertoire. He particularly likes working with sets which enable him to stage related scenes simultaneously. He can make collective processes visible by co-ordinating starkly defined scenic elements. Again and again he uses erotic moments in the story to achieve dramatic and dynamic effects. Especially in historical plays he leads his actors through stylistic gradations so delicately balanced that they both portray the character and criticize it at the same time. Stein's theatre is powerfully dialectical not least because a sharp intelligence and a powerful and sensitive sensuality form a tangible union in his work.

9. PETER ZADEK (born 1926) emigrated in 1933 with his Jewish parents from Germany to England. His theatrical work still shows evidence of the fact that his career began in England (1949–60). Zadek's concept of theatre is better described with words like 'entertainment' or 'show business' than with *Bildung* or *Kultur* or *Aufklärung* (enlightenment). His intellect and wit are sophisticated rather than teutonically serious. He is not in the least given to solemn musings.

Since 1960, however, he has been working almost exclusively at German-speaking theatres—for a considerable time as a travelling director, with a prolonged stay in Bremen (1964–7). Since the autumn of 1972 Zadek has been Generalintendant at the Schauspielhaus Bochum. His unconventional attitude, which led him to open his theatre to the people at large, offering it as a place of entertainment for everybody, speedily made it into one of the most successful theatres in the Federal Republic.

From England Zadek brought not only his feeling for the theatre, but also his predilection for Shakespeare and his love of writers like Behan and O'Casey. Their plays were among his best productions: Behan's *The Hostage* (Ulm 1961, Bremen 1962); O'Casey's *The Silver Tassie* under the title *Der Pott*, 1967 in Wuppertal, 1970 in Stuttgart); Behan's *The Quare Fellow* (Bremen 1964)—about which Ernst Wendt wrote: 'Zadek showed a play about human beings and humanity, deeply moving with all its bitter gaiety'.

For a time, and especially in the mid-sixties, Zadek had the reputation of being the most provocative among the younger producers. He himself confesses that at that time his work was intended for a handful of friends and critics, and that he had purposely stressed the sensational aspect of a play, using spectacular scenery and effects. At the same time he also presented less spectacular, completely concentrated, strictly controlled and realistic productions. His *Cherry Orchard* (Stuttgart 1967) depicted the comic and banal aspect of the characters soberly and without pathos. It seemed to be an almost deliberate antidote to Noelte's *Three Sisters* (1965, at the same theatre). Zadek further developed his Chekhov style in his Bochum production of *The Seagull*, achieving an unforced gaiety, in which the tragi-comedy was presented without constraint and with gentle irony.

Despite its radical individualism, Zadek's theatre has never failed to be political. But his political attitude cannot be separated from theatrical effects; for this reason it lays itself open to misunderstandings and suspicion from every side. For example he made O'Casey's *The Silver Tassie* into a 'show' about football and war, using music-hall and cabaret effects and slapstick comedy. The play's pacifist emotions were expressed with a shocking facetiousness. This apparent tastelessness (which suited the material very well) caused a scandal, and the production was attacked from the right (and left).

Zadek's greatest recent success also used vaudeville techniques.

Hans Fallada's novel *Kleiner Mann—was nun?* (*Little Man—What Now?*) was made into a revue : around the story of the minor official Pinneberg and his loyal, brave wife, Lämmchen, Zadek and Tankred Dorst arranged a framework of numbers, songs, dances and short humorous sketches from the so-called 'roaring twenties'. Zadek handled the story of Pinneberg and Lämmchen with great tenderness and empathy. These scenes stood in contrast with the noisy, garish revue numbers. The contrast set up an emotional conflict in the spectator, pin-pointing the political implications of the production. Was the gaudy glitter of the twenties contrived to gloss over the wretched state of the masses? Was the rise of Fascism closely connected with the easily satisfied lower-middle-class mentality?

The two productions showed the unmistakable beginnings of a new and ambitious people's theatre, were adapted by Zadek for television and—characteristically both his *Silver Tassie* and *Kleiner Mann—was nun?* were exhibited to mass audiences. (Of all nine directors, Zadek is the only one to work regularly and successfully with the mass media.)

His most recent productions prove that he not only takes the public seriously, but positively needs it for his performances, which become complete only in the minds of the spectators. Zadek has in fact shown himself to be a radical, both theatrically and politically, in violating two taboos of Federal German society : in *The Merchant of Venice* he depicted Shylock (played by Hans Mahnke) as malicious, mean and negative, the personification of all the clichés of anti-semitism; and in Tankred Dorst's *Eiszeit* (*Ice Age*) he portrayed an elderly, reactionary writer, who had collaborated with the Fascists, as a fascinating and humane character, in harmony with himself. (O. E. Hasse played the old man.) Both plays were meant to provoke the public into examining its repressed prejudices. Zadek takes it upon himself to pose the question to what extent today's philosemitism is a reversal of the former antisemitism, and how far official anti-fascism merely cloaks attitudes which still persist. It is extremely risky to take such liberties in the West German society of today : the danger of complete misunderstanding cannot be ruled out. But in trying to stir the public's conscience and to give his theatre a utopian dimension, Zadek fills his stage plays with a vitality that communicates itself across the footlights—to the minds of the audience, to the town and the people.

(Translated by Claudia Rosoux)

SELECT BIBLIOGRAPHY

General

Garten, H. F., *Modern German Drama.* London 1964.
Natan Alex (ed.), *German Men of Letters, Vols. 1–6.* London 1961–72.

Knudsen, Hans, *Deutsche Theatergeschichte.* Stuttgart 1970.
Kunisch, Hermann (ed.), *Handbuch der deutschen Gegenwartsliteratur,*
2 vols. Munich 1965.
Schöne, Günter, *Tausend Jahre deutsches Theater (914–1914).* Munich
1962.

Chapters 1–4

Boyd, James, *Goethe's Knowledge of English Literature.* Oxford 1932.
Garland, H. B., *Lessing. The Founder of Modern German Literature.*
London 1962.
Garten, H. F., *Gerhart Hauptmann.* Cambridge 1954.
Gillies, A., 'Herder's Essay on Shakespeare: "das Herz der Unter-
suchung",' *Modern Language Review* 32 (1937).
Osborne, John, *The Naturalist Drama in Germany.* Manchester 1971.
Pascal, Roy, *Shakespeare in Germany 1740–1815.* Cambridge 1937.
Spalter, Max, *Brecht's Tradition.* Baltimore 1967.
Stahl, E. L., *Friedrich Schiller's Drama. Theory and Practice.* Oxford
1954.
Stern, J. P., *(Georg Büchner: a World of Suffering in) Re-interpretations.*
London 1964.

Bauer, Gerhard and Sibylle (eds.), *Gotthold Ephraim Lessing.* Darmstadt
1968.
Girard, René, *Lenz 1751–1792. Genèse d'un dramaturge du tragi-
comique.* Paris 1968.

Grimm, Reinhold (ed.), *Episches Theater*. Cologne and Berlin 1970.

Gundolf, Friedrich, *Shakespeare und der deutsche Geist*. Berlin 1911.

Guthke, Karl S., *Geschichte und Poetik der deutschen Tragikomödie*. Göttingen 1961; *Richtungskonstanten in der deutschen Shakespeare–Deutung des 18. Jahrhunderts*. Shakespeare Jahrbuch 98. Heidelberg 1962.

Hilscher, Eberhard, *Gerhart Hauptmann*. Berlin 1969.

Klotz, Volker, *Geschlossene und offene Form in Drama*. Munich 1972.

Kreuzer, Helmut (ed.), *Hebbel in neuer Sicht*. Stuttgart 1963.

Price, Lawrence Marsden, *Die Aufnahme englischer Literatur in Deutschland, 1500–1960*. Berne and Munich 1961.

Rohmer, Rolf, *Lessing und Shakespeare*. Shakespeare Jahrbuch 103. Weimar 1967.

Rothe, Friedrich, *Frank Wedekinds Dramen: Jugendstil und Lebensphilosophie*. Germanistische Abhandlungen 23. Stuttgart 1968.

Stahl, Ernst Leopold, *Shakespeare und das deutsche Theater*. Stuttgart 1947.

Symington, Rodney T. K., *Brecht und Shakespeare*. Bonn 1970.

Szondi, Peter, *Theorie des modernen Dramas*. Frankfurt 1959.

Voigt, Felix A. and Reichart, Walter A., *Hauptmann und Shakespeare*, 2nd ed. Goslar 1947.

Wiese, Benno von, *Friedrich Schiller*, 3rd ed. Stuttgart 1963.

Chapter 5

Bablet, Denis, *Edward Gordon Craig*. London 1966.

Eisner, Lotte, *The Haunted Screen. Expressionism in the German Cinema and the Influence of Max Reinhardt*. London 1969.

Fuerst, W. R. and Hume, S. J., *Twentieth Century Stage Decoration*, 2 vols. New York 1929 and 1967.

Kenworthy, B. J., *Georg Kaiser*. Oxford 1957.

Knight, A. H. J., *Georg Büchner*. Oxford 1951.

Lindenberger, H., *Georg Büchner*. Illinois 1964.

Macgowan, K. and Jones, R. E., *Continental Stagecraft*. New York 1922.

Mortensen, B. M. E. and Downs, B. W., *Strindberg*. Cambridge 1965.

Moussina, Leon, *The New Movement in the Theatre*. London 1931.

Ritchie, J. M. (ed.), *Periods in German Literature*. London 1966.

Samuel, R. and Thomas, R. H., *Expressionism in German Life, Literature and the Theatre (1910–1924)*. Cambridge 1939.

Sokel, Walter H., *The Writer in Extremis—Expressionism in 20th Century German Literature*. Stanford 1959.

Willett, John, *Expressionism*. London 1970.
Willibrand, W. A., *Ernst Toller and His Ideology*. Iowa 1945.

Bablet, Denis and Jacquot, Jean (eds.), *L'Expressionisme dans le théâtre européen*. Paris 1971.
Rühle, Günther, *Theater für die Republik*. Frankfurt 1967.

Chapter 6

Hern, Nicholas, *Peter Handke—theatre and anti-theatre*, Vol. 5 of Modern German Authors Series. London 1971.
Hilton, Ian, *Peter Weiss—a search for affinities*, Vol. 3 of Modern German Authors Series. London 1970.
Subiotto, A. V., *German Documentary Drama*. Birmingham 1972.

Hinck, W., *Das moderne Drama in Deutschland*. Göttingen 1973.
Koebner, T. (ed.), *Tendenzen der deutschen Literatur seit 1945*. Stuttgart 1971.
Rischbieter, H. and Wendt, Ernst, *Deutsche Dramatik in West und Ost*. Velber 1965.
Taeni, R., *Drama nach Brecht*. Basle 1968.
Weber, D. (ed.), *Deutsche Literatur seit 1945*. Stuttgart 1970.

Chapter 7

Breicha, Otto and Fritsch· Gerhard (eds.), *Aufforderung zum Misstrauen. Literatur, Bildende Kunst, Musik in Österreich seit 1945*. Berlin/ Frankfurt 1970.
Spiel, Hilde, *Welt im Widerschein. Essays. (Die österreichische Szene)*. Munich 1960.
Suchy, Walter, *Literatur in Österreich von 1945–70. Strömungen und Tendenzen*. Vienna 1973.

Chapter 8

Askew, Melvin W., 'Dürrenmatt's *The Visit of the Old Lady*', *Tulane Drama Review*, June 1961.

Klarmann, Adolf, 'Friedrich Dürrenmatt and the Tragic Sense of Comedy', *TDR*, May 1960.

Natan, Alex (ed.), *Swiss Men of Letters*. London 1970.

Rogoff, Gordon, 'Mr Dürrenmatt Buys New Shoes', *TDR*, October 1958.

Wellwarth, George, 'Friedrich Dürrenmatt and Max Frisch: Two Views of the Drama', *TDR*, March 1962.

Chapter 9

Theater in der Zeitwende, 2 vols. Berlin 1972.

Chapter 10

Esslin, Martin, *Brief Chronicles*. London 1970.

Hayman, Ronald, *Techniques of Acting*. London 1969 and 1975.

Chapters 11–13

Deutscher Bühnenverein, *Theater-Statistik 1971–72*. Cologne 1973.

NOTES ON CONTRIBUTORS

CLIVE BARKER has directed plays in England and Germany and lectured for the Drama Department of Birmingham University. He is now Associate Director at the Northcott Theatre, Exeter.

VOLKER CANARIS has worked for the West German Radio, Cologne, and contributed to *Theater Heute* and *Die Zeit*. He has worked as a Dramaturg for Suhrkamp Verlag and his books include *Jean Anouilh*.

PETER FISCHER is a London-based theatre and art critic who writes for German, Swiss and Austrian newspapers, as well as broadcasting for German radio stations. He has translated British and American novels, and he is the author of *Mosaics*.

RONALD HAYMAN has directed plays by Brecht, Grass, Handke, Walser and Fassbinder. His books include *Techniques of Acting, Samuel Beckett, Harold Pinter* and *The Set-Up, an Anatomy of the English Theatre Today*. He is a regular contributor to the arts page of *The Times*.

NICHOLAS HERN is the author of *Peter Handke—Theatre and Anti-Theatre* in the series Modern German Authors—Texts and Contexts. He has lectured for the Drama Department of Glasgow University and he is now Drama Editor at Eyre Methuen.

T. M. HOLMES is a lecturer in the German Department at the University College of Swansea.

LADISLAUS LÖB is a lecturer in the School of European Studies at the University of Sussex and author of *From Lessing to Hauptmann—Studies in German Drama*.

GERTRUD MANDER has lived in London since the early sixties and contributed regularly to *Theater Heute* and various German newspapers. Her books include *Shakespeare's Zeitgenossen, Shaw* and *Molière*.

JOHN OSBORNE is a lecturer in the School of European Studies at Sussex University and author of *The Naturalist Drama in Germany*.

STUART PARKES is a lecturer in German at Sheffield Polytechnic. For his doctorate he wrote a thesis on Martin Walser and he has written a number of articles on West and East German literature.

HILDE SPIEL was born in Vienna and has been living there again since 1953, after periods of working in London and Berlin. She has contributed to *Theater Heute* and *Die Welt*, and her books include the novel *The Darkened Room* and *Fanny von Arnstein oder die Emanzipation*.

ARRIGO SUBIOTTO has been Professor of German at Birmingham University since 1971. He is preparing a book on Brecht and is the author of the study *Bertolt Brecht's Adaptations for the Berliner Ensemble*.

KLAUS VÖLKER's books include *Frank Wedekind, Yeats und Synge* and *O'Casey*. He has contributed to *Die Zeit* and he is co-editor of *Spielzeit*.

H. M. WAIDSON is Professor of German at the University College of Swansea. His books include *The Modern German Novel 1945-65*.

INDEX

Der] Abstecher, 129, 137
Achleitner, Friedrich, 165
Ackermann, Konrad Ernst, 219
Adorno, Theodor W., 136
Agathon, 29
Agnes Bernauer, 78 f
Ahlsen, Leopold, 130
Aichinger, Ilse, 164 f
[Der] Alpenkönig und der Menschenfeind, 154, 258
Andorra, 172 f, 184 ff
Antigone
    Sophocles, 255
    Hasenclever, 121
Antoine, André, 98
Anzengruber, Ludwig, 157
Appia, Adolphe, 116–18
Arden, John, 9, 207 ff
Aristotelean "rules", 7, 16, 18, 27, 63
    rejection of, 87–105, 114 f
Artmann, H. C., 165
Asmodi, Herbert, 141
[Der] aufhaltsame Aufstieg des Arturo Ui, 51, 191
Austieg und Fall der Stadt Mahagonny, 104 n
Auschwitz, 132, 136

Baal, 128 n
Babel, Isaak, 266
Bachmann, Ingeborg, 164 f
Baden-Baden, 223
Bahr, Hermann, 158, 160
Baierl, Helmut, 197
Barbarians, 266
Barlach, Ernst, 120, 260
Barlog, Boleslaw, 236, 249, 261
Barrabas, 163
Basle, 245 f
Bassewitz, Henning Adam von, 60
Bauer, Friedhold, 197
Bauer, Wolfgang, 166, 169
Bauernfeld, Eduard von, 75
Bayer, Konrad, 165
Bayreuth
    Markgräfliches Opernhaus, 218
    Festspielhaus, 223
Beckett, Samuel, 176 f, 179
Beer-Hofmann, Richard, 160
[Der] Befehl, 164
[Die] Befristeten, 167
Behan, Brendan, 272
Benrath, Martin, 260 f
Berg, Alban, 104
Berghaus, Ruth, 194 f
Bergman, Ingmar, 247
Berlin, 223, 227, 235 f
    Berliner Wettbewerb, 256
    Freie Volksbühne, 240, 263
    Grosses Schauspielhaus, 117
    Hebbel-Theatre, 163
    Königsstädtisches Theater, 220

    Opera House, 218
    Proletarisches Theater, 123
    Royal Theatre, 215, 220
    Schaubühne am Halleschen Ufer, 230, 241, 252,
        255, 269 f
    Schiller- und Schlossparktheater, 228, 230, 258,
        260, 268
    Schumann Circus, 117
    State Theatre, 248
    Theater am Schiffbauerdamm, 240
Berlin, East, 52, 189 ff, 250
    Deutsche Staatsoper, 238
    Deutsches Theater, 196, 198 f, 237
    Komische Oper, 194
    (*See also* Berliner Ensemble, German Democratic
        Republic)
Berliner Ensemble, 7, 9, 52, 87, 189–210 *passim*, 230
    241, 250 f, 265 f
Bernhard, Thomas, 167 ff, 254, 268
Besson, Benno, 194, 199, 247, 251
[Der] Besuch der alten Dame, 172–9 *passim*
[Der] Bettler, 120, 127 n
[Der] Biberpelz, 100
Biedermann und die Brandstifter, 172 f, 184 f
Biel, Achim von, 236
Billinger, Richard, 158, 163
Biografie, ein Spiel, 173, 187 f
Birch-Pfeiffer, Charlotte, 75
Bleibtreu, Carl, 99
Bleiwe lasse, 145
Blut am Hals der Katze, 145
Bochum, 225, 232, 255, 272
Boeck, Johannes A., 164
Bolt, Robert, 207
Bond, Edward, 200, 216, 261 f, 268 ff
Borchert, Wolfgang, 129 f
Bornemann, Fritz, 240
[Die] bösen Köche, 140
Bostroem, Annemarie, 192
Brahm, Otto, 98, 117
Bräker, Ulrich, 35
Brandes, Johann Christian, 72
Braun, Felix, 160
Braun, Voiker, 197
[Die] Braut von Messina, 88
Brecht, Berthold, 7, 9, 18, 23, 25 f, 52, 87, 104, 131,
    137, 140, 174, 184, 189–210, 230, 236, 240,
    249 ff, 254, 258, 265 f
    and Shakespeare, 49 ff, 56
    (*See also* titles of plays)
Bremen, 254, 255, 272
    Theater am Goetheplatz, 240
    Concordia, 240
Bremer Freiheit, 145
Brenton, Howard, 210
Bronnen, Arnolt, 162
Bronner, Gerhard, 163
[Der] Brotladen, 194
Bruckner, Ferdinand, 160, 162
[Ein] Bruderzwist in Habsburg, 42, 156

Brus, Günter, 166 f
Büchner, Georg, 9, 43 f, 77 f, 82, 87, 95 ff, 101, 104, 105 n, 108 f, 115, 126, 131, 172
Buchreiser, Franz, 166
[Die] Büchse der Pandora, 103, 110, 126 n
Buckwitz, Harry, 242 f, 249
Bunuel, Luis, 168
Bürger Schippel, 112 f
[Die] Bürger von Calais, 121
[Der] Bürgergeneral, 71
Bury, John, 203

Cabinet of Dr. Caligari, 115
[La] Cagnotte, 271
Calderon, 38, 48, 155 f
Canetti, Elias, 167, 169
Canut, 65
Cardenio und Celinde, 65
Carstensen, Margit, 254
Cement, 200
[Les] Chaises, 260
Change, 166
Chekhov, Anton, 264, 272
Chéreau, Patrice, 247
[The] Cherry Orchard, 264, 272
[Die] chinesische Mauer, 184
[The] Churchill Play, 210
Clarissa Harlowe, 65
Claudel, Paul, 260, 262
Clavigo, 71
Clément, Pierre, 59 f
Clever, Edith, 254, 269
Cologne, 256 f
Coriolanus
  Shakespeare, 43, 52 f
  Brecht version, 52
  Lenz version, 89
Corneille, Pierre, 8, 16 f, 27, 88, 96
Court theatres, 13, 24, 34, 37, 98, 217, 219 ff, 227
Craig, Edward Gordon, 116 f
Crime and Crime, 111
Csokor, Franz Theodor, 161 f

Dalberg, Freiherr Friedrich von, 221
Dance of Death, 126 n, 264
Dantons Tod, 44, 78, 96 f, 115, 131
Darmstadt, 227
  Landestheater, 244 f
  Orangerie, 245
Daubeny, Peter, 201
Deichsel, Wolfgang, 145
Denger, Fred, 192
Des Meeres und der Liebe Wellen, 42
Des Teufels General, 129 f
Deutsche Bühnenverein, 222
[Le] Diable et le Bon Dieu, 9
Dialect writing, 165 f
Dichterleben, 40 f
Dichtung und Wahrheit, 89
Diderot, Denis, 15, 60, 62 f, 66, 68, 85
Dietrich, 122
Don Carlos, 72
Donadieu, 164
Donnerstag, 164
Dorst, Tankred, 142, 232, 257, 267, 273
Dostoevsky, Feodor, 82
Drach, Albert, 167
Draussen vor der Tür, 129 f
[A] Dream Play, 111 f
Drei Akte, 142 f

Dresden, 189
  Schauspielhaus, 127 n
  Opera House, 218
Düggelin, Werner, 245 f
Dürrenmatt, Friedrich, 9, 53 ff, 171–82, 188
  Monstervortrag über Gerechtigkeit und Recht, 181
Düsseldorf, 228, 248
Dymchitz, Alexander, 237

Early Morning, 209, 269 f
Easter, 111
Edward II, 49 f, 258
Egmont, 33 ff, 70 f
Eiche und Angora, 137
Ein Tag mit Edward, 164
Einen Jux will er sich machen, 155
[Der] Einsame, 128 n
Einsame Menschen, 83
Eiszeit, 142, 273
Ekhof, Konrad, 220
Electra (Hofmannsthal version), 117
Elisabeth von England, 162
Emilia Galotti, 18, 21 f, 66 ff, 72, 83, 96
Engel, Erich, 199, 201
English travelling companies (17th century), 7, 13, 27 f, 57 n, 216 f
[The] Entertainer, 206
Enzensberger, Hans Magnus, 131, 136
Epitaph for George Dillon, 205
Erdgeist, 102 f, 110, 126 n
Erfurth, Ulrich, 243
[Die] Ermittlung, 132, 249
[Die] Ermordung des Aias, 138 f
[Die] Erneuerung, 126 n
Erwachen, 120
Eschenburg, J. J. 35
[The] Eternal Road, 162
Experimenta, 143
Expressionism, 107–28, 162
  in films, 115 f, 127 n
  in painting, 115, 117

Fallada, Hans, 232, 273
[Die] Familie Schroffenstein, 41
Farquhar, George, 202, 204
Fassbinder, Rainer Werner, 145, 231, 254
[The] Father 126 n
Faust (Goethe), 9, 17, 45, 71, 114
Faust (Lessing), 17
Fegefeuer in Ingolstadt, 269, 271
Fehling, Jürgen, 127 n, 263
Felsenstein, Walter, 194
[Ein] Fest für Boris, 168, 268
[Das] Fest zu Kenelworth, 40
Feuchtwanger, Lion, 50
[Der] Fisch mit dem goldenen Dolch, 141
Fleisser, Marieluise, 269, 271
Florian Geyer, 101
Foreign plays in Germany, 215 f
  (See also individual playwrights)
Forte, Dieter, 136 f, 257
Das Fossil, 113
Frank der Fünfte, 53, 174, 176, 179
Frankfurt am Main, 31 f, 231, 251
  Schauspielhaus, 242 f, 255
  Stock Exchange theatre, 242
  Theater am Turm, 231, 267
Franziska, 126 n
Frau Flinz, 197
Frau L., 143

Freiligrath, Ferdinand, 43
French Revolution, 38, 69, 76, 78
Freytag, Gustav, 97
[Das] Friedensfest, 83
Frisch, Max, 9, 171 ff, 182–88, 237, 242
Frühlings Erwachen, 10, 102 f, 109 f, 126 n, 255, 266
Führmann Henschel, 83
Fürth, 223
Furttenbach, Joseph, 217 f

Galileo, 49, 206
The Gamester, 62
Ganz, Bruno, 254, 268 f
[Königs] Garten, Hugo F., 163
Gas I, II, 122
Gaskill, William, 204, 209
[Die] gefesselte Phantasie, 154
Gemmingen, Otto Heinrich von, 72
Genet, Jean, 260 f
Genossenschaft deutscher Bühnenangehörigen, 221
George, Stefan, 48
[Das] gerettete Venedig (Hofmannsthal), 48
German Democratic Republic, 9 f, 56, 189–200, 250 f
Gerstenberg, H. W. von, 31, 35, 88
Gervinus, Georg, 43
Gesang von lusitanischen Popanz, 133
[Die] Geschäfte des Herrn Julius Caesar, 52
Geschichten aus dem Wienerwald, 161, 259
[Ein] Geschlecht, 121
[Die] Gewehre der Frau Carrar, 195
Ghiese, Therese, 269 f
Glaube, Liebe, Hoffnung, 266
Glaube und Heimat, 158
Goering, Reinhard, 121
Goethe, Johann Wolfgang von, 8 f, 17 f, 20, 25 f, 31 ff, 36 f, 43, 45, 47 f, 70 f, 76, 79, 85, 89, 96 f, 114, 221
    and Shakespeare, 9, 32 ff, 47, 89
    (See also titles of his works)
Gorki, Maxim, 266
Gottes Tod ein Unfall, 167
Gotthelf, Jeremias, 171
Göttingen
    Deutsches Theater, 223
Gottsched, Johann Christoff, 8, 14–16, 19, 57 n, 63, 65
    Versuch einer Critischen Dichtkunst, 61
Götz von Berlichingen, 8 f, 32 ff, 79, 89 f, 97
Grabbe, C. D., 43, 87, 104 n
Graf Oederland, 242
[Der] Graf von Charolais, 160
Grass, Günter, 52 f, 56, 140
Graubner, Gerhard, 225, 244
Graz, 165 f
[The] Great Highway, 111 f
Griem, Helmut, 261
Grillparzer, Franz, 10, 25, 39, 42 f, 76, 146 n, 154 ff, 169
Grimm, Reinhold, 87
Gropius, Walter, 225
[Der] Gross-Kophta, 70
Grosse Schmährede an der Stadtmauer, 142
Grosser Wolf, 267
Grossmann, Gustav Friedrich Wilhelm, 72
Grüber, Klaus Michael, 243, 251, 254
Gründgens, Gustav, 236, 248 f
Gruppe 47, 164, 167
Gryphius, Andreas, 8, 27, 65
[Die] Guerillas, 135 f
Guinness, Alec, 205

[Der] Gute Mensch von Sezuan, 242
Guthke, Karl S., 61, 76, 87
Gutzkow, Karl, 42, 77
Gyges und sein Ring, 78 f

Hacks, Peter, 56 f, 195 ff, 199
Hafner, Philipp, 153
Hall, Peter, 203 f, 247
Halle, 198
Halm, Friedrich von, 75
Hamann, Johann Georg, 88
Hamburg, 16, 24 f, 219, 248
    Deutsches Schauspielhaus, 228, 260, 268
    Opera House, 218
    Thalia Theater, 259
Hamburgische Dramaturgie, 21 f, 24 f, 29 f, 64
Hamlet (Shakespeare), 44, 47 f, 204, 255, 266
    (Freiligrath), 43
    as character, 42 f, 50, 55
Hamlet in Wittenberg (Hauptmann), 46 f
Hamlet in Wittenberg (Gutzkow), 42
Handke, Peter, 9, 143, 167–9, 254, 262, 267 f
Hands, Terry, 207
Hanneles Himmelfahrt, 101
Hannibal, 104 n
Hanover, 218
Hansel, 166
Hardenberg, Prince, 215, 217
Hasenclever, Walter, 120 f, 127 n
Hauptmann, Gerhart, 10, 44 ff, 82 ff, 87, 98 ff, 157
Hauser, Arnold, 59, 69, 77, 82
[Die] Hebamme, 135 f
Hebbel, Friedrich, 39, 78 ff, 84, 97, 156 f, 257
[Das] heilige Experiment, 164
[Die] Heilige Johanna der Schlachtöfe, 105 n, 242 f
Heimarbeit, 144
Heins, Wolfgang, 199
Hello Dolly, 155
Helm, 143
Henrichs, Benjamin, 264 f, 271
Henry V, 255
Henz, Rudolf, 160
Herakles 5, 197
Herbert, Jocelyn, 203
Herder, Johann Gottfried, 22, 30 ff, 35, 37, 39, 70, 88, 90
Herodes und Mariamne, 78
[The] Heroic Life of the Bourgeoisie, 113
Herr Karl, 164
Herr Peter Squentz, 27
Herrmann, K. E., 269
Herzog Theodor von Gotland, 43
Hettner, Hermann, 97 f
Hey, Richard, 141
Heyme, Hansgünther, 255 ff
Hidalla, 126 n
Hildesheimer, Wolfgang, 139 f
Hilpert, Heinz, 223, 237, 249
[Der] Himbeerpflücker, 164
Hinkemann, 124
Hirche, Peter, 140
Hochhuth, Rolf, 132, 135 f, 171, 249
Hochwälder, Fritz, 164, 169
Hochzeit, 167
Hofmannsthal, Hugo von, 47 f, 117, 156, 158 ff, 169
[Der] Hofmeister, 70, 87, 91 f, 103
Hoger, Hannelore, 254, 266
Holberg, Ludwig, 8
Hölderlin, Friedrich, 45, 134
    Hölderlin, 134, 258, 267 f
Hölle Weg Erde, 122

Hollman, Hans, 251, 254 f, 258 ff
Holz, Arno, 82
Homo Faber, 185
Hoppla, wir leben! 125
Horváth, Ödön von,187, 144, 161, 169, 254, 259, 266
[*Die*] *Hose*, 112
[*The*] *Hostage*, 272
Hotel de Commerce, 164
Hübner, Kurt, 240, 254 f, 269
[*Der*] *Hund des Generals*, 134
Hurwicz, Angelika, 203 ff
[*Die*] *Hypochonder*, 143 f

Ibsen, Henrik, 7, 10, 82 f, 98 f, 109, 252, 257, 263, 270 f
Iffland, August Wilhelm, 75
[*Der*] *Ignorant und der Wahnsinnige*, 168 f, 268
[*Die*] *Illegalen*, 192
Im Wirbel der Berufung, 47
In der Sache J. Robert Oppenheimer, 132, 134 f, 249
Ingrisch, Lotte, 167, 169
Indipohdi, 45 f
Ionesco, Eugène, 179, 260
Iphigenie auf Tauris, 36 f, 45, 70 f, 89
Ironhand, 9
Italienische Nacht, 161, 259

Jagdszenen aus Niederbayern, 144
Jahnn, Hans Henny, 242
Jakobovsky and the Colonel, 163
Jans der Enenkel, 151 f
Jeanne 44, 164
Jedermann, 48, 113 f, 160
Jessner, Leopold, 117, 127 n
Johst, Hanns, 128 n, 163
Jonson, Ben, 7
Juarez und Maximilian, 162
[*Die*] *Juden*, 20
Judith, 78
Julia, 78
Julius Caesar, 33, 37, 51 f, 89
Jung-Wien, 157 f, 160
[*Das*] *junge Deutschland*, 76 f, 127 n
[*Der*] *junge Gelehrte*, 13, 20
[*Die*] *Jungfrau von Orleans*, 72
[*Der*] *jüngste Tag*, 161

Kabale und Liebe, 72 ff, 83, 115, 258
Kaiser, Georg, 121 f, 126 n
Kaiser, Wolf, 199
Kant, Immanuel, 71
Karge, Manfred, 195
Kasimir und Karoline, 161, 259
Kaspar, 167, 267
kasperl am elektrischen stuhl, 165
Kassel, 227
   Ottonium Theater, 217
[*Die*] *Kassette*, 112, 264
Katzengold, 197
[*Der*] *kaukasische Kreidekreis*, 49, 92, 201, 242
Kayser, Wolfgang, 87
Kehlmann, Michael, 163
kein pfeffer für czermak, 165
Keller, Gottfried, 171
Kerndl, Rainer, 197
[*Die*] *Kette fällt*, 192
Kilger, Heinrich, 202
[*Die*] *Kindermörderin*, 69 f
King John (Dürrenmatt version), 53 ff, 181

Kipper Paul Bauch, 197
Kipphardt, Heinar, 87, 132, 134 f, 171, 196 f, 249
Kleiner Mann, was nun?, 232, 273
Kleist, Heinrich von, 9, 25, 39, 41 f, 76, 98, 252, 261, 271
Klinger, Friedrich Maximilian, 8, 32, 69, 91, 114 f
Klinger, Kurt, 164
Klotz, Volker, 87
Kokoschka, Oskar, 119 f, 127 n
Komödie der Eitelkeit, 167
König, Michael, 254, 269
König Nicolo, 103
König Ottokar, 42
Königsberg, 219
[*Das*] *Konzert*, 160
[*Die*] *Koralle*, 122
Kornfeld, Paul, 114, 120, 126 n
Kortner, Fritz, 240, 242, 249, 256, 269
Kotzebue, Ferdinand von, 75
Krankheit der Jugend, 162
Kraus, Karl, 155, 160 ff, 167
Krefeld, 262
Krejca, Otomar, 247
Kreuzer, Helmut, 87
Kroetz, Frank Xaver, 144 f
Kühnelt, Hans Friedrich, 164
[*Die*] *Kurve*, 142

Labiche, Eugène, 113, 271
Lampe, Jutta, 254, 269
Lange, Hartmut, 138 f
Langhoff, Matthias, 195
Langhoff, Wolfgang, 199, 237, 249
Laokoon, 21
Laube, Heinrich, 77
Lear (Bond), 209, 261
[*The*] *Legend of the Dead Soldier*, 128 n
[*Die*] *Leiden des jungen Werthers*, 17 f
Leipzig, 189
   Neubersches Theater, 13, 19 f
Leisewitz, Johann Anton, 69
Lenau, Nikolaus, 154
Lenz, 43, 95
Lenz, Jakob Michael Reinhold, 8, 35, 70, 87, 89 ff, 95 f, 101, 103 f, 114 f
Lenz, Siegfried, 138
Leonce und Lena, 44, 78, 105 n
Lernet-Holenia, Alexander, 162
Lessing, Gotthold Ephraim, 8 f, 13–27, 57 n, 59 f, 63 ff, 68, 70, 72, 83, 85, 88, 96, 192, 219, 235
   and Shakespeare, 28 ff
[*Die*] *letzten Tage der Menschheit*, 160 ff
Levetzow, Ulrike von, 46
Lietzau, Hans, 255, 260 f
Lighting and stage effects, 115–18, 126 nn, 194, 202, 210, 218 f, 226, 242 ff
Lillo, George, 59, 61 f, 64, 68
Littlewood, Joan, 202 f, 207
London
   Laterndl (Austrian exiles), 163
   National Theatre, 228
   Palace Theatre, 201 f
   Royal Court Theatre, 203, 209
   Theatre Royal, Stratford, 202
[*The*] *London Merchant*, 59, 61 f, 64 f, 68, 76
Look Back in Anger, 203, 206
[*Der*] *Lorbass*, 197
Lucie Woodvil, 65
Ludwig, Otto, 39
Luft, Friedrich, 236
Lukács, Georg, 60

Lulu, 102, 104, 110
Luther (Osborne), 206 f
Lysistrate und die NATO, 136

Macbeth (Shakespeare), 39, 50, 255
  (Schiller version), 9, 34 ff
  (H. Müller version), 199 f, 258
Macbird, 258
Magdeburg, 198
Magic Afternoon, 166
Man of Straw, 113
Mann, Heinrich, 113
Mann ist Mann, 125, 194
Mannheim, 25, 231
  Opera House, 218
  Nationaltheater, 221, 241 f
Marat/Sade, 132 f, 210, 257
Maria Magdalena, 78 ff, 84, 156
  (Kroetz version), 144 f
Maria Stuart, 72
Marius und Sulla, 43
Marlowe, Christopher, 7, 49 f, 258
Marowitz, Charles, 216
[Der] Marquis von Keith, 103, 126 n
Martin Luther und Thomas Münzer, 136 f, 257
Martini, Christian Leberecht, 65
Marya, 266
[Die] Maschinenstürmer, 105 n, 123
Masse-Mensch, 123 f
[The] Matchmaker, 155
[Die] Matrosen von Cattaro, 192
Measure for Measure, 42, 48, 51, 255
Med ana schwoazzn Dintn, 165
Mehring, Franz, 99
Meiningen (Court Theatre), 98, 221
Mell, Max, 160, 163
Mercier, Louis Sebastian, 68 f
Merry Wives of Windsor, 207
Merz, Carl, 163
[Der] Messingkauf, 49
[Der] Meteor, 180
Metropolis, 122
Meyer, C. F., 171
Meyer Helmbrecht, 164
Michael Kramer, 101
Michelsen, Hans Günter, 142 f
[A] Midsummer Night's Dream, 27, 48
Minetti, Bernhard, 264
Minks, Wilfried, 240, 254 f, 265 f, 269
Minna von Barnhelm, 20, 23, 66
Miss Julie, 126 n
Miss Sara Sampson, 60, 65 f, 68
[die] missglückte luftreise, 165
[Der] Mitmacher, 177
Molière, 15, 20, 113, 264
Monk, Egon, 251
Moore, Edward, 62
Mörder, Hoffnung der Frauen, 119 f, 127 n
Morhof, D. G., 27
Moritz Tassow, 197
Mueller, Harald, 267
Mühl, Otto, 166 f, 169
Müller, Heiner, 195, 197, 199 f, 258, 261
[Der] Müller von Sanssouci, 195
[Das] Mündel will Vormund sein, 168, 267
Munich, 105 n, 109
  Cuvilliés-Theater, 218
  Deutsche Kammerspiele, 50, 241, 258, 269
  Nationaltheater, 223, 238
  Opera House, 218
  Residenztheater, 127 n, 260, 264

Musik, 104
[Die] Mutter, 252, 270
Mutter Courage, 49 f, 194, 201 f, 205, 237

Nachrichten aus der Provinz, 145
Nachsaison, 141
Nachtstück, 140
Nathan der Weise, 23 f, 66, 192, 235
Nationaltheater (proposed), 24 f, 219
[Die] natürliche Tochter, 70
Neher, Caspar, 203
Nestroy, Johann, 154 f, 161, 169
Neuber, Karoline (Die Neuberin), 13, 20
[Der] neue Menoza, 91
[Die] neuen Leiden des jungen W, 198
Neuenfels, Hans, 243, 251, 254 f, 262 f
Nibelungen trilogy (Hebbel), 156
Nietzsche, Friedrich, 44, 114
Nitsch, Herbert, 166 f, 169
Noch zehn Minuten bis Buffalo, 140
Noelte, Rudolf, 255, 263 ff
Nun singen sie wieder, 183

O'Casey, Sean, 262, 272
[Der] öffentliche Ankläger, 164
Olivier, Laurence, 204 f
Ollapotrida, 162
Optimistische Tragödie, 269 f
Orth, Elisabeth, 260
Osborne, John, 203, 205 ff
Österreichische Komödie, 162
Ottfried, 77
Otto, 8, 32
Otto, Teo, 202, 242
Otway, Thomas, 48, 60, 117

Pacifism, 121 f, 183, 255
Palitzsch, Peter, 202, 243, 250 f, 254 f, 262, 265 ff
Pandämonium Germanicum, 91
[Les] Paravents, 261
Pascal, Roy, 33
Pastorale, 139
Pauken und Trompeten, 201, 204
[Le] père de famille, 63
Peymann, Claus, 254 f, 267 f
Pfeil, Johann Gotlob Benjamin, 65
Philemon und Baucis, 130
Philoctetes, 261
[Die] Physiker, 172–80 *passim*
Pikulik, Lothar, 60
Pinter, Harold, 179, 186
Pirchan, Emil, 117
Piscator, Erwin, 123, 131 f, 191, 240, 242 f, 249, 256
Planchon, Roger, 247
Planspiel, 143
Platz, 122
[Die] Plebejer proben den Aufstand, 52 f, 140
Plenzdorf, 198
[The] Plough and the Stars, 262
Portner, Paul, 146 n
Porträt eines Planeten, 177, 180
Poss, Alf, 144
Prange, Rolf, 244
Prinz Friedrich von Homburg, 42
Professor Mamlock, 192
Publikumsbeschimpfung, 262, 267

Qualtinger, Helmut, 163 f
[The] Quare Fellow, 272

Racine, Jean, 8, 17, 96
Raimund, Ferdinand, 154, 258
[Die] Ratten, 84 ff, 101
[Der] Raub der Sabinerinnen, 235
[Die] Räuber, 25, 35, 72, 91, 253, 255, 261
[The] Recruiting Officer, 202, 204
Redl, Wolf, 261, 267
Regensburg, 218
Rehberg, Hans, 163
[Das] Reich Gottes in Böhmen, 162
Reinhardt, Max, 50, 111, 113 ff, 117, 126 n, 127 nn, 162
[Der] Retter, 127 n
Rhynsolt und Sapphira, 65
Richard III (Shakespeare), 37, 50 f, 199
    (Weisse), 29 f
Richard Savage, 77
Richardson, Tony, 204, 206
[Der] Ritt über den Bodensee, 167, 268
Robert Guiskard, 42
Robertson, J. G., 27 f
Roggisch, Peter, 263, 266
Romeo and Juliet, 34, 40, 89
Romulus der Grosse, 179 f
Rose Bernd, 83 f
Rose, Jürgen, 254, 261, 269
Rosenkavalier, 159
Rostock, 189
Rousseau, Jean-Jacques, 68, 71
Royal Shakespeare Company, 203, 207
rozznjagd, 166
Rudolph, Niels-Peter, 251
Rühm, Gerhard, 165
rund oder oval, 165
[Die] Rundköpfe und die Spitzköpfe, 51

Salomon, Horst, 197
Salzburg, 113, 268
Samuel Henzi, 20
Sartre, Jean-Paul, 9, 132
Saunders, James, 216
Sauschlachten, 166
Saved, 209, 262, 269
Schaer, Wolfgang, 75 f
Schäfer, Fritz, 225
Schall, Ekkehard, 190 f, 265
Schalla, Hans, 249
Scherenschnitt, 146 n
Schiller, Friedrich von, 8 f, 25, 71 ff, 76, 83, 85, 87 f, 91, 94 ff, 98, 115, 233, 253, 255 f, 258, 261
    and Shakespeare, 9, 34 ff
[Die] Schlacht bei Lobositz, 195
Schlaf, Johannes, 82
Schlegel, August Wilhelm, 34, 37 ff
Schlegel, Friedrich, 38, 42
Schlegel, Johann Elias, 35, 38, 57 n, 65
Schluck und Jau, 44 f
Schnitzler, Arthur, 157 ff, 169
[Die] schöne Helena, 196
Schönemann, Horst, 198
Schönemann troupe, 220
Schönherr, Karl, 157 f
Schreyvogel, Friedrich, 163
Schröder, Friedrich Ludwig, 16, 25, 75
Schröder, Rudolf Alexander, 48
Schubart, C. F. D., 36
Schubert, Heinz, 203 f
[Der] schwarze Schwan, 55, 137 f
Schweikart, Hans, 249
Schwenter, Daniel, 27
Schwerin, 220

Schwiedrzik, Wolfgang, 270
[Der] Schwierige, 159
Scofield, Paul, 205
Scott, Walter, 9
Scribe, Eugène, 7
[The] Sea, 268
[The] Seagull, 272
Seeschlacht, 121
Sellner, Rudolf, 249
Seneca, 8
Shakespeare, William, 7 ff, 15 ff, 19, 21, 27–58, 63, 70, 88 f, 98, 114, 178, 216, 259 f, 265 f
    (See also titles of plays)
Shakespeare dringend gesucht, 196 f
Shylock, 273
[The] Silver Tassie, 272
[The] Skin of our Teeth, 222
Snob, 264
So ein Theater, 143
[Der] Sohn, 120, 127 n
[Die] Söhne des Herrn Proteus, 140
[Die] Soldaten (Hochhuth), 135 f
    (Lenz), 70, 87, 89, 91 ff
    (Zimmermann), 104
Sommer, Harald, 166, 169
Sonnenfels, Joseph von, 153 f
Sophocles, 37, 178, 255 f, 261
Sorge, Richard, 120, 127 n
[Le] Soulier de Satin, 260, 262
Soyfer, Jura, 162
Spalter, Max, 87, 109, 128 n
Sperr, Martin, 144
Spitteler, Carl, 171
Spitz, Rudolf, 163
Staiger, Emil, 39
Stanislavsky, Konstantin, 98
[Der] staubige Regenbogen, 242
Steckel, Frank, 270
Stein, Gisela, 261
Stein, Peter, 230, 240 f, 247, 252, 254 f, 261, 268 ff
Stella, 71
[Der] Stellvertreter, 132, 135 f, 249
Sterbender Cato, 65
Sternheim, Carl, 86, 108, 112 f, 118, 264
Stifter, Adalbert, 154, 159
Stoppard, Tom, 204, 210
Stramm, August, 120
Stranitzky, Josef, 153, 156
[Die] Strasse nach Cavarcere, 164
Strauss, Botho, 143 f, 267, 269, 271
Strehler, Giorgio, 247
Strindberg, August, 10, 108, 110 ff, 118, 120, 126, 264
Stroux, Karl Heinz, 236, 249
Sturm, Dieter, 269
Sturm und Drang, 8
Stuttgart, 251
    Württembergische Staatstheater, 268
Subsidized theatre, 189 ff, 215–34
    (See also Nationaltheater)
Sudermann, Hermann, 82
Szondi, Peter, 62

[Die] Tage der Commune, 194 f, 258
[The] Taming of the Shrew, 44
Tasso, 255, 269
[The] Tempest, 45, 48
Thate, Hilmar, 194
Theatre of the Absurd, 26, 125, 130 f, 137, 139 f, 142, 146, 179
[The] Three Sisters, 264, 272

Tieck, Ludwig, 40 f
Titus Andronicus, 43, 54, 89
To Damascus, 111 f
Toller, Ernst, 122 ff, 142
    Toller, 142, 257, 267
Tolstoy, Leo, 82
[*Der*] *Tor und der Tod*, 48, 159, 168
Torquato Tasso, 70 f, 89
[*Der*] *tote Tag*, 120
Touring companies (after 1945), 224, 228, 233 f
[*Ein*] *Trauerspiel in Sizilien*, 78
[*Der*] *Traum ein Leben*, 155
Treibjagd auf Menschen, 164
Trissenaar, Elisabeth, 263
Troilus and Cressida, 262
Trommeln in der Nacht, 124 f
Trotzki im Exil, 134
[*Der*] *Turm* (Hofmannsthal), 160
    (Weiss), 132
Turrini, Peter, 166, 169
Tynan, Kenneth, 202, 204

Ulm, 217 f, 225, 254
[*Der*] *Unbelehrbare*, 141
[*Der*] *Unbestechliche*, 159
[*A*] *unhamlich stoaka obong*, 166
Unruh, Fritz von, 114, 121 f

Vanillikipferln, 167
Vega Lope de, 10, 157
Venice Preserv'd, 48, 117
[*Die*] *Verführung*, 120, 126 n
[*Das*] *Verhör von Habana*, 131, 136
[*Die*] *Verschwörung des Fiesco zu Genua*, 72, 94 f
[*Die*] *Verspätung*, 139
Victor, 262
Vienna
    Burgtheater, 154, 220
    Cabarets in, 162 f
    Hof- und Nationaltheater, 154
    Opera House, 218
    F. Schlegel in, 38
    Theater in der Josefstadt, 163
Viertel, Berthold, 236
Viet Nam Diskurs, 133, 146 n, 269
Vitrac, Roger, 262
Volksbühne, 232
Volksstücke, 144 f
Voltaire, 21, 59
Von Morgens bis Mitternachts, 121
Vor Sonnenuntergang, 45 f, 82
[*Der*] *Vortritt*, 167

Wagner, Heinrich Leopold, 68 ff, 91 f
Wallenstein trilogy, 9, 37, 72
Walser, Martin, 129, 137 f, 143
    Hamlet als Autor, 55 f
[*Die*] *Wandlung*, 123
[*Die*] *Weber*, 82, 100 f
Weber, Gerhard, 241
Weber, Max, 62

Wedekind, Frank, 9 f, 86 f, 101 ff, 108 ff, 118, 120, 126, 255, 266
Weh dem, der lügt, 146 n, 156
Weh dem, der nicht lügt, 141
Weibsteufel, 158
Weichert, Richard, 127 n
Weiffenbach, Klauss, 269
Weigel, Hans, 162 f
Weigel, Helene, 237
Weimar, 35 ff
    Goethe in, 34, 70, 221
        Weimar Classicism, 35, 63, 71
    Deutsches Nationaltheater, 198
    (*See also* Court theatre)
Weisenborn, Günther, 192
Weiss, Peter, 9, 131 ff, 146 n, 171, 210, 249, 257 f, 267 ff
Weisse, C. F., 29 f
Wekwerth, Manfred, 192, 194, 199, 247, 251, 265
Wendt, Ernst, 260
Werfel, Franz, 114, 160, 162 f
Werner, 77
Wie ein Auto funktionierte, 144
Wieland, C. M., 28 f, 35, 42
Wiener Gruppe, 165
Wiener, Oswald, 165, 167
Wiesbaden, 223, 227
    Hesse State Theatre, 256
Wilder, Thornton, 155, 184, 222
Wildgans, Anton, 160
Wildgruber, Ulrich, 262, 268
Wilhelm Meisters Lehrjahre, 34, 38, 42, 48
Wilhelm Tell, 37, 72
Willett, John, 108, 111, 114, 201
Wir heissen Euch Hoffen, 192
[*Die*] *Wirklichkeit und was man dagegen tut*, 167
Wischnewski, Wsewolod, 269 f
Wolf, Friedrich, 192
Wölfflin, Heinrich, 91
Wondratschek, Wolf, 143
World War I, 107, 119, 121, 160 f
Woyzeck, 44, 78, 96 f, 108 f
Wozzeck, 104
Wünsche, Konrad, 140 f
Wuppertal, 244

Zadek, Peter, 232, 240, 251, 254 f, 271–3
Zeit der Schuldlosen, 138
Zelinda and Lindoro, 258
Zero Zero, 166
Ziem, Jochen, 145
Zimmermann, Bernd Alois, 104
[*Die*] *Zimmerschlacht*, 138
Zola, Emile, 82, 101
Zuckmayer, Carl, 10, 129 f
Zürich, 269 f
Zusanek, Harald, 164
[*Die*] *Zwillinge*, 32, 91

1003, 164
1913, 112
3. November 1918, 161